# PRAISE FOR
## *IN THE SHADOW OF THE VALLEY*

"In sobering detail and with open palms, Bobi Conn mines the depths of her desperation to earn love from a sadistically cruel father and an abused mother, from the boys and men who darken her path, from friends who betray her, and from a God who seems to have turned away from her. Conn's honesty is heroic and heartbreaking as she shares her story of enduring the stigma of poverty and abuse, claiming her self-worth, and discovering the limits of forgiveness. A necessary and timely read."

—Susan Bernhard, author of *Winter Loon*

"This important and necessary debut memoir explores the rich beauty and disturbing tragedy of Appalachia, how the people, like the land, have been exploited by corporate greed. Bobi Conn is a masterful storyteller weaving a tale of extreme poverty; an abusive, drug-addicted father; and a devoted grandmother's love into the wider tapestry of an entire at-risk population's lives. *In the Shadow of the Valley* is like the hollers that pockmark the land; the beautiful and haunting words will echo in your heart and mind long after the final page."

—William Dameron, author of *The Lie: A Memoir of Two Marriages, Catfishing & Coming Out*

"In her memoir, *In the Shadow of the Valley*, Bobi Conn recounts the nesting doll of her life, from growing up in a Kentucky holler to eventually becoming a mother of two. But before the promised land, the route there is labyrinthine, complete with moving walls and trapdoors. Even so corralled in these pages, it's clear that Conn's aptitude for survival is enviable. Yet, her strength is that writing has become, for her, a kind of performance art. She wields her own experiences without romanticization or adding shock value for effect, which makes her voice accessible whether she's speaking of exposure to trauma at an early age or grappling with the implications of her upbringing as an adult. In that sense, she has crafted a relatable memoir where she reaches the reader wherever they are and reminds us, 'The hero of the story is always the storyteller. The storyteller is the one with power.'"

—Bianca Spriggs, Affrilachian poet and author of
*We're Still Big Banging*

# In the Shadow of the Valley

# In the Shadow of the Valley

## A Memoir

## BOBI CONN

Little
a

Published by Little A, New York

www.apub.com

Amazon, the Amazon logo, and Little A are trademarks of Amazon.com, Inc., or its affiliates.

ISBN-13: 9781542004169 (hardcover)
ISBN-10: 1542004160 (hardcover)
ISBN-13: 9781542004176 (paperback)
ISBN-10: 1542004179 (paperback)

Cover design by Laywan Kwan

Printed in the United States of America
First edition

*I dedicate this book to my children, who have taught me everything I know about giving, and to my granny, who taught me to receive. I love you all more than words can tell.*

# Contents

Author's Note   xi

Prologue   1

Chapter 1: The Commandments   7

Chapter 2: Gravel   13

Chapter 3: Leaving Now   23

Chapter 4: Sunday Morning   33

Chapter 5: Gifted   39

Chapter 6: The Dark of Night   45

Chapter 7: What We Can Fix   53

Chapter 8: Spare the Rod   61

Chapter 9: Holy Vows   69

Chapter 10: Fish out of Water   75

Chapter 11: A Long Way from Home   81

Chapter 12: Out Loud   91

Chapter 13: Hunger   101

Chapter 14: Happy Now   109

Chapter 15: Love and Marriage   117

Chapter 16: A Pretty Smile   123

Chapter 17: The Walking Wounded   129

Chapter 18: Holding On   135

Chapter 19: Letting Go   141

Chapter 20: Say It Right   147

Chapter 21: To the City   153

Chapter 22: Faithful   159

Chapter 23: With You   165

Chapter 24: The Cathedral   169

Chapter 25: The Canary in the Coal Mine   175

Chapter 26: About Love   183

Chapter 27: The Gift   191

Chapter 28: Cyclical                                    203
Chapter 29: The Whore                                   209
Chapter 30: Pretending                                  217
Chapter 31: Handwritten                                 227
Chapter 32: Silver Dollars                              235
Chapter 33: The Brokenness of Everything                243
Chapter 34: Strangers                                   251
Chapter 35: That Would Be Good                          263
Chapter 36: Patron Saints                               269
Chapter 37: The Long Night                              277
Chapter 38: Defiance                                    283
Chapter 39: Out of Line                                 293
Chapter 40: In the Holler                               297
Epilogue: Endless Revision                              301
Acknowledgments                                         305
About the Author                                        307

# AUTHOR'S NOTE

I wrote this book to tell a story that I believe to be both important and good, and the best stories are true—the truth is complicated, compelling, and moving. At the same time, memory is fallible, and some of the material for my book derives from events that happened several decades ago; some of my stories are based on what I have been told by others, and that material has been identified as such. I have told each story with careful attention to the objective truth as I know it and with the utmost care for the people involved. I have changed the names and identifying features of characters in this book to help protect their privacy.

# PROLOGUE

Life was different in our holler, I came to learn. And we were definitely living in a holler, not a *hollow* like you might read about in the dictionary or see on a fancy map. *Merriam-Webster's* will tell you it's *a small valley or basin.* The dictionary can also tell you it's *a depressed or low part of a surface; an unfilled space.* But what it can't tell you is what that means, where the depression becomes visible in the land, what is inhabiting all that unfilled space.

Only people who were raised in hollers can do that.

A holler is a place where you very likely grew up in spitting distance of a relative, or at least close enough to see their house when the leaves had fallen for the year. It's a place where the sun takes a little longer to show itself in the morning and falls to sleep behind the hills a little sooner. Someone's always discovering the treasures buried in hollers—lumber, mineral rights, gas rights—and when they're not ravaging the forests we explored as children, unsupervised and unafraid, or muddling the clear streams where we splashed and found fossils and learned to pick up crawdads without getting pinched, when they're not ravaging our minds with OxyContin and cheap heroin and low-paying jobs and Mountain Dew and broken schools, it is us doing the ravaging: pulling our guns out or throwing fists, taking a beating in front of the kids, or searching desperately through Dad's dresser while he's gone, knowing there's something in there that will get us high.

But the holler is more than that, too. The holler is quintessential Appalachia—the perfect symbol for this complex physical and cultural landscape. Here, the word is everything—it is saturated and dripping with history and sorrow and, still, beauty—a living paradox of place wrapping its arms around you in verdant honeysuckle vines that hold you close, that never let go.

Before my dad's friend burned our house down, I could have taken you to the holler where I grew up. We could have stood on our old front porch to witness the Appalachian Eden sprawled around us, a patchwork of color and beauty and memory. If we looked to the left, toward the mouth of the holler, we would catch a glimpse of the white boards of Granny's house, especially in the winter when the two pawpaw trees shed their exotic leaves in her cow field. Up the road was the head of the holler, but nothing really seemed to exist past the sycamore tree that towered over the corner of our yard.

I used to stand on the porch when the rain poured down, all other sounds drowning in a symphony of water that beat the tin roof. In the spring, the frog songs reminded me that the land was waking up, and the whip-poor-will sang its refrain—always, it seemed, a love song. A few months later, the cicadas would buzz and hum and an ominous feeling hung in the air between them. It was the sound of summer in our holler and I loved it, though I troubled over how those strange creatures knew to break their slumber and join the rest of us aboveground.

Most of this land is the Daniel Boone National Forest, but Granny had a hundred acres tucked into it, and she had given my parents one of them. We had a small yard in front of the house—big enough to play and ride bikes, and even let hogs root around in, for a time. A page-wire fence ran the length of the yard, and a one-lane gravel road lay just beyond the fence. A narrow ditch separated Mill Branch Road from a hillside that came out of nowhere, and I explored that landscape without end.

I came to understand that the blackberry brambles by the side of the road appeared in the same places every year, as did the Indian paintbrush flowers—the brightest splash of red I ever found in a forest dominated by the green of living leaves, and the brown of the dead. The blackberries were sometimes as tart as they were anything, but it was worth the risk when you bit into a sweet one, its juice exploding onto your tongue while the skin surrendered to your teeth. Those wild berries were so good, you might not notice you had also eaten a sugar ant that was trying to get its own fill. Every year, I looked for two patches of purple phlox, one on the hillside across from where our wooden picnic table sat and one in the shady part of our yard, behind the old smokehouse. I found the little flowers, so perfect in their symmetry, blooming again and again in the same places—born and bound to this land, like me.

Although I spent a lot of my time alone as a child, I felt surrounded by figures that I couldn't see. I wondered where I came from, *who* I came from, because I somehow knew there was more to my story than what I saw each day.

My father had told me that our Irish ancestors were sent to the States as the English emptied the Irish prisons of debtors and violent criminals; our family were terrorists, he said. I like to think they caused trouble for the colonizers, just as a lot of the Irish did on the southern plantations where they were sent to work as indentured servants. According to some accounts, the Irish and Scots-Irish prisoners escaped from plantations and trekked north into the Appalachian Mountains, where the southerners would not follow.

I grew up thinking *Kentucky* meant *dark and bloody ground.* I believed the popular myth that claimed Native Americans never lived in Kentucky but used it as a hunting ground. That epithet, *dark and bloody ground,* is often attributed to Dragging-Canoe, a Cherokee chief, who either warned or promised the whites that this land would be stained with their blood. Other sources say our state name is from an Iroquoian word that means *land of tomorrow* or from a Wyandot word for the geographic *plain*. Regardless, the violent colonization of Appalachia at large—this place many have used as a way to describe heaven itself—began centuries ago.

And this land *is* heaven on earth, pulsing with life and beauty. But there is darkness in this unyielding, incomparable landscape that is saturated with tears and blood and forgotten roots that lie beneath the ground, now soft, now decayed. Whether we are bound to some bright tomorrow or the failures of yesterday is yet to be seen.

Most of my family members either can't or don't want to talk about their histories. My father, though, loved to tell me stories about my great-grandfather Conn, the moonshiner. My father valorized him and had helped him make moonshine until the old man died. Papaw Conn wouldn't talk about him, and Granny said it was because my great-grandfather was a drunk and habitually imprisoned, so Papaw was raised by his grandparents. Though my great-grandfather wore a suit and a fedora during the Depression, my great-grandmother couldn't feed all her five children.

What is history anyway? A story: *The last man standing holds the pen.* A sense of place: *I am on this path that is hardly comprehensible.* A birthright: *I may be from, but I am not of that world.*

I grew up idolizing the flawed people of my history. The cheaters, the drunks, the mean men and their women. They were my first heroes, and they lived their hard lives surrounded by the unspeakable beauty of the land that I call home. But the older I got, the less clear it was where my home could be. Not the holler I was born to, which I finally stopped visiting even for Christmas because Dad still might shoot someone, and I would have only myself to blame if I was there. Not the college town where everyone knows every mistake I have made but none of the reasons for them, and where men I once loved tell stories with their accounts of my flaws and faults. Not out West—Lord no, there aren't enough hills, and the whole place seems naked. Not down South or up

North, because I've always been in this in-between state and that suits me. But there is no comfort here.

*Home*—can anyone define that? For some, it's simple: *Where the heart is.* Cross-stitch that and hang it on a wall. For the rest of us, it's a negation: *Where I've never been.* Perhaps it is, after all, that one place to which we can never return. I left my home and grew up, carrying my child self everywhere I went, full of longing and fear and memory. I couldn't stay there and survive, but now Granny is gone, and I can't drive to her house and eat the best chicken and dumplings you ever had. There is no creek to keep me company, us running wild together behind the house and wandering through the holler. No hills to hike up so I can check on the spring and get a good drink. No trees to hide me. All the things I loved, I had to leave.

# CHAPTER 1

## *The Commandments*

My father ordered me one warm afternoon—I must have been five or six—to walk the half mile to Granny's and call her a whore. This remains my sole memory where my father knelt down and held my shoulders, speaking to me at eye level. Kneeling there, he calmly told me that the church my granny took me to was all a lie. God was dead, he died a long time ago, and he wasn't coming back.

I had been going to the First Church of God with his mother, *Granny* not only to her grandchildren but to her own children and husband, since I was born. She wrapped me up and carted me off as soon as it was decent, and we went every Sunday morning, to the holiday services, and on Wednesday nights when I was old enough to go to youth group. Every once in a while, I had to go on a Sunday night, when there were few kids and there was nothing to do but wait for it to be over. At the end of the Sunday evening service, though, the men would sometimes stand around whoever sat on the front pew in the middle aisle, lay their hands on that person, and pray in a babbling, overlapping way that made me think they might do something even stranger.

Still, I knew that my father had things mixed up—it was Jesus who died, not God, and he did come back, and God never went away at all. We didn't spend much time on that topic once my father was sure the message was clear. His attack on the church and God didn't bother me too much. I somehow knew it was retaliation for something Granny had done or said, like daring to voice her disapproval of his booze, his pills, his fighting-man ways.

At five, it never occurred to me that I could refuse the task he assigned to me. I nodded a *Yes, I will do that*, sensing his rage would quickly be redirected toward me if I showed any emotion. Nothing he ordered us to do was ever optional, and I wouldn't have the audacity to refuse his commands for a long time to come. I understood that I did not own the word *no*.

What does *no* mean? What do we accomplish when we speak it? It is a refusal: *I do not accept this dubious gift*. Self-protection: *You will not violate my sovereignty*. Denial: *I am not these things that you name me*. Children learn the word at a young age, as they test the limits their parents set for them and the boundaries the physical world imposes upon them. As frustrating as it is to accommodate the child's *no*, that word is essential. *No* functions in a way that *please don't* never has, in a way that tears and cries never will. It took me many years to learn the word *no*. I do not remember ever saying that word to my parents in defiance: *You cannot make me do this*. Or in resistance: *I will no longer be subjected to* . . .

In fact, I do not remember speaking much at all as a child. I may have—my mother claims I did—but I remember so much more the quietness that engulfed me, shame and fear twisting my insides. I waited for moments to pass, for the confusion to subside, for the adults around me to say, *Everything is okay*. No one ever did. Words were weapons, just another form of violence that I hid from. I hid myself deep so that on the surface, people would see *quiet* and *good girl*. I thought I could control their understanding of me, keep my inner torment a secret—it seemed like another sin to be so angry—but I did not realize how much my sense of self was controlled by all that *hiding*.

As a child walking down that one-lane gravel road, I thought I understood the word *whore*. I had heard it before, growing up in a home with few attempts to censor the vulgarities of the world. I had probably already heard it screamed at my mother, who never denied any curse but who seemed to think her motherly arms would somehow protect her face and her *self* from what rained down. Somehow, I knew it was a word for women, and I knew it was something to be ashamed of. It was also a word for girls—girls who had been molested or maybe wore short shorts, as I was to discover soon enough. I was scared to call my granny such an ugly name.

It was not my word, but it came to be mine before many others. It was roughly akin to *little slut*, which I learned around the age of nine, when I was wearing a floral shirt that tied at the bottom. I thought it was fashionable, though I had no way to know such things. It came from a real clothing store—not a Big Lots or a consignment shop—so I prized it above my other shirts and felt just the faintest hint of being pretty when I wore it. But my dad caught a glimpse of skin between the bottom of the shirt and the top of my shorts. When he first told me I should cover up, I laughed, thinking it was a joke—after all, I was nine, and who sees a nine-year-old's stomach and thinks *little slut*?

*You think that's funny? You want to walk around looking like a little slut? Don't you ever laugh at me again.*

The smile stole from my face as I began to learn that if I felt *pretty* or *stylish*, something was wrong. That if I wanted to look cute—like everyone else always seemed to look with their nice clothes and nice hair and nice smiles—shame would follow.

I walked down to my granny's house—it was always *down*, since we were closer to the head of the holler—knowing that what I was about to do was wrong, maybe even a sin, though it was not specifically mentioned in the Bible, as far as I knew. I walked without seeing the blackberry brambles I searched through at other times, when I was on my way to ask Granny for some eggs, onions, or tomatoes. I didn't see the creek I spent countless hours poring through, catching crawdads whose pincers I feared, watching always for copperheads that might be aroused by my presence, ready to strike.

When I walked through the kitchen door, she looked up and asked right away what was wrong. I burst into tears and told her that I was supposed to tell her she was a whore, knowing I was taking a risk by not actually calling her that name but hoping it was close enough. Granny wrapped her arms around me, telling me everything was going to be all right and not to worry. Through my hot tears, I told her I was so sorry, and she pulled me to her and *shushed* my cries. I was relieved that there was no anger on her face, grateful that she knew this wasn't my idea.

I wonder now how she sorted through that heartache, the grieving for her broken granddaughter, for her broken son, for her own fractured dream of family and answered prayers. Maybe she saw God's will at work, some infallible plan that played out while I wept. Did she have faith that this, too, had its divine purpose and that obedient children would inherit the earth some fine day? She had faith, to be sure. But that's not what I saw on her face that day.

Before long, that same look would cross my own face more than once, as tragedies piled onto one another and I slowly came to realize I could not change that grim reality. I grew familiar with a feeling of dread that was nearly eclipsed by weariness. A heartache that could no longer cry out. But before I ever felt the same pain that Granny must have felt that day, I knew that she ached for me and for what was unfolding. I knew that this hurt her, too, and that we grieved together.

In that moment, perhaps like me, she wondered what else would be lost that day, what punishment would come for us all. Maybe she feared my father and what had come from her birthing bed. Maybe there was a story I didn't know, a history of transgression that rested in her memory in which this day was just another turning page. Maybe she clung to the love we had, the desperate devotion I felt for her, the need that only she could fill.

Maybe she didn't know what to think. How to feel. What she did know was that the child in front of her needed her, and that her own grief would have to wait.

She drove me home and responded to his insult while I stood there. *You leave her alone,* she said. *Don't you do that to my little girl again.* I was scared for her and awed as she spoke without fear, not knowing what he might do. It was the first time I had ever heard anyone defy him. It was the first and last time I ever heard anyone tell him not to hurt me.

It made sense to me then that he needed someone to tell him that, because in fact even I didn't understand that it wasn't okay to hurt me, whether it was my heart or my mind or my body at stake. I would spend much of my childhood quietly enduring whatever there was to endure, keeping my face still so my rage and fear did not betray me, so whoever it was would not punish me further.

When a teenage boy took me to an empty classroom in the basement of our church, I sat quietly on his lap like he told me to. I said nothing as he pulled my shirt out from under the waistband of my skirt. I stayed silent while his hands moved around my five-year-old body. When he was done, I went into the bathroom just like he said and fixed my clothes without a word. I never told Granny or Papaw Conn what the boy had done in the basement at church. I never told my parents. I don't know what he said to me to keep our little secret safe, but it didn't matter—I already knew how important it was for girls to keep our mouths shut.

No one thought to tell me when I became an adult, *It's okay now, you're allowed to say no.* I went from being a child who did not speak up, to being an adult who did not. Before I knew how to protect myself, I had to watch best friends turn away in disdain when I answered yes, the bruise on my neck was probably from my boyfriend. I had to hear a lover say things like, *How could you let those men do that, I don't know any other women who would let that happen.* I had to watch my friends become my ex-husband's friends and feel their affection for me diminish. Since I hadn't told stories about him, they believed all the stories he raced to tell.

I had to unlearn the most important lesson I had learned as a child, the most important rule of survival—to *be quiet.*

I asked my mom once whether she had ever told her father—kind, gentle Papaw Wright, who lived on the road we took to town—what my dad did to her. *Lord no, your dad wouldn't be able to drive past their house if I did.* It made sense at the time—we don't inconvenience a man who terrorizes his wife and children. We don't bother a kind, protective father with the knowledge of what his son-in-law has done and maybe watch that good father reveal a violence of his own. We don't want any trouble.

And besides, *You knew he was like this when you married him.*

# CHAPTER 2

## *Gravel*

It took a long time for me to understand that most people couldn't relate to the things I took for granted as a child. Things like how we had a cup of copperhead venom in the refrigerator for several years, how I watched my father tease and taunt the caged snake until it struck the Saran Wrap he had stretched over a plastic cup, how that cup sat beside our hot dogs and mustard and lifeless iceberg lettuce. For a while, whenever I looked through the refrigerator for something to eat, I thought to myself, *Better not drink the venom.*

What did he even want it for? There was probably a plan to use it against someone, or maybe he wanted to have it on hand just in case. I don't remember my parents ever warning us not to touch it. But we knew—we knew well that to get ourselves hurt by doing something stupid would only lead to a whipping.

We were tucked so far away in our holler, our own small, unbothered wilderness that the outside world could hardly reach, for better or for worse. My brother and I occupied ourselves in the ways that children of our sort did. We ran through the woods, we waded through creeks and climbed around on barbed-wire fences, we picked up empty corncobs that had been gnawed clean by the rats who lived in the corncrib long after my dad gave up on raising hogs. We knocked wasp nests down and picked up odd mushrooms we found growing. We used hammers and nails and climbed into the loft of the barn by scaling the uneven boards that jutted out along the corner, scraps of wood and dusty wood planers waiting to break our fall. In some ways, we were so very free.

But we were not free to speak our minds—our voices did not belong to us. There was no room to say, *I don't deserve this,* or *You are hurting me,* or *Please, no more.* Only one person had the power of language in our home, and words were just as potent as his other acts of violence.

Worse than being cussed at or belittled, though, was how he forced us to say cruel things and laughed at the spectacle: *Tell your mother to lay down and let her pups suck.* It made my stomach quiver to say it, though I did not know what it meant. He would tell me to say that to her, and I was too scared to say no, though I could sense it was wrong and somehow dirty. It was his way to shut her up, putting his words in our mouths, where they tasted like sawdust and liquor and muddy water. I didn't even wonder how my own words would feel when they rose up from within my quivering belly and came charging out.

Our father played strange games with us, all of us. He would grab my mother's hand and pull one of her fingers back, forcing it into an unnatural bend while she would cry out, *Please stop, no, you're hurting me, come on this isn't funny,* and he would grin and look at us kids, standing there with confusion and alarm on our faces, and then he would chuckle. He might let go long enough for her to sigh with relief, and I would think everything was okay until he bent her fingers in the wrong direction again. Sometimes he would do that until she buckled to the floor, begging on her knees for him to stop, almost crying, with my brother and me not knowing what was happening—could it really hurt when our father was smiling and laughing? Those two things did not make sense together, and I thought everything had to make sense, somehow.

At some point, I stopped trusting myself to know the difference between what made sense and what did not. I learned that when things looked wrong, felt wrong, there had to be something I didn't understand. I learned I should trust the man telling me to trust him, to accept whatever he was doing, no matter what my own good sense had to say. I learned to ignore my own judgment, and for a good long time, I had no idea that I could trust myself.

We used to go out to this man's house, an old man out in the country—Earl. Earl did not have indoor plumbing or electricity, but he did have a lot of empty metal Prince Albert Tobacco cans. Sometimes he would give one to my brother, and I wished he would give me one because they seemed precious and rare. Earl's skin was brown and wrinkled, and one of his eyes was smaller than the other. It looked like his face had been injured long ago, maybe in a war. The man raised hogs with my dad. We used to have hogs in our yard, and at one point, they stayed across the creek at the corncrib, but now the hogs were at Earl's place, where the hills were too steep to play on, and there were no woods in sight.

During one of our visits, my father called for me to come to him while I was walking around the fields, looking at the cows and trying to find a way to have fun. I went to him, and standing beside Earl, my father held out a long, thin red pepper to me.

*Eat this,* he said.

I told him I didn't like hot peppers.

*The red ones aren't hot,* he said. And though he was smiling, I knew I did not have a choice in the matter. I wanted to believe him and thought maybe this was a different kind of pepper than what I had tried before. I bit off the end, and instantly, my mouth was on fire. My father laughed at the joke as I rubbed my shirt on my tongue over and over, desperate to cool it down. I was embarrassed that he had made a joke of me in front of Earl, who I don't believe laughed, but I was in too much pain to care about much else. It was still burning when we left, and on the ride home, sitting in the back of the pickup truck, I wondered how long some pain could last.

I couldn't accept that my father would hurt me for fun, humiliate me for his pleasure and maybe the amusement of another grown man. All the things that I heard and saw and felt fell onto and into one another, clanging in a relentless, deafening echo that demanded my constant vigilance.

He talked about the bank and how they were going to take the house. He told our mother he would burn it down with all of us in it before the *goddamn bankers got their hands on it*. He talked about the Social Security office, the settlement that he deserved, the paperwork that needed to be done, and the appointments he had to go to. I heard the state attorney's name over and over, and I heard about the crooked doctors who wouldn't refill his prescriptions. I knew in my child's heart that when those people finally left him alone, his back injury would get better, and we could keep our house, and the settlement money would make up for him not working.

It was the lawyers, the bankers, the system—they were working against him, against *us*, and keeping me from having a dad who loved me and who could go fishing and grow a garden and put corn out for the wild turkeys in the hills behind our house, a dad who could just be happy to have us and our beautiful holler and the Daniel Boone National Forest all around us, bathing us in beauty each day, all day long, instead of a dad who sometimes turned to rage for no reason at all and left bruises on us or called us *little piece of shit* or woke us at night while he did awful things to our mother.

At the time, he was also still a drinker, and Dad liked to give me beer starting from a young age. I think I was around five when I stumbled into the corner of the refrigerator, off balance, and I heard him laughing. Much later, rummaging through the thousands of pictures my parents took—why did they take so many pictures?—I found one of myself in nothing but a diaper, sitting on a yellow lounge chair in front of our trailer that we lived in before they built the house, grasping a cold Stroh's with both hands. A can of lighter fluid completes that composition, the picture of white trash.

Mom told me later that the picture was staged, but she also told me in complete seriousness that they used to put beer in my bottle to make me sleep. Either way, I drank beer whenever they let me and liked it until I was nine years old and my Sunday school teacher said alcohol was bad for the liver. The next time my father offered me a drink of his beer, I told him, *I don't want any*, even though I was scared to death I would get into trouble for saying no. It turns out that the only thing I feared more than my father was going to Hell, because the God I learned about didn't take sin lightly.

It is a wonder we had so many pictures lying around, just like it is a wonder we were able to afford a Nintendo at some point. Just that one system—nothing fancier—and I don't remember us getting any games besides the first Super Mario Bros. and Duck Hunt. But why would such poor people spend their money like that? The time would inevitably come when we really needed that money for food, for the electric bill. They could have taken us to the dentist or saved up for the next disaster they surely knew was coming. But we lived the poverty boom-and-bust lifestyle. In a landscape littered with disappointment, immediate gratification seems to make sense. In a region defined by broken promises, you might as well take the safe bet, the pleasure of a moment that might never return. There is no promise of tomorrow, and there's a damn good chance tomorrow will be worse than today. Most of these crises can't be fixed with $300 anyway. Let's have some fun while we can.

Considering how little love there was to go around in our house, and how keenly I felt the shortage, I blamed my little brother in some way for the pain that set in at an early age. I took out all of my hostility and aggression on him, and if I had not been able to do that, I probably would have turned it all inward even more fervently than I did. We were Irish twins—he was born one year and four days later than I was. I was named after our mom's father, and my brother was named after our paternal grandfather. Junior was my playmate, my victim, and my witness, someone who shared my fear and my anger, at least until he found a way out of all that *feeling*.

The one and only time I ever heard my brother defy our father was during dinner, when he was about six years old. We were eating, and suddenly, my brother was crying. My father had either ridiculed him or harassed him for some little thing, but, still, he demanded to know why Junior was crying. I was proud and horrified when my brother responded, *Sometimes I just get so sick of you.* We all sat in perfect silence for a moment, which my father ended with a sweep of his arm, sending his plate full of food and glass full of milk into a kitchen cabinet and onto the floor. My brother sobbed over his plate, and my father thundered out of the kitchen, ordering our mother to clean up the mess.

Part of me was thrilled that Junior felt brave and confident enough to say those words—words I would have never said. As much as I resented him for seeming to be so much more lovable than I was, I felt a deep need to protect him as well. The other part of me wanted him to keep his mouth shut and not make our father angry, because Dad's anger never stayed contained. I just sat there, fear knotting itself inside me as I waited for Dad to come back into the kitchen, and watched Mom clean up the mess on her hands and knees.

Those were the kinds of scenes that could happen in the solitude of our holler. The slow realization that we were poor and sure did look it became entwined with stories about the needy I sometimes read or heard at school. I began to understand that things were different at our house, but I was smart enough not to tell my teachers or the police officer who came to school to teach us the names of all the drugs and how bad they are. I always knew we didn't have money, but it wasn't a lack of money that made me feel poor, worthless, *dirty*. I didn't know the word *poverty* yet, but there was a poverty that made our home feel so different from our granny's.

Poverty was the cheap meat we ate with boxed macaroni and cheese, but it was also the food my dad flung to the floor. It was the picture I found of my father's handiwork, a picture he took after he tore the kitchen faucet loose and hurled it through the kitchen window. It was the dentist appointments we never had, the coal stove spewing fine black soot onto our clothes, into our hair and our noses; it was the fire dying in the coal stove; it was my mother slammed into the coal stove. It was the ear infections that kept me from hearing every first insult, every first command. It was the electric going out during every storm, but it was also my father turning the meter upside down so it would run backward and we could pay the bill. It was the creek water we weren't supposed to drink, the same water we mixed into Kool-Aid. It was watching my dad shoot his gun at a dog by the creek. Watching him whip a dog with his belt. Watching him dump a dog's body in the woods. It was riding in his truck to another man's house, where he left me sitting as he took his rifle to the man's front door. It was the truck getting repossessed and the bank's men loading the truck with our trash at gunpoint before they could drive it away.

It was complicated. It refuses to be defined.

In my childhood fairy-tale world, my father was misunderstood. Not even he understood himself like I did. I hurt for him—his pain, the oppression of living poor and being a man who felt too small. I grew up in fear of this man I loved, ready to forget his transgressions in an instant. There were so many, it seems he killed the part of himself that might have claimed redemption.

I waited for the moment when we would wake up and realize that it was all a bad dream, that my father loved us and was there to protect us, that my mom was strong and worthy of his adoration. We would share a laugh at the odd dream that seemed so real and then go about being our true selves—selves that smiled because we weren't afraid, and our teeth weren't rotting, and no one would whip you because they thought maybe you were mocking them.

That moment never came, though I was *so sure* it would—I had faith that the father I loved would someday see himself as the good man I wanted him to be. I told myself it was only a matter of time, just around the corner. But those fairy tales don't end when you turn eighteen. You become a woman looking for another man who just needs your love, your devotion, your endless forgiveness. You keep stubbornly trying, waiting for dictators to become benevolent kings.

We didn't have central air-conditioning in the house and only had a window air conditioner in the living room when I was older. We kept the doors open when it was warm, the screen doors almost keeping the bugs out. There was a door at the side of the house, in the corner of the kitchen. Sitting at the kitchen table, you could see out the door to the creek and our trash bin beside it, an open, rusted metal container where we put bags of garbage until they started to pile up, and then we would burn them, plastic and all. Junior and I usually got to burn the trash, and it was especially fun when there was a Styrofoam plate in there. We would twirl the melting Styrofoam around a stick and watch it drip, like a liquid that didn't know what it was.

One morning while we were eating breakfast, Junior and I heard screams from outside. We jumped up from the kitchen table and went to the back door, where we stared through the screen. Our father had our mother's hair in one hand, and he was using it to pull her down the road toward Granny's house—they were at least to the first post of Granny's fence that marked the boundary and kept her cows in. We watched as he used his other fist to hit our mother over and over on her head, face, whatever he could get to. It was mostly her screams that we were hearing, though his were mixed in, too. For some reason, far away as they were, he suddenly noticed us, though he didn't stop dragging her.

Time stood still. The sound of his rage and her cries tore the leaves from the trees. His fist beat her head and her back and the sun beat down the gravel road and lit our faces and their bodies, and the water glittered in the creek just steps away from where we stood, motionless. My mother hit the gravel and the gravel hit back, both of them giving up something along the way. The sun shining hard, the air still, everything coming apart then—cells, neurons, shafts of light, all broken and breaking. Something was breaking inside of me, too, something I didn't even know I needed yet.

# CHAPTER 3

## *Leaving Now*

I was twenty-five when I asked my mom why she had stayed with my father for so long. *For you kids.* I asked whether maybe it would have been better for us if she hadn't stayed with him so long. *Yeah, I can see that now,* she said.

What is it that convinces so many women—and men as well—to endure destructive relationships *for the sake of the children?* My mother must have performed some painful mental calculations to measure the devil she knew against the one she did not. How could the fear and uncertainty of what *might* happen to her children compare to what *was happening* to her children? Of course, most parents don't want to deprive their child of the other parent. But maybe the other parent is cruel every once in a while—how does that weigh against every kindness that came before it? Maybe there are certain things within a person that only come out when they are responsible for a baby or arguing with a teenager, they're out of a job, or the burden of survival is just too much. Sometimes it feels impossible to weigh the potential loss of a parent against the pain that parent might inflict. And then there are the good times—those fleeting moments when you let yourself relax, when things suddenly seem to slide into place, when you finally think, *Things are getting better.* Maybe you do that for years.

I think now that my mother believed she was staying for us kids, but where would she have gone if she *had* tried to leave? She didn't have a full-time job for most of the eighties, and no safety net of friends or family who were ready to take her—*us*—in. My father habitually recorded phone conversations and rigged doors so he would know whether they had been opened. It didn't seem like any secret was safe from him, and there would have been no mercy if he had caught her planning to leave. We weren't living in the digital age—the only technology she had to work with was whatever dilapidated car she was driving at the time. And before she could overcome those challenges, she first had to escape the mental prison that he had built around her with every insult, every threat, every beating. Somehow, she had to convince herself that despite all evidence to the contrary, she was not powerless.

But why was she there with him in the first place? Why did she endure so much, sacrifice so much? Maybe she didn't know any better. Maybe she didn't like herself enough to demand better. Maybe she told herself things were going to be okay and one day woke up to find they certainly were not but that she had nowhere to go. Does it matter?

When I was around five, my uncle showed up at our house one day, and my dad accused my mom of flirting with him. I remember my uncle had a strange look on his face, and I didn't know why he looked so calm when my dad seemed to be on the verge of wanting to fight him. Maybe it was because they were both up for a good fight. But all of a sudden, my dad rode off in my uncle's truck with him, and Mom grabbed us kids and took us through the barbed-wire and electric fences into Granny's cow field. We ran to the creek that cut through the field and got down in it to hide when my uncle's truck drove back to our house and then left again. We waited until Mom said to run, and then we ran through the creek, trying to stay low and hidden, until we were close to Granny's house.

We got there and Papaw Conn loaded us into his pickup truck, where we all bent over as far as we could so nobody could see us through the windows. On the way out of the holler, we met my uncle and dad on their way back to the house. They hadn't stayed gone long, so they must have gone about halfway up the holler, to a neighbor who sometimes grew weed with my dad. Papaw stopped to talk to them, as you always do on country roads, and we stayed crouched down and quiet. Granny sat on the far end of the truck cab, her face betraying nothing. I learned so much from watching her but never stopped to wonder where and why she had learned to show so little emotion. I was just trying to survive, and maybe she was, too.

We finally drove on to Papaw and Grandma Wright's house. We may have been there a night—it's hard to keep all that leaving straight.

I think that was the time when Mom finally told my dad he needed *help* and she wasn't coming back until he got it. The next day, he went to the sixth floor of St. Claire Regional Medical Center—the psychiatric ward—and stayed there for two weeks. We visited him, and he introduced us to a woman with dark hair and wide eyes who would trade him cigarettes for pills. He showed us what he worked on while there, plaster-of-Paris fruits that he had painted with circus hues and cartoon smiles that didn't stay in their neat lines. The orange was my favorite, with its soft peach color, but the banana was too yellow and the apple too red, their smiles too white. When he came home, he hung them up above the kitchen stove, where they stayed until the house burned down. Looking at them always unsettled me, a constant reminder of his time on the *crazy floor*, when people started using the phrase *mildly schizophrenic*, whatever that meant.

It seems like we left a lot, but the worst time for me began at the IGA grocery store in town. We often brought Ale-8 bottles there to return for ten cents apiece, which added up to quite a bit when we hauled in cases at a time, all covered in the tiny ants that invaded our kitchen whenever it was warm, forming a marching line toward the trash can. We would store the Ale-8 bottles on the front porch, where the ants had all the access they could hope for to the sweet residue in the bottom of each bottle. I have pictures of me, three years old or so, holding a Pepsi bottle up to send the last of the pop into my mouth. I have a lot of pictures of myself from that age and onward to when my two front teeth visibly decayed. For the rest of my life, the sugar and the phosphoric acid from those pops changed the way I smiled.

It was usually my mom and us kids who hauled the bottles to the window in the corner of the store, where some man would take them to the back and give Mom the voucher for the cash. I watched, wondering whether the man minded all those ants and what happened to them once they were taken to the back of the store. Did they escape? Did they settle there, in the mysterious dark room in the back of the IGA, to live a comfortable life? Or did the man kill them, angry that we had brought them out of the holler?

For a few years, Mom would drive Junior and me everywhere in our brown Chevette. It often wouldn't start right away, and Mom would have us kids push it for a bit, and then she could pop the clutch to get it running. Junior and I would run to the car and hop in with it still moving. It was usually easy for us to push the car when we started at our driveway, since the road from our house to Granny's traveled on a slight downward slope. It was a little tricky to open the doors and hop in with the car moving, but we learned. As an adult, I learned to pop a clutch myself, even pushing a pickup truck while alone and pregnant, with the driver-side door open, until I had enough momentum to jump in and roll downhill with the clutch down and to hit the gas at just the right moment. As a kid, though, it was not so easy when the county roads department laid fresh gravel, since the thick, loose rocks were difficult to run on and we slipped more often. Much of the time, the road was worn smooth where the car and truck tires rolled over it, and a narrow path of rough gravel marked the center of the road.

One time in the IGA parking lot, a man noticed us, my brother and I still in grade school, trying to push the car fast enough for Mom to get it started. It was harder in the flat parking lot, without gravity on our side. The stranger came and helped, which struck me as odd at the time, and the look on his face told me he thought something was odd, too. As a kid, I couldn't push as fast as he could, so when he told us to get in the car and let him push, I did, and we rolled away. I'm sure Papaw Wright could have fixed the car with no problem. He owned and ran a successful garage all my life, and most of my mother's life, too. I imagine he would have wanted to fix it, knowing she was driving around with us children. I imagine it was my father who liked the car that way, always leaving my mother uncertain and with the threat of being stranded looming over her.

But once, there was a glimmer of something else in her when we arrived at the IGA. We didn't make it out of the car. Instead of opening her door, Mom stopped us with a strange look on her face. *Do you all just want to leave?*

I didn't know what she meant. I knew we were there for groceries, maybe some macaroni and cheese, and I didn't quite like the idea of whatever she was saying. She added, *I've saved up some money. We could just leave your dad. We don't have to go back.* I was the last to say *okay.* We went to the Super 8 Motel by the interstate, which was pretty nice because it had two beds and a color TV. Soon, we were on the phone with Dad, telling him we weren't coming back. He talked to Mom first and then to my brother, neither of them showing any emotion. They handed the phone to me and Dad was crying, begging me to come home, he would be different, everything would be different. He claimed he needed us, and that's all I needed to hear. I couldn't believe how callous my mom and brother had been, knowing Dad was *so sorry* for everything. Mom asked what I thought we should do, and I told her we should go back, Dad *promised* things would be better, and how could we leave him like this? We went back that night.

I had learned by then that his feelings were the most important in the family, that his moments of regret—authentic or not—were more important than whatever we felt at any time. I needed to forgive him like God forgave me for being such a sinner. None of us deserved forgiveness from our *heavenly father*, so who was I to withhold it from my *earthly father*? Who was allowed to be vengeful? Who was allowed to be angry?

I knew later that it was my fault, that Mom and Junior were ready for it to end, but I had dragged us back. The next time he beat her or made us cower or threatened someone, I knew I had let that happen. I had fallen for it, foolishly, when Mom and Junior knew better. But I wanted him to love us, and so when he cried, I thought it was the moment I had been waiting for—the moment he finally wanted us and knew how important we were to him.

I wanted to please, to avoid wrath. It was a devastating alchemy of abuse and religious fear, and I accepted my constant inner hell as punishment for how unworthy I was. Desperate to earn God's love, my father's love—anyone's love—I forgave in an instant, full of hope for some imaginary future. Like so many women before me and since, I learned that you go back, you stick it out, you love the man until he is saved by your sacrifice. It's the kind of thing you can always see going so badly in someone else's life, but not in your own.

～

Each time we went back, things were good for a few days, and sometimes for as long as a week. There were roses one time, and I told Mom, *That was nice of him.* She snorted a laugh and replied, *Sure, I'm the one who will have to pay for them.* My guess is that we all paid for them, in one way or another.

I thought my mom would leave us all only once. I was about six. My brother and I were playing outside and ran into the house when we heard her screams. I thought Dad was killing her, it was so much louder than the normal screaming. Instead, I found them squared off on either side of the kitchen table, and she was armed with a heavy antique kitchen scale. She was raging. I had never seen her so angry. She usually only looked scared when they fought. When he noticed us, my dad took the opportunity to mock her. *Look, kids—look at your mother. She's crazy, she's fucked up.*

His laughter was derisive and shook me. I didn't know what to think, how to make sense of her rage, her impending violence. Then he said the most shocking thing of all: *You'd better straighten up, or I'm going to take these kids and leave.* He had never threatened to take us before, and I implicitly knew he didn't want us. I was begging *please no* in my mind when she screamed, *Take them! Take them and get out of here, just leave me alone! I don't care anymore!*

I wondered in horror what would happen to us if he took us away. He might kill us, he might whip us, we might never see anyone we love again. I was more frightened then than ever, thinking she would sacrifice us for good, one last time, and we would be lost to the world. It didn't happen, of course. My father sent us to the car and we waited there for about fifteen minutes, but it was my mother who came and told us to get out, that we weren't leaving. I searched her face for some explanation, but it wasn't there. I never asked her what had happened, how it was that she was ready to watch us leave. I don't know who backed down first, but I imagine it was her. And I imagine that it was not my father's love that made her change her mind but that he spelled out the consequences for her if she didn't *put that fucking scale down right now*, and she started seeing things his way.

There was another time when she talked back to him, and I watched him grow more agitated. I wasn't even ten, but I asked her, *Why don't you just go along with what he says, make him happy?* It wasn't really a question—I was agitated, too. I knew that she knew what to do, how to survive—we all did. What was the point of fighting back? There would only be hell to pay. Some part of me knew that he was still in the wrong, of course, and that my mother had every right to stand up for herself. But I didn't care. I didn't have the emotional resources to always care about what was wrong or right or fair—I just wanted things to be bearable. I didn't want to wonder again what he was going to do to her, to us, to anyone we loved.

All that time, I was going to church every Sunday morning with Granny. Between church and God and all the uncensored reading I did, I developed my own superstitious faith in the unseen. Grandma Wright didn't go to church but chain-smoked and gave me grocery bags full of her tabloids—usually *Star*, which I would read cover to cover, intrigued by the lovers and wives, the breakups, and the scandalous red-carpet outfits. One time, there was a *Sun* in a bag she gave me, and I read it thinking it would be like *Star*. I found out pretty quickly it was more like the *National Enquirer* that sometimes appeared at Grandma's house but that I usually saw at the grocery checkout lines.

But in that issue of *Sun*, there was a set of instructions on how to make your deepest wish come true. In the lower right-hand corner of one of the pages, the tabloid gave directions to fold a new one-dollar bill in a particular order, place it in a new white handkerchief, put the handkerchief under one's pillow, and imagine what it was one longed for the most. And then, the instructions claimed—*abracadabra*—the wish would be granted.

It seemed so simple, but I wondered what exactly they meant by a *new* dollar bill. I could not find one in our house that was less than a few years old, but I thought I would give it a try anyway. My father had lots of handkerchiefs that he carried with him. None of them were in new condition, though. I went into my parents' bedroom as nonchalantly as I could and picked one that looked the whitest, thinking it would have to do. Back in my bedroom, I followed the directions for folding the dollar bill and handkerchief exactly so and looked forward to lying down that night.

I was not sure what I would wish for, but as I thought about it in the dark, I quickly started dreaming. *I am sleeping in a large white bed, covered by a pristine white comforter. My bedroom has beautiful wooden walls. My father walks in and I sit up, propping myself with the thick, soft pillows behind me. He is wearing a white suit and looks strong, healthy. He sits on my bed and says,* I just want to say thank you—thank you for showing me the light. *And I am relieved, proud, knowing I have finally saved him.*

Many years later, a boyfriend would tell me that it was *dark magic,* that my father's white suit marked him as a deceiver, that Lucifer was the *light bearer,* and that it was a spirit trying to trick me. For years, I just waited to see whether it would come true.

I didn't know yet that his cruelty and coldness never had anything to do with us, with how lovable we were, how good or bad we had been. As an adult, I could intellectualize it. I could talk about his own self-loathing, about projection, about abuse and cycles and emptiness, etc., ad infinitum. Eventually, I came to have a little more compassion for myself and for my life, which always seemed to be more difficult and a little more ugly than other people's lives. I realized how hard it is to manage a bank account and bills, and not smoke cigarettes or drink or some other form of self-medicating, when you still carry that feeling from childhood that tells you death is near, and you very well might die at the hands of someone you love, someone you need. And besides, I was reminded every Sunday in church that the world would end in decidedly unpleasant ways—probably any minute now—and that I was most likely going to Hell. It is hard to get your act together when you are waiting for the Apocalypse.

But inside, even at twenty, thirty, thirty-five years old, after becoming a mother myself and finding pity for my father who could not love us nor be loved, I still found myself hoping that before he died, I would know how it felt to have a father who loved me.

# CHAPTER 4

## *Sunday Morning*

Everyone knows, of course, that the only father you really need to worry about is the one in Heaven. He's the one whose judgment really matters, the one who can make Hell last forever. Half the time in church, that's what I thought about, full of fear and trembling—that some pain is endless, that some things burn relentlessly. That my heavenly father could hate me, despise me, revile me no matter what I did, because I was born into sin, and damn if nothing seemed to help, no matter how hard I prayed.

That's the only thing that made sense after I had learned so many Bible verses and cleaned my room and even made the teachers at school proud, but still felt like something was tearing me apart from within. All the awful things I felt inside must have been because I was such a sinner, even though I wasn't sure exactly what I had done wrong. I just *knew* that something was terribly wrong inside me. The hell I was in was just a promise of what was yet to come, if I didn't fix myself. If I didn't make it right.

But half the time, there was Jesus and the New Testament with its relative gentleness. I read most of the Bible alone, sometimes fervently preparing for Sunday school so I could win a mini-Snickers candy bar for memorizing my verses—which I was particularly good at—but mostly so I could go to Heaven, or at least have a fighting chance.

We read only from the King James Version of the Bible, which was so full of poetic language, so many *thou*s and *breadth*s, I was fully prepared to study philosophy and poetry in college but didn't know that yet.

Learning Bible stories from soft, old women with white hair made it easy to believe in Heaven. But then that older boy took me downstairs to a Sunday school classroom while everyone else listened to the sermon upstairs. He took me to the room I was supposed to go to after kindergarten and sat me on his lap as he pulled my shirt out from my skirt.

The skirt was dark blue, with a red hippopotamus embroidered on it. My shirt was light blue, a button-up, and had a scalloped collar. It's the same outfit I am wearing in a picture taken of my brother and me, a picture that hung in my granny's house for as long as I can remember.

The boy's grandparents were friends of my grandparents, and they called each other *Brother* and *Sister* in church. His grandfather had worked with my papaw Conn. The grandmother sang in the choir, and I loved the way she stood in front of the whole church sometimes, singing in a trembly voice: *Amazing grace, how sweet the sound, that saved a wretch like me.*

I saw the boy again when I was seventeen and attending church with my granny in a rare effort to please her with my potential to go to Heaven. He sat by his pretty wife in church; she held their baby. I watched them, wondering whether he remembered that day and recognized me. I prayed that whatever had led him to touch me had faded long ago, was forever extinguished, that his baby was safe.

I don't know that he didn't do more on that Sunday morning. I don't remember any physical pain or exactly what I felt other than a great, uneasy fear. I avoided that church classroom afterward, going so far as to stay in the younger Sunday school class for a year, rather than sit with the other kids my age in that room. My granny tried to convince me to go to the next class, but I claimed I just loved my Sunday school teacher too much and didn't want to leave her, which everyone eventually accepted. I wouldn't attend activities in that room and instead lingered elsewhere, around other Sunday school teachers, whenever all the other young children were gathered there. At the time, I didn't consciously think about what had happened, but I knew I didn't like the way I felt in that room. I still remember the way the tables looked, where the door was situated, the coolness of the air around us when he pulled me to him.

My parents didn't go to church with my granny except sometimes on Easter, and they encouraged us to pray in only one situation. They would tell us to go to one of our beds—mine or my brother's—and, in the dark, put our faces down to the bed and close our eyes. Then, as sincerely and excitedly as possible, we were to pray for Reese's Cups. We obeyed, and you know how God is good and if you ask, you will receive? Well, within just a few minutes of our praying, Reese's Cups would suddenly come raining down from above, and we would gather them up and take them to the living room. Our parents would ask, *Did God answer your prayers?* And we would say, *Yes, look at our Reese's Cups!* I didn't know whether they realized we knew they threw the candy in through the open door, and I never began to understand why they wanted us to pray for such a thing. Maybe there was some satisfaction in watching us ask for something they could deliver. I was embarrassed by the whole charade but kept it up, just like they told us to.

Despite my parents' lack of interest, I still wanted to be a good Christian. When I was nine, I decided to get baptized—I had been saved countless times at the altar, and I thought maybe going a step further with baptism would make the good feeling last longer. I wore a flowery dress, and in front of the whole church, our preacher, who looked a little like someone from *The Munsters*, dunked me backward into what was basically a large bathtub with a nature scene behind us.

Granny was waiting for me when I walked out sopping wet into the back room, and she asked me how I felt. I answered her, *Perfect,* and she assured me, *You are.*

But even after being baptized, I couldn't shake the feeling that something was terribly wrong. After a couple of weeks, I found myself listening intently to the sermon, straining to hear God's voice. All that happened, though, was that at the end of each service, the preacher would beseech all the sinners to *give it up, walk down that aisle, and give yourselves to God.* He was waiting for us, waiting to welcome us into the Kingdom of Heaven, and all we had to do was ask.

I thought he was talking to me because we both knew I was so awful inside, something wasn't right. Maybe the devil had gotten me, or I had committed so much sin without even meaning to. So again and again, I asked. I walked down the aisle, sick with fear, and cried at the altar beside my granny, who knelt and cried there every Sunday. Sometimes we prayed together. Sometimes she gave me her wet tissues to blow my nose into. I begged to be forgiven for my sins, for all the impurities that must have been making me feel like I was being torn apart nearly all the time. Sometimes the preacher came over and laid his hand on our shoulders and prayed with us, and I thought that might help. Sometimes he didn't, and we made our way back to the pews at the end of the service, but nothing felt different. After a while, I realized that the preacher knew my granny didn't need to be saved. Somehow, he knew she was there for the people she loved.

I wonder now whether anyone was puzzled by my weekly trek to the front of the church—there certainly weren't any other children up there. Did they think I was a zealot? That I was a child of God and able to hear him so clearly? Or perhaps, like my friends' mothers and some doting teachers, they simply thought that despite their concern, there was nothing they could do for me.

Growing up in a holler as we did in the 1980s and in eastern Kentucky, it was perfectly normal to get whipped as punishment. Dad often used his leather belt, but both our parents would sometimes make us go pick our own switches, and the only ones nearby were from those thorny black locust trees. The sting of the switch was accompanied by thorns tearing the skin of our legs or bare bottoms, so my brother and I were both pretty set on avoiding switchings and whippings as much as possible.

Sometimes I would stare out the kitchen window at the big black locust tree that grew there, thinking how uninviting it was with its thorns and hardness. Not the weeping willows of my fantasies, where I imagined that one day I would live with the tree spirits, despite never having been told a story about tree spirits or, at that point, having seen an actual weeping willow.

We ate like poor people in that kitchen. Lots of baloney sandwiches, lots of Kool-Aid. Sometimes, when Dad wasn't home and we had very little, my mom, brother, and I would share a can of beans for dinner. When Dad was there, we ate cautiously, hoping not to arouse his ire. That took some finesse, though, since there really was no predicting his anger.

But I use the word *poor* as if it were a simple word, as if you should understand. Being poor will always be married in my mind to the other, intangible sorts of poverty that infused my childhood. One night, the large black locust tree became a site for my knowledge of poverty when my mother, my brother, and I crushed aluminum cans beneath it. I started to stomp them onto one of the cinder blocks that formed our back steps, since that was easier than crushing them on the wet ground. My mother corrected me and had me move my cans back to the ground, saying we needed to mash them where some of the mud would get into them. That way, she said, they would weigh more when we took them to the aluminum recycling place.

I didn't know exactly what that meant about us, but I remember feeling ashamed when the large, dirty-looking man weighed our bags of cans. Surely he knew that part of the weight was from something other than aluminum. I avoided looking at my mother's face, hoping she wouldn't also have to feel the shame if she didn't see it in me. After all, we needed the money to buy milk.

We always knew someone poorer than we were, though. A family who lived in a bus. A little girl who had worms coming out of her nose, she was so infested with parasites. A man who liked to burn his son's arms with a lighter and then pull the scabs off and cover them with shaving cream. There was always something worse.

Ten years after my last whipping, a friend came to my house before we went to a party. We cooked steaks—she was on her period and craving meat. I watched them sizzle in the pan as my thoughts drifted, until I heard the zipping sound of her belt as she pulled it from her belt loops, frustrated with the constriction around her stomach. The look on my face when I wheeled around, still flinching, told her everything.

*Easy, girl,* she said. *I'm not your daddy.*

It was nice, in a way, to have someone who in that moment knew what had happened inside me, without me having to explain. Most people would have responded with a blank look, and then some sympathy after I explained my reaction with nervous laughter. If you don't know how it feels, there is no understanding that kind of fear. She was also the first person who knew, before I even said it, that it was hard to date a man with money, someone from a different class.

The day I agreed to call my granny a whore, I didn't get a switching, but I knew I had traded on something precious to save my *self*, my skin, my body. It was an impossible choice, at that age: to face my father's rage with no one to defend me, wondering how far he would go, or to insult my grandmother, the one person who made me feel safe and loved and seen. There was shame at either end, and a great question about who I was, who I could be in such a world. About why everything was so pretty around me, yet I felt so ugly inside.

# CHAPTER 5

## *Gifted*

One day in first grade, I shuffled to the balance beam in dejection. My best friend was playing with another girl who was younger and seemed to smile and laugh a lot. Even then, I had a sense that I wasn't as happy as other children, and most of them had a carefree air that I couldn't quite understand. Like they weren't always watching, on alert and taking note of the world around them.

My friend came to me and asked me what was wrong, and I told her how sad I was that she had another friend. She comforted me but told me that she could have other friends and still like me. That didn't make sense to me, though—I knew the world as a place where there is only so much love to go around, a finite amount of attention and care that any one person can give. My friend had dimples and a sweet smile, and her blue eyes lit up easily. I had felt lucky that she liked me, and it seemed that this was the end of my good fortune.

In fact, she did continue to be a friend, but I never again felt sure that any friend was there for good. It would take years—decades, even—to understand that all my relationships perfectly met my low expectations. That it was not bad luck or a curse that doomed me to feel constant loss, but that my beliefs about the world would shape everything around me, that my childhood trauma would render it all as if *through a glass, darkly.*

Still, as a child, I loved being at school, and when I look back to those early years, I remember laughing with my classmates and feeling like we were all friends. In second grade, a boy in my class and I came up with nicknames for ourselves by spelling our names backward. His worked out to something that sounded like *Carrie*, and mine was pronounced *E-bob.*

Almost twenty-five years later, I looked at the county jail website and saw that he was there, still in our hometown. He probably did not do as well in school as I did and likely had a hard time finding a decent job. His parents may have abused him, or he may have been raised by grandparents, or he may still live with his parents when he's not in jail. Whenever I look up inmates in the county jail, I inevitably see former classmates in there for burglary, robbery, methamphetamine manufacturing, narcotics trafficking, driving while intoxicated, and so on. I see grown boys I had crushes on, and I search their faces, looking for their stories.

This particular boy was a quiet, good-natured friend who had slightly chubby cheeks and a matter-of-fact air about him. In his mug shot, he stands in front of a cinder-block wall and stares straight into the camera, revealing nothing in his gaze. I search his eyes for some detail, some betrayal that will tell me how he got there. I wonder whether he is still kind or if he has come to hate the adults who failed him and now hates everyone else and himself in turn. I wonder whether he will find his way out or trudge along in a cycle of incarceration, joblessness, desperation, drug abuse, and, finally, a lonely death.

Or, I wonder, could he become a brilliant engineer or poet? Where does his passion lie? What is the spark inside him that gives him hope life is worth living and, even more, life still holds a promise of happiness in some unwritten future? I think about touching his soft cheeks and reminding him how we sat in the hallway in our elementary school, how I was studying spelling bee words, how we didn't think of ourselves as being any different from anyone else. How laughter came so easily, how we enjoyed that moment, no matter what else was haunting us from home and no matter the nightmares that would not stay put in the darkness, where they belonged.

In fourth grade, I entered the county school system's *gifted* program and was the only person from my school to do so at the time. I rode the bus alone from our little school, which sat near the same creek that flowed by my house, to the combined elementary and middle school in town. For one day a week, I went to this new place, meeting strangers and suddenly surrounded by throngs of people. I had no idea how to do anything I was supposed to do—I was constantly afraid I would get on the wrong bus and end up in another town, or I would go to the wrong room and be lost forever.

There were about fifteen other kids in the program, all from various schools in the county, and we would have our weekly gifted school day in a room adjacent to the basement library of the elementary wing. I thought all the other kids knew each other, though they probably did not. Almost everyone, though, seemed to possess a sort of ease, a self-assurance that they knew what to do and they were certain that what they were doing was good. We had Spanish lessons, and we learned about current events. It was the first I ever heard of the Soviet Union and the man with the strange red birthmark on his forehead. We learned about other cultures and had international food days, where our teacher made a Japanese chicken dish and we all said *konnichiwa*.

Early in the school year, we were given "About Me" sheets to fill out so we could get to know each other. It was a list of our favorites—favorite song, favorite television show, favorite food, etc. At that time, I had never heard any music except what played on the one country music station that reached our holler, and a few of the records my parents owned—a lot of country, a little Janis Joplin. My favorite musician was Ricky Skaggs or George Jones—people my classmates had never heard of.

When I took that sheet home from my gifted class to try to tell my classmates "About Me," I sat in my father's recliner and read the sentences and thought about the blanks we were supposed to fill in. *Tell them about me.*

One of the questions asked, "If you could be any other person, who would you be?" My immediate thought was that I didn't want to be anyone else, because if I was someone else, someone else would have to be me, and nobody else could do it. I was nine, and I gave it no further thought. I don't remember whether I filled in the blanks so my teacher would be happy with my effort, but in that moment, it seemed imperative that I be *me*, and accept being *me*, so I could do whatever it was I needed to do. So it would all make sense in the end, this unbearable life I had.

Though I tried my best to figure out what I was supposed to do in my gifted class and did well in my work, I did not have what it took to succeed socially with the other students. I continued the program in the fifth grade—we all rode a bus to the board of education building, where we held our weekly class in a large conference room. Like dogs, wolves, and flocks of chickens, the kids had figured out a pecking order where I was at the bottom. They particularly enjoyed calling me *Boobie*, which tormented me to the point that my mother wrote our teacher a letter and told her I wanted to quit the program. The teacher took a few of the kids aside and told them to stop, and for a while it seemed they gave up that particular way of taunting me.

At one point, I told them about my nickname from grade school, *E-bob*, thinking it would be a preferable nickname to hear from them. I didn't realize, though, that anything they did or said would take on a hurtful edge, and the silly nickname that I had helped create and laughed about with my friend became the subject of songs, chants, and endless cruel jokes in my weekly gifted class. They seemed to take a lot of pleasure in provoking me, though most of the time I either glowered silently or cried with frustration and exhaustion.

Once, as we waited for the bus to take us to the board of education building, I sat on the front steps of the elementary school in town with my *science project*. We were given pretty loose parameters for constructing a science project, and I had no idea how to do one. My mother bought me a figure of the Statue of Liberty from the dollar store that, when placed in water, would expand over several days. I had never seen such a thing, and though I had a nagging doubt that it did not qualify as a scientific experiment, I did my best to make it work. I carefully cleaned an empty glass Tang jar from Grandma Wright's house and peeled the label off, then placed the figure in it and measured the amount of water I could add. I also measured the figure as it expanded, but before long, it outgrew the jar and sat contorted, the substance all soft and grotesque and Miss Liberty looking anything but regal. But I had nothing else to use, so I took it to school and hoped it would be acceptable to my teacher.

My fears about my misshapen Statue of Liberty were quickly confirmed by the other students, who began making fun of me in earnest while we waited for the bus to take us to class. I felt my face grow hot, and I tried to ignore them for a few minutes, but they were standing in front of me as I sat on a step at one side of the school entrance. They didn't seem likely to grow tired of their game that particular morning. I couldn't think of anything else to do, so I moved from one side of the school door to the other, desperate to get away from them and their mockery. When I sat back down on the steps, I slammed my Tang jar onto the concrete in rage, and the glass shattered while I was still holding on to it. Pieces of the jar flew away from me, and my swollen Statue of Liberty fell out, all her water lost around us. My classmates were suddenly silent and stared at me with wide eyes, and I ran into the school toward the bathroom, afraid of what I had done but relieved that they were finally quiet.

The tears fell hot down my face, and a man in the hallway looked at me, asking, *How are you doing today?* I didn't recognize him and assumed he was a teacher. I paused for a second and responded, *If I was any better, I would be dead.* He gave a concerned, *Aw, don't say that,* but I was already walking again. I rinsed my red face in the bathroom and ignored the girls who came in, too angry to feel embarrassed in that moment. When I went back outside to catch our bus, my classmates had gathered my things together, picked up the broken glass, and salvaged what was left of Miss Liberty. I was surprised by their rare kindness but got on the bus silently and did not acknowledge it. When my anger subsided, we were right back to the same roles.

I understand now that there were, in fact, other children like me—though they weren't likely to be in the gifted classes with me. The gifted program was full of kids whose parents liked them, or at least signed them up for gymnastics lessons and took them to get their teeth cleaned and all the things that were foreign to me. On normal school days, I was around other kids whose parents drank too much or did pills, who hit them with belts and mostly just didn't want to hear the kid make any noise. Not all of them were like that, but because we were in a poor part of the county, I didn't stick out like a sore thumb. There were plenty of other kids with their own personal hell burning inside them as we tried to memorize capital cities and the names of all our presidents and multiplication tables.

My little elementary school was mostly a haven, where my teachers liked me and I didn't stand out too much. Some days, though, after I turned in my work and was drawing or reading while the other kids finished, in my head I would hear my mother screaming like she was in two worlds at once, being beaten by my father some two miles away and coming to me at the same time, reminding me that something was always wrong. I didn't stop to think about it, but I somehow knew that the other kids weren't torn apart by what came from finishing their work and sitting in stillness, no longer distracted from their mothers' distant screams. I knew I wasn't like them.

# CHAPTER 6

## *The Dark of Night*

Growing up, I learned that although holidays were the best thing ever, there was also a very real chance that something would go wrong anytime we gathered for a family meal or opened presents. We went to Grandma Wright's on Christmas Eve, but we went to Granny Conn's house for most other holidays. Granny cooked all the food you could ever want in eastern Kentucky: turkey, ham, chicken and dumplings, mashed potatoes, corn bread, Stove Top stuffing, green beans from her garden, corn that she grew, and macaroni and tomatoes (made with her own canned tomatoes).

She insisted on giving me her canned vegetables long after I stopped appreciating them, and then after I started again. I remember the day I opened the last Mason jar of tomatoes she ever canned and gave to me. I held on to it like the treasure it was and still thank whoever is listening that I had sense enough to know its value.

On Christmas Eve, Grandma Wright usually baked a ham with pineapple rings—we didn't have pineapple anywhere else—but there was pizza, too. Nobody would deliver up in our holler, so we usually had pizza only at Grandma's. They got normal television, so Papaw Wright would be watching racing, wrestling, or *The Andy Griffith Show*. I always gave Grandma chocolate-covered cherries and gave Papaw a tin of cashews or walnuts still in the shell. I wrapped them with care, each time so proud I could give them something they loved.

I walked to my bedroom door one day not long before Christmas to find that my bed and floor were covered with plants, drying and sending off a scent that reminded me of the smell that came from my parents' bedroom sometimes.

My dad told me not to go in—*That's your Christmas.* And he laughed often about the way Christmas came for us, a good harvest that was quickly spent on the things we couldn't afford the rest of the year. Tax returns were like that sometimes, too—we got the Nintendo that one year, and my brother and I played Duck Hunt as much as we could stand it but played Super Mario Bros. until we beat it. Every time we went to a grocery store, I searched the magazine aisle for a cheat book and could usually memorize one cheat to use once we got back to the looming violence of our home.

When I was around six years old, Christmas Eve came, and my brother was eager to open a gift—*Just one,* he said—and my mother said we could. Dad wasn't home. I admonished them: *How could you all think of opening presents while our dad is out there working to make money for us on Christmas Eve?* My mother was as disgusted with me as I was with her: *Your dad's not working—he's drinking with his friends. Do you want to open a present or not?*

I opened the gift she handed me, but I was too young to pretend I wasn't crushed. That night, I slept on the couch until he stumbled through the door. He went to wake up my mother while I pretended to sleep in case he started hitting her.

My brother and I would get up in the mornings and check with each other. *Did you hear it?* I'd ask him. *Yeah. Did you?* We didn't really discuss the details. One night, I awoke to her cries, and I heard the sound of his fists. Then, *If you wake those goddamn kids up, I swear I will kill your fucking parents, you hear me?* He threw open my bedroom door, flipped the light on, and stood above me, looking for a flicker of awareness to betray me. After a minute—a few minutes? a lifetime?—he turned off my light, shut the door, and went to do the same thing in my brother's room. I knew Junior must be pretending to be asleep, too, fearing for our lives, her life, our grandma's and papaw's lives.

It is remarkable how good I became at hiding my feelings. I learned to keep my face blank, hold back tears, lower my eyes, and to lie when it really mattered. You would think this kind of skill would come in handy later in life—I could be an expert poker player, or an actress, or maybe even a politician. But still, I felt things too deeply—the hiding never lessened the intensity of all that *feeling*. As I grew older, I hid my emotions and pushed down my feelings in all my relationships, which was actually somewhat beneficial since I kept finding myself surrounded by people who reminded me of my father in some way. But all that hiding, all that silence, makes you vulnerable in a different way.

My six-year-old Christmas Eve, though, ended up being less violent than those kinds of occasions often were. Dad told us all to wake up, and as he fell to the floor and into the coffee table, as he cussed and pushed and threatened, we got our coats on. He wanted to go to the little country store owned by a woman named Birdie. That little country store should be on a calendar somewhere, one that depicts the simplicity of quiet country living. There was room for only two or three cars to park at one time, and you walked up worn wooden steps to get to the front door. Weathered wooden slats covered the outside, and white paint chips fell from the boards in a year-round, lead-based snow. Inside, it was just one room that held a child's dream of candy. All the pops were in hard glass bottles, and on the counter sat two obscenely large jars, one filled with giant pickles, the other with unnaturally pink pork franks. Birdie had white hair even when I was young. She seemed soft, like old age was treating her mercifully.

I still think of Birdie and that little store, and I long for the moments I remember in there, picking out candy cigarettes—the best ones had a bit of color at the end, which made it easier to pretend you were really smoking.

Everything was dark and closed, but Dad wanted a pop from the machine on the front porch of the store. Mom drove, and Dad grabbed the steering wheel over and over, pulling our long yellow Buick toward the creek, into the other lane, everywhere, as Junior and I sat silent in the back seat, at a time before children wore seat belts. There was the creek that bordered our one-lane gravel road, and then there was another creek across from Birdie's. I don't know how Mom kept us out of either one. Somehow, we did not die, and Dad got the Grape Crush he wanted. The next day, we waited until the afternoon to open our presents. From his bed, we heard him: *Tell those little motherfuckers to be quiet out there. My head hurts, and I don't want to hear a fucking sound.* I was still young enough to be surprised, at that point. Still young enough to think, *Surely he doesn't mean that.*

~

The holiday I looked forward to the most was the Fourth of July. My dad's cousin would bring his family from Tennessee, including a daughter close to my age and a son close to my brother's age. Their middle child, a girl, had the hard lot of trying to fit in somewhere, anywhere. They would show up with a trunk load of fireworks that were illegal in Kentucky, and we would grill hamburgers and hot dogs and fry potatoes in aluminum foil, waiting for the sun to set. The adults would drink their cheap drinks, and my dad would give us liberal sips of beer or hard liquor while his cousin wasn't looking. Then they would slip off to smoke a joint or maybe snort some pills while we caught lightning bugs, impatiently passing the time until we could watch the jumping jacks burn up the grass and experience the pure novelty of the Roman candle. The next day, we'd all go camping on the other side of Cave Run Lake, the biggest tourist attraction from there to Winchester.

The lake was built by flooding part of the Daniel Boone National Forest, but it happens that my great-grandmother—Granny's mother—owned land down there, too. The Army Corps of Engineers dammed the Licking River after paying, I'm sure, a terribly fair price for her land. By the 1960s, when the project began, the US government had watched while speculators bought the lumber and mineral rights from Appalachians, and those robber barons left the region polluted and broken. Even as a child, I knew we weren't supposed to trust politicians.

I grew up knowing that fact in the same way we knew not to pick up a snake—not because someone told me, but because it was necessary to survival. Listening to the news that Papaw Conn sometimes watched, I heard about promises of a brighter future, good jobs, better pay—but those things just didn't seem to make it to the poor people around me. How would someone like my father get a good job anyway, without a high school diploma?

The politicians who made these promises didn't look like us or talk like us. They always seemed to be talking out of both sides of their mouths—saying whatever they thought their audience wanted to hear and changing the message accordingly. Besides all that, it would have taken sacrifice to truly address the reality of poverty and the many kinds of despair in this country. Despair takes on a different look, depending on where you go, but those who have lived it can see it in others. No, the kind of sacrifice it takes to make real change isn't glamorous, and it's not a sure bet you'll get reelected or even recognized. Why would anybody want to stick their neck out for some ungrateful rednecks? At some point in my childhood, it seemed like the long-standing cultural disdain toward Appalachia became mutual.

None of that bothered us kids, of course, as we swam in the lake that drowned my great-grandmother's home, as we ran through the tame forest, picking up sticks for the grown-ups to build a fire. In retrospect, those vacations seemed to always go so well because the adults had plenty of beer, weed, and pills on hand. If it could have been that simple all the time, I would have loved to have seen my dad drunk and high. At home, though, he wasn't prone to being jovial unless someone else was around, and if he just couldn't get what he was looking for—well, we all suffered with him.

One particular year—1987?—something went wrong as we waited for our cousins to arrive for what was usually a whole week of Dad being mostly bearable. Junior and I were playing in the front yard when he yelled for us to come to the living room, and right away we recognized that as a bad sign. Sitting in his recliner, he was holding a tape recorder, one that my brother and I used to make recordings of ourselves telling stories and talking in funny voices, and sometimes my brother would record the sounds of our parents having sex. I thought we were going to be in trouble for something my dad had found recorded, but instead, the battery cover was missing from the back of the tape recorder, and the batteries along with it. He started out asking us, with unusual calm, *Who did this? You're not in trouble, just tell me.* Neither of us said anything. *Was it you?* He asked us both, and we each denied removing the battery cover. *Who was it then?* One of us offered that maybe it was our cousin, the daring one, the one who got whipped a lot. Dad didn't think it was him.

The more he asked, the more his voice betrayed an agitation that told me we were, in fact, getting closer to trouble. Still, we both denied removing the battery cover until he was calm again and said, *Fine, I'll whip you both and send you to bed, and there will be no fireworks for either one of you.* I knew he would follow through on the threat, and I looked at my brother, my one confidante and fellow prisoner there. I always felt like Junior was nicer than I was, and maybe more fragile, for some reason. He grew up to be nearly a foot taller than me and by no means a scrawny man, but back then, I wanted to protect him and thought I could maybe take a whipping better than he could, maybe it hurt him more since he was smaller. It also seemed terribly unjust that neither of us would get to see the fireworks, when both of us were innocent.

I took a small step forward and told our father, *I did it.* His calm gave way to rage, and he demanded over and over to know why I did it, but I couldn't answer him and didn't know what to say, so I stood there saying, *I don't know,* which might have been his least favorite thing. After a few more minutes of demanding that I explain myself, he finally got to the whipping, bringing his belt across my bottom and wherever else it landed. Was it three times? Four? More? It was excruciating. I knew the Bible said it was good for me, but I wasn't sure my father did it out of love. Could he save my soul even if he didn't mean to?

The worst part about my father's whippings was that afterward, we were not allowed to cry in his presence. If we cried, he said, *Dry it up, or I'll give you something to cry about.* And my brother and I would suck it all back in—the tears, the cries, the yelps—so he would not be further enraged. I held in my cries until he sent me to my room, where I threw myself on my bed and sobbed into my pillow as quietly as I could.

When my mother came to check on me, I told her I hadn't done it. She said she knew, so I asked her why she let him whip me. *You know how your father is,* she said. At that moment, I began to understand how each of us—my brother, my mother, and myself—were very much alone in that house. In my child's mind, I felt the most alone of all.

I didn't know why I wanted to protect my brother, and why no one could protect me. I didn't understand what happens to people when they are just trying to survive. I couldn't have told you that, as a girl, I felt like I had a duty to my family, a responsibility that was God given or something close to it. As if I was the only one who could save us.

# CHAPTER 7

## *What We Can Fix*

On our one-lane gravel road, my brother and I had more freedom with cars than most. From the time we were three or four, we were often allowed to sit on our parents' laps and steer the car as they drove from our house to Granny and Papaw Conn's, since it was such a short distance and there was so little traffic on our road. Of course, there were no police patrols and no neighbors close enough to see anything that happened at our house. The best treat was when our father would let us sit on the hood of the car, which he started letting us do when I was about six, and we would press ourselves against the hood or windshield, hanging on to nothing as he drove.

Those adventures usually seemed safe enough, as even our dad must have decided it was best not to lose a kid off the hood of a car. Sometimes, though, when there was a dog around, the dog would somehow get in front of the car, and suddenly Dad would accelerate. The car would be right on top of the dog, who was by then running as fast as he could. Junior and I would scream and yell for our dad to slow down and be careful, and Dad would just laugh and gun it a little, bringing us even closer, I was certain, to the dog's demise. We never ran over a dog, though, and we never fell off the car. On those days, it was a relief to reach our driveway and see the dog run safely into the yard, away from Dad's laughter and our racing hearts.

Other than the beagle named Daisy that one of Dad's friends gave us, dogs never lasted long enough at our house for me to remember their names, so I did not grow attached to them. Most of the time, strays showed up out of nowhere, and we fed them table scraps when we had them to spare. I'm certain we never bought a bag of dog food. They wandered up the gravel road or out of the woods like some unfortunate fairy-tale child who stumbles upon a suspicious gingerbread house.

I didn't realize people took animals to vets until I was much older, and later in life, it was still difficult to understand why people bought lamb-and-rice dog food or spent money on medicine for dogs or booties for their paws. Those are the kinds of things you buy when you have so much money, you don't have to worry anymore about how many times your children have eaten hot dogs this week, or how they're behind on their shots, or whether their clothes are looking too small or too stained so maybe someone's going to call social services on you.

Even after growing up and getting a job and being able to buy organic food and the name-brand clothes for my kids that I wore only as hand-me-downs from friends, I struggle to imagine how we could take care of a dog like a family member. It seems that my guilt and worry about all the dogs I saw mistreated come out in subtle cues to them now, as they sniff me and I tense up, suddenly filled with the same fear I had as a child, wondering what awful thing is going to happen next.

When I was about eight years old, we had a dog around for a while—whether it was one my dad chased down the road with us on the car, I couldn't say. Looking back, I can tell you it was about the size of a Lab and completely black. I don't think we gave it a name. Once, it followed me to Granny's house when I walked there to get some onions and tomatoes for my dad on a sunny afternoon. Granny and Papaw Conn were not home, but the chickens were out, pecking away at the dirt and grass, minding their own business. The dog got excited about the chickens and lunged for them, and my shouts could not stop him from chasing them in earnest. He finally caught a baby chick and crushed it in his jaws, dropped it and sniffed, then walked away. I was devastated by the chick's death and walked back to our house sobbing, tears rolling down my face.

My father was standing outside, and when he saw me approaching, he demanded to know what was wrong. He already seemed angry, and my sorrow gave way to another feeling, a caution. I tried to catch my breath and, through choked sobs, told him that the dog had killed one of Granny's baby chickens. I thought I might get in trouble, and some little part of me wondered whether he might tell me everything was okay, but he just grew angrier, and it seemed he was impatient, or unhappy that I interrupted him, or some other undefinable emotion. He unbuckled his belt and slid it out of his belt loops.

I thought I was going to be whipped for not controlling the dog, but he grabbed the dog by the scruff of the neck and yanked it into the air—all fifty or so pounds. The dog yelped at being jerked off the ground, but when my father whipped it over and over with the belt, the dog's cries shocked me into silence. I could not cry for myself anymore and just stood there watching, wishing I had known to protect it. When he dropped the dog, my father turned to me and told me to stop crying, or he'd give me something to cry about. But my tears had already stopped.

When I was older, I found that some of my friends would laughingly recall their mothers coming after them with a wooden spoon. They spoke of things like being *spanked*, which I didn't quite understand—it didn't seem to have any impact on them, and it was more like a joke shared between the children and parents, an act of authority and submission that was almost a charade.

My father's leather belt, though, fell on us without mercy, without reason. I was a Girl Scout for some of my grade school years, and one late fall, as winter darkened toward us, we picked paper angels from a plastic tree somewhere in town. The angels bore the names of children whose parents declared themselves unable to buy a doll or underwear or shoes for their children that year. Each of us Girl Scouts picked an angel from the tree and vowed to buy a gift or two for the unlucky child. Mine wanted a doll, and one afternoon, while my mother worked, my uncle came to get me, my brother, and our father to go to the dollar store and buy the doll. I think that was around the time that Dad no longer managed the gas station, but Mom still went there to do the bookkeeping. Dad had a pretty steady flow of people in and out of the house, and he was always *wheeling and dealing*, as he put it. Selling pills or the weed he grew meant we didn't have to put our own names on an angel tree.

As we started to pull out of the driveway, my father noticed that my brother had chocolate around the corners of his mouth. Dad told my uncle to stop the truck just as we were pulling away, and he sent us back inside. I wasn't quite sure what was going to happen until my dad started whipping Junior in the living room. After a few hits, he sent Junior to his room and turned toward me. I realized that he was about to make a mistake—his frustration had been with Junior, not with me, and I had done nothing to anger him. I thought he must have forgotten what upset him, and in a moment that stands out as the first and only time I tried to defend myself, I started to speak: *Wait*— But before I could explain, the belt hit my back, my ass, my legs, and my words were gone. What was I going to tell him? In that moment of clarity, I saw his unhinged rage and thought I could make him see it for what it was. For a moment, I knew I was innocent.

When my mother came home that evening, she went into the bathroom with me as I showed her the bruises on my body—somehow asking her, perhaps because of something I had heard at school, whether this was abuse. She murmured a dismissal, and I asked her whether he had told her what happened. She said *yes*, he told her we refused to clean our rooms, so we were punished. And that was all.

It was especially ironic that he told her we wouldn't clean our rooms. I cleaned constantly, always thinking that with a little more effort, everything would be perfect, and Dad would have nothing to be angry about. By the time I was seven, if we children were left alone for a few hours, I often set out to get the laundry folded, the floors vacuumed, the coal stove cleaned, and the coal buckets filled. I washed dishes, I organized my books alphabetically, I made my bed. I swept the coal-dust-covered cobwebs from the corners of our living room. Nothing worked, but I kept trying. I brought home report cards filled with As and teachers' praises, but Dad always pointed out with a laugh that while it was good, any A should have been an A+.

Looking back now, I can see that anxiety fueled my feeble attempts to fix the broken world around me, and that anxiety didn't go any damn where as I grew older and grew up. I would have to have children of my own and see their messy bedrooms and the toothpaste on the bathroom sink and some crumbs forgotten on the kitchen table. I would have to find myself back at the edge of panic and fear, not knowing what was happening inside me but knowing something bad would happen because of the mess, finding myself angry that someone else was sending me back to my childhood hell. I would have to see the hurt or anger in my children's eyes to slowly understand that no one was going to punish me anymore. To understand that if I didn't fix myself, I would pass my brokenness on to them—the burden of my anxiety and fear and heartache would somehow become theirs, no matter how hard I wished and prayed otherwise.

My brother didn't respond to all that fear and anxiety like I did. Instead, he would shove everything under his bed when he was supposed to clean his room. I told Mom once, thinking they were fooled, and she explained that he was younger and not as good at cleaning as I was. Junior made terrible grades, so when he brought home Cs and the occasional B, he was rewarded. One time, I mentioned how unfair it was that I got rewarded for only the highest grades, and Mom said since

I was capable of making the higher grades, that was what I should do. I was disappointed that I couldn't seem to win my parents' love that way, but making good grades was easy for me, and getting positive feedback from teachers was enough to keep me motivated to do well in school. That turned out to be very lucky for me, since it's a lot easier to claw your way out of poverty with scholarships and a college degree.

But I kept searching for ways to convince my dad to love me, and I finally thought I had figured something out—I could make him laugh. I began imitating one of the radio DJs we heard on the station our radio was always tuned to, the only station that reached us so deep into the holler. I tried to learn jokes so I could come home and tell them to him, and I thought for a short time that I had made myself good enough, that he finally loved me. It wasn't long, though, until he no longer laughed at my jokes. The happiness I felt lasted for such a brief time, and I was desperate to earn it again, to deserve his affection once more.

I began seeing my ugliness in the mirror. The more I looked at it, the more repulsive I found the face looking back at me, until it felt like torture to be in my own body. I already knew how to punish myself for everything that was wrong with me—I learned it from the adults—and so my self-loathing ate at me. I was certain my father didn't love me because I was unlovable, undeserving, unworthy. I could feel it in my body, which longed for safety.

But no matter what he did, I kept wanting life to be better for my father. I felt his rage and pain as if they were my own, and sometimes it seemed like I alone could fix it all. I never thought it was his fault that he was cruel or unloving—I thought it was the rest of the world, I thought it was the pills he had to take for his back, his back that got hurt at work, and he tried to get workers' compensation for it, but they screwed him over, and he was left with a bad back and nothing to show for all his hard work. And there he was, with a taste for painkillers and all that pain, and disks in his back that always needed surgeries he didn't get and some of those disks having just disappeared altogether. It was this sad mess, this chain of events that led him down the path of self-destruction, and it was the doctors and the lawyers and the banks, and it was not being able to make a living and support his family—that's what drove him to the point of no return.

I spent most of my life believing that, until I was twenty-seven. That's when I asked my mother what had happened to his back while managing the gas station, what injury had caused the pain that spread from him through our family and into the world, and she said it was something minor, something inconsequential. That he didn't get screwed by the workers' compensation office—he just didn't turn the paperwork in on time. That he came home with his minor hurt and tried to make it worse by bench-pressing their bed. So he could go to the doctor and get some good pills.

I knew then that I would never get him back, that maybe he was never there to lose in the first place. I had been dreaming of the man I knew he could be, that I just *knew* he wanted to be and surely would *choose* to be someday. For the first time, I was struck with the understanding that as hard as I had tried to make sense of the whole mess, it was time to give that up.

# CHAPTER 8

## *Spare the Rod*

We barely got television reception through the huge antenna that stood next to our house, reaching beyond the roof. On Saturday mornings, my brother and I would take turns twisting it around in the ground, moving it slightly so its futuristic rods pointed this way and that. Eventually, we would settle for the least fuzzy version of the cartoons we could manage and tried to watch them with the distortion intermittently blurring the picture completely. Sometimes the picture was tolerable but there was no sound. The one channel that came in clearly almost all the time was Kentucky Educational Television on the Public Broadcasting Service. There were no cartoons, but we loved *Sesame Street*, and at some point, I got to see enough of *The Electric Company* to fall in love with it.

*Mister Rogers' Neighborhood* came on right after *Sesame Street*, and we watched it to make fun of Mister Rogers, with his dull sweaters and unfamiliar calm demeanor. He gave out unsolicited advice, and even compliments, all while going through the same routine of changing from one nice pair of shoes to another, from a sport coat to a cardigan and back. I didn't understand why he felt the need to change his shoes when he walked into the house, and who on earth has an inside sweater. I had never seen someone wear a cardigan or sport coat or be so optimistic for no reason. Everything about him grated on my nerves, though I felt a twinge of guilt for mocking him in our little house filled with cigarette smoke and heartache.

I suffered through the educational bits and cheerful assurances so I could watch his model train go to the Neighborhood of Make-Believe, where I was enthralled. Daniel Stripèd Tiger was my favorite puppet, and my mother and I would sometimes rub our noses together like he and Lady Aberlin, saying, *Hugga wugga,* which is what I thought they said on the show. In that land of make-believe, everyone was basically good, and stories felt important. I tried to understand their world, and while watching the puppets, I felt a comfort that disappeared each time the red-and-yellow trolley headed back to Mister Rogers's tidy house.

I also loved *Reading Rainbow*—I read all the time, and though I didn't go find the books LeVar Burton talked about on the show, it was a world I could understand. I threw myself into books as much as possible. I would walk down to Granny's house while reading a book, reasonably sure I wouldn't get hit by a car. Sometimes I tried to ride my bike down there while reading, which was a little trickier. Sometimes, when I couldn't run to the forest while my dad was shouting, I would close the door to my room and open a book, forcing myself to read the words, pulling my mind away from the sounds in the next room over and over, willing myself to go into someone else's world, where fathers weren't nightmares.

To watch just about anything, my brother and I would sit together in our dad's recliner, which was placed close to the television at an angle, near the front door. For most of my young life, my dad kept a gun loaded and leaning against the wall by the front door. I learned to shoot a .22 rifle early on, but I knew this one was more dangerous—maybe a more powerful rifle, or a shotgun. I also knew I was never to touch it, and as I grew older and heard stories about other kids getting their fathers' guns and accidentally shooting someone, I marveled that they were so daring as to touch the guns. I don't remember ever being told not to touch it, but I never did, and the possibility never crossed my mind. I had a vague sense that if I touched a gun, I might die, but I was certain that if I touched it without permission, I would get a whipping that would make all the other whippings seem like a joke.

I saw my dad use his guns several times. He owned quite a few and would sometimes show them to me, saying things like *SKS* and *AK-47* and names of foreign countries I had never heard of. I fired a shotgun once and never forgot how it kicked, bruising my bony shoulder, but the only one I could identify by sight was the sawed-off shotgun.

My father once pointed a rifle at his father, my quiet, church-going papaw, in our driveway. I hardly ever heard an angry word from Papaw, and his prayer before meals always began, *Dear Heavenly Father,* and almost always ended, *Thank you, Lord and Granny, for the food.* Papaw stood there, his face perfectly expressionless, while his son shook with rage. I couldn't hear what my father said as I watched from the porch, but I saw the words twist his mouth and a darkness cross his face. Finally, Papaw got to leave, and the gun came inside.

Before I could tell the difference between abuse and discipline, I asked Granny why my father turned out like he did. *We let him get away with too much,* she said. I thought I understood that—*spare the rod and spoil the child.* But I wondered where he learned to use the belt he turned on us with cruelty.

I woke up one night to hear loud voices in our driveway. I looked out my window, and from a hard angle, I could see my father standing in the driveway with a man from down the road. The man was leveling a rifle at my father, who seemed oddly calm standing there, as though violence was his resting point. The man yelled for a while, and my mother was out there, and I could hear her plead with him. This man had the nicest house on our road, and we would sometimes go there to pick cherries from his cherry tree. He finally left, and the next morning, I asked my mom why he had done that. She told me he was drunk and angry that one of my dad's friends had driven past his house too fast.

Later, my father told me that the neighbor never knew Papaw was lying in the field next to our driveway, looking through his own rifle scope and aiming at our neighbor's head.

I would have thought that the neighbor's reaction was excessive if my father had not already outdone that himself. The neighbors at the head of our holler—the last family on the road—had a boy who was probably eight years older than me. One day when I was about five, he drove by our house too fast to suit my father, who said he was concerned that one of us kids would get hit by a car. By that time, we had a page-wire fence that ran the length of the yard, but still—I suppose Dad wanted to err on the side of caution. So, my father told me, he took two five-gallon buckets of oil from the gas station and brought them home, then spread the oil over the road that ran along our fence. For good measure, he scattered screws and nails over the oil. *That will slow him down,* he said. Years later, he told me about another young boy—sixteen or so—who drove past the house too fast. On the boy's way back down the road, my dad stopped him and used a baseball bat to bash in his windshield, headlights, and side-view mirrors.

On another night, I awoke to the sound of guns. I remember I was about six, and they were right outside my bedroom window, in our front yard. I looked out my window and saw my uncle firing a handgun toward our driveway, where my mother ran and jumped into our long yellow Buick, an atrocity with two doors and a brown roof. My father was in that direction, too, firing a gun back at my uncle—his brother. I could not see what kind he held in his hand, but he almost never showed me a handgun, so I assumed it was a rifle. I wondered what would happen to us all, and it occurred to me that something might kill me that night. My window was open because it was warm outside, and I got back in the bed, as close as I could to my headboard, and held myself tight, waiting for it to pass.

The next day, I saw several bullet holes in our car. Nobody had gotten shot, but apparently my father filed a charge against my uncle, because several days later, my parents took my brother and me with them to the courthouse, where we went to an office, and my father told them he wanted to drop the charges.

*Drop the charges? For attempted murder? Are you sure?* the woman asked.

*Yes, I'm sure,* my dad told her.

I heard the shotguns and rifles many other times, mostly used on the stray dogs that we would adopt for a short time but that inevitably wore out their welcome somehow. We never asked what happened, and I was never told there was something wrong with the dogs or given any notice they were about to be executed. I would be sitting in the house, reading or watching one of our home-recorded VHS tapes once again, and I would hear the blast. The sound would echo all around as it bounced between the hillsides, while I ran to the front or back door depending on where the sound came from. I would hope that I wouldn't get shot and hope that my mother wasn't dead in the yard and wonder whether my father killed someone or killed himself or was finally just going fucking nuts and was going to kill every goddamn one of us.

Despite everything, I think my brother and I were raised to be responsible with guns. Our father told us never to point a gun at someone, even if we thought it wasn't loaded. Junior and I used BB guns and the .22 rifle to shoot pop cans lined up on the picnic table. We learned guns were fun, but first they were for survival.

I grew up thinking there was a difference between the way guns are used in cities and how people in the country think of them. My papaw Conn hunted squirrels, and there was always talk of hunting for deer. My dad sometimes shot copperheads in the front yard and, as they came out of the Daniel Boone, he fired bird shot toward hikers he suspected of hunting ginseng. But mostly, the guns were there to protect him from the nameless enemies he talked about when he was high and telling us seamless, endless stories of what he had seen and done. He never went hunting. Maybe he was more like the city folk than he thought.

After he started taking pills in earnest, my dad was pretty concerned about cleanliness and swept the porch constantly. Or maybe he was just wrestling with the demons that inevitably reawakened every time the pills wore off—he always told me that the Lortabs he snorted were the *poor man's cocaine*. When he finished with the porch, he would sweep the ground in front of it, where the rain dripped into shallow puddles from the grooves in our tin roof. Junior and I sometimes collected the water for no apparent reason, and I would watch the rain drip from the roof in waterfall curtains, mesmerized by their sure and steady paths. When Dad swept the ground, though, Junior and I would take the rare opportunity to laugh at him quietly, mocking him when we were out of earshot.

His approach to cleaning was all his own—he never came close to crossing any gender boundaries. He never washed the dishes or laundry—in fact, when Mom bought her first book telling women how to leave their abusive husbands, she hid it in the laundry basket in the bathroom, just below a soiled shirt or two, knowing he would never find it there. I came across it and asked her about it, and she assured me he would never see it in such a hiding place.

While I imagine he never cleaned the toilet, and I know he gave my mother crabs from some woman he fucked in the back of the gas station he managed, he watched me carefully when I set the table, chastising me if my hair hung over his plate at all. When he sat in his recliner, he inevitably found crumbs in it and accused my brother and me of eating in his chair. But we hardly ate in his chair at all, knowing that if we spilled something, he would be furious and our punishment would be thorough.

I daydreamed, though, of rubbing grape jelly all over his recliner and tying him down in it. I thought that being sticky would be the worst experience for him, and though occasionally my mind wandered to the idea of what it would be like to hit him while he was tied down, something about that fantasy seemed wrong. I ultimately decided that just being restrained would be torture enough for my father.

My mom and dad and a lot of their friends smoked cigarettes, so sometimes Dad would make us go outside and pick up all the cigarette butts that were strewn around the yard but that were especially prevalent around the front porch. We picked them up dutifully, careful not to overlook a single butt from the porch to the driveway. It almost made me feel proud, knowing how careful I was.

Once, he told us to start picking them up while he was talking to his buddy in the front yard, both of them smoking. I thought that surely he would put the butt out and throw it in the coffee can we were dropping the butts into, but when he was done, he flicked it to the ground near me. I don't remember who the friend was, and I don't think it was someone I really cared about in the first place, but I was again surprised that our dad would treat us with such disregard—*like dogs,* I thought. I think the friend had a strange look on his face when his eyes met mine, and I wondered what he would do with his own cigarette butt. I'm nearly certain he didn't throw it on the ground, since I don't have a special disdain for him that would have lasted all these decades.

That disbelief turned out to be a big part of the problem in growing up with an abuser. There were constantly things I just couldn't believe because they made no sense—so many illogical experiences that defied reason and basic decency. By the time I became a young adult, I had grown suspicious of my intuition, my judgment, even my own feelings. I became the perfect target for the kind of people who like to undermine, ridicule, or control another person—except then, they were usually the same people I slept next to at night.

When I was about eight, after Dad started building a two-story addition onto our house, my mom loaded us kids into the car in a rush to get away from him. I heard him from the open window of the second-floor bedroom that was going to be mine, and he stuck his rifle out the window. For a moment, I thought he might shoot us, but he started screaming at my mother that if she left and took us, he would kill himself. I didn't know what to do or which would be worse, but we ran to the car anyway. I asked her as she backed out, *What if he shoots himself?* She answered, *I hope he does.* There was nothing else to say.

The door to our new addition faced the creek behind our house and was solid wood, about six inches thick. It didn't have a doorknob or lock but instead had three makeshift bolts that we had to slide deep into the door to close it. I never understood why it was so very thick, but it seemed meant to protect us. It was a beautiful door, clearly made by hand, and I can only assume he acquired it by trading pills or something he'd stolen. Outside that door, only a few feet of yard lay between the doorway and the bank of the creek, which edged closer to us each year. The creek ate away at the bank closest to the back corner of the house until the corner had only a couple of inches of dirt left. When I noticed these things, it would fill me with a concern that I never shared with my parents. My fears about the house falling into the creek never did come to fruition, though—instead, it met a fiery end before the creek had enough time to eat its way to the house.

# CHAPTER 9

## *Holy Vows*

I've often wondered what happened that made my mother so easy to abuse, so helpless in the presence of my father. I grew up knowing that I had to be ready to leave a man—my husband, a lover, the father of my children—and that I had to mean it. I grew up knowing how my children would someday look at me, how their contempt and disgust would spread toward me despite the undying love we might share, if I let them hear and see me being belittled one too many times.

Of course, being a single mother was a different undertaking in the 1980s, when my mother first should have left. When I did my leaving decades later, I'd had ample opportunities for education, I'd had easy employment solutions, I'd had scores of women before me who left men and became single mothers and redefined that concept, who paved the way for single mothers to be allowed to be sexy and free and independent. But it still takes a good twenty years to pull yourself out of poverty, as I came to find out. And that's if you're lucky—no medical crisis, no new traumas that make *mental health* seem like some silly fairy tale, the realm of princesses and parents who somehow manage to give just the right amount of support to their children.

If you can survive the weight of bills you can't pay and the emotional demand of children who you know deserve to be loved better than you know how to love, and if you can endure the loneliness and the panic that takes your breath away when you imagine what would happen to your children if you died or someone took them from you, then you just might make it, eventually. So I hear.

I have also learned a thing or two about loving the wrong kind of men, about staying too long. I listened to the things that broke inside when boyfriends and husbands named me *worthless* and *weak*. And when they spoke with their hands, I excused the marks they left as a one-time thing—a different kind of thing, something we didn't even talk about. I've stood staring at the door like so many women do when they think about leaving, counting the large and small things I would have to account for: money, shelter, the ire of an entire community, a ride out of town, a safe place to land. After making my way out, I counted the things I left behind: a home in an idyllic forest, a bed frame, the baby's favorite stuffed giraffe.

I rented grungy apartments that permanently smelled of the sad meal someone cooked there before we arrived. I put my mattress on the floor for the next ten years. I tried to make it all better.

I've come to believe that one of the defining moments of adulthood is the moment at which we recognize our parents as the overgrown children we all are, running around and reacting to each other as we learned to from our parents. Enacting our *oldest child* or *baby of the family* roles, our *good girl* and *troubled child* titles. Proving over and over that we are either the pieces of shit our parents resented and could not raise or the angels they adored who could do no wrong.

I thought something must have changed my father, that he had to have been different at some earlier point. I wondered whether he was kind in his younger days, or charming, just trying to decipher exactly what would have led my mother to marry him. *No,* she says, *he was not.* He would storm away from her house if she could not come with him, threatening to find other girls. He would drive another girl by her house for her to see. He had been cruel and hateful always.

Had either of my husbands been kind to me before I vowed myself to them? I never thought to ask myself.

My mother has had false teeth for many years. When I was little, I was fascinated by her jaw popping when she yawned and her teeth that looked so pretty until she pulled them out, leaving her smile half-empty. She told me she was in a motorcycle accident when she was seventeen, and her teeth were knocked out and her jaw broken. For days, she lay in the hospital with her mouth wired shut, and no, it does not hurt now, but her jaw has popped ever since.

Years later, it struck me that my mother had been on a motorcycle with someone other than my father—who was he? Did she like him? Did he like her? Did the accident bring their perfect love to an untimely end? Could he have been my father if she had stayed with him?

*He was a boy I liked,* she said, *but your dad was jealous that I went out with him sometimes. Someone loosened the lug nuts on one of the motorcycle wheels, and as we gained speed going down US 60, the wheel came off and we crashed. I'm pretty sure it was your dad who loosened the wheel. I never dated the other boy again. I married your father soon after.*

As she told me this story, the history of my parents fell into place in a new way. I knew how it felt to want his love—a love that was always so impossibly close. I understood how she must have pushed all her words down when he threatened to find someone else, just as I swallowed my anger with each insult, afraid to lose him forever. My mother had lost her words, her ability to define *herself* to herself or anyone else, for so long. Like many in abusive relationships, she had paired with the person who was happiest to exploit her vulnerability. And with each cruelty, with each torturous moment, her voice was quieted. Whatever weakness first made her tolerant of his abuse had been replaced by her need to survive and, soon, to protect her babies—as well as she could.

In an alternate universe, I see her closing the door the first time my father threatened to storm off and find another girl. She shakes her head over it, whispering with her sisters that night as they daydream about the colleges they will go to. They aren't marrying poor, bad-tempered boys in hollers. They aren't trying to feed babies on a man's gas station job. They aren't having babies in trailers and crushing aluminum cans in the mud for milk money. They aren't smoking cigarettes in the kitchen while their husbands snort pills with their buddies in the barn, hoping their husbands will pass out as soon as they come in, hoping their moods do not darken as they walk toward the house.

In this alternate universe, those daughters of the sixties are listening to their Tom Jones and Smokey Robinson records—still making their own clothes from Simplicity patterns, sure, but after high school, they attend the local university or work in a shop in town. They marry young men and live in real houses and probably still get divorced, but there are no broken jaws. Almost everyone remains intact, more or less.

In real life, Dad never seemed to mind us knowing how reckless he could be, how casual his regard was for others—for us. He loved telling stories, and I was an avid listener, at once horrified and mesmerized as I tried to stitch a coherent narrative from the pieces I collected. When he was about nineteen, he worked for the hospital in town, delivering oxygen to bedridden patients at their homes. Dad was always a master in the black market, always trading something for something else, always procuring weapons and tools and drugs with his skills in negotiating, or perhaps in coercion.

He told me a story that while he was an oxygen deliveryman, he convinced a janitor at the hospital to steal a tank of nitrous oxide for him, since the janitor had the key to the room where the tanks were stored and locked away from people like my father. As soon as he got the tank, Dad took it with him to the delivery truck and hooked it up to a mask that he strapped to his face. He said that he turned the nitrous on full throttle—not mixing it with oxygen, as your local dentist would do to prevent a massive loss of brain cells—and drove down the road with his usual supply of oxygen tanks in the back.

Then, my father told me, as he drove down the road and crossed into the other lane, he hit a woman, and they had a terrible crash that left the woman paralyzed for the rest of her life. I don't know why my father did not go to prison but somehow got out of the charges with perhaps a misdemeanor, perhaps some community service, maybe probation? No punishment or injury worth including in the story he told.

I think about her sometimes, that woman, and wonder whether she is still alive. I wonder what she was doing before she was paralyzed, whether she had a job or children or was a student at the university in town. I wonder where she was driving to before the crash, and did a sense of foreboding puzzle her while she listened to the radio in her car? I wonder whether she somehow found strength and inspiration to redefine herself after the accident, perhaps to become an Olympic swimmer or to reach out to children in wheelchairs so they would have a role model who showed them anything is possible. I wonder, if she didn't have children, whether she could have and who they would have been, whether she would have loved them and raised them to be gentle people or would have someday despaired that her children had gone astray.

I wonder whether she ever had an orgasm after that, or thought about my father and hated him, or found Jesus and thought it was a divine intervention. I wonder whether she lived in our town the whole time, whether I ever saw her in a store or on a sidewalk, and whether she knew who I was. I wonder whether she saw him in me, hated me for what he had done, resented him surviving and going on to make babies who could be like him. I wonder whether she was happy to be alive after that, or not.

I wonder how on earth he has survived for so long, and why.

While I was learning to survive being me and interrogated my mother about her young life and how it felt to be her, she told me another reason why it took her so long to leave my father. She had eloped with my father at the age of seventeen, crossing the Tennessee border, where they could get married without any parental interference.

I still have the picture of them on their wedding night—my mother in a pink dress, my father wearing the same smile I have always feared.

After she came back and moved into the holler with him, she eventually complained to her own mother about how he treated her. Grandma responded with the old adage, *You've made your bed, now lie in it.*

I imagine I know how Grandma Wright felt when she said that. Angry at a daughter who didn't listen, who snuck off with the bad boy. Not ready to rescue a grown woman, not sure whether that woman is ready to rescue herself. Not knowing what has happened to her daughter's children, what *is* happening, what comes next.

# CHAPTER 10

## Fish out of Water

One of my friends in grade school lived in a new double-wide trailer on a hillside—her family seemed to have lots of money, and they gave her clothes to me when she outgrew them. I was always excited when I went through the garbage bag of hand-me-downs, knowing I would have something that had been in style. One time, I discovered her leather jacket in the bag, and I wore it to school with excitement, although it turned out no one else was still wearing them that year. Instead of making me look more like them, the jacket marked me again as the one who did not belong, who could not be like the others.

This friend's family let me spend the night often throughout grade school and middle school, though I don't remember her spending the night at our house much. She liked doing her hair and putting on makeup, which were things I was not good at or interested in. Sometimes I tried to pretend I enjoyed it, but I felt like it sucked the life out of me to watch her paint her fingernails, and I sure as hell didn't want to paint mine.

When I spent the night with friends or cousins, there were times we heard their parents argue. I still remember several of those moments vividly, though with a little more experience under my belt, I can now safely say they were minor arguments.

At the time, I was alarmed, and while my friends said, *I hate it when they argue,* they looked confused when I asked, *Is he going to hit her?* And they would say *no* with a strange look, as if they didn't understand the language I was using, as if the question made no sense, while I found a place to make myself small in case the screaming came close, in case the anger exploded and suddenly we were all potential targets, in case men were all the same, everywhere. My friends would continue playing or watching cartoons while everything tightened inside me, while I prayed and took shallow breaths and feared for our lives.

My child world grew stranger, more uncertain and complex, but remained that esoteric place of meaning and simplicity. Maybe the living world around me—the forest, the streams, the breathing plants and animals—pulled me back from becoming too lost in my confusion. I thought the story of *Hansel and Gretel* got it backward—you don't get lost in the woods, because that's the safest place to be. No one eats children or lays traps for them out there. The real danger is where people are comfortable and cloaked and never truly laid bare—in their homes, in their cities, in their churches.

I began hiding food in my dresser drawers—candy bars and bags of chips—thinking I could prepare myself in case we ran out of food again. I alphabetized my books and carefully arranged my treasures on my bookshelf. The plastic monk piggy bank—mostly empty—I had found at Great-Grandma's old house. The 1905 *Sears, Roebuck & Co. Catalogue* I found there as well, full of toys and advertisements that even I could recognize as quaint. The rock I found in our creek, completely covered in imprints of fossils, more beautiful than anything else I owned.

I found that I had a ritual for entering the bathroom, touching the bathtub and the sink and the toilet-tank lid just so, in perfect order. And the towels—the stack of dingy towels had to be touched, too. When I walked into the house, I tapped my fingers in a pattern on the back of my father's recliner, each time daring myself to break the pattern, skip a tap, but always returning to the chair to finish the pattern if, in a moment of bravery, I tried to defy it.

At night, I lay in bed unable to sleep, trying to count sheep, which seemed like something from a silly fairy tale, but I couldn't stay focused. I wondered who came up with counting sheep and how on earth that was supposed to help anything. So I memorized the alphabet backward night after night, until I could say it as quickly that way as I could say it forward.

When I closed my eyes to surrender to dreaming, refrains from songs started playing themselves over and over. I tried to end the incessant-but-broken singing by imagining a record needle dragging across the album, stopping the sound, silencing everything, but that didn't work, and I heard the same phrases from songs playing over and over, a torture that twisted melodies into taunts and jeers. *He stopped loving her today / he stopped loving her today / he stopped loving her today / he stopped loving her today.*

When we did have a window air conditioner, we weren't allowed to keep our bedroom doors open. That way, the cool air would stay in the living room, and Dad could be more comfortable. For most of my young childhood, there was no cool air in the living room, either. I remember lying in the heat of my bedroom, the still air sitting outside my open window as if it were waiting for something. No breeze flew over me, no fan was there to cool me. I lay there and cried, no longer struggling against the heat but knowing there was nothing for me to do, no respite to be found.

Sometimes my dreams were not like dreams at all, but empty spaces that I was drawn into. There were sounds like whispers that reverberated through my mind, excruciating in their quietness. I woke up feeling broken, like I had been lost in another world, a fun-house world without color or depth or dimension, but where every moment was cruel.

In one nightmare, my father is dragging my mother into their bedroom, and she is pleading with me to help her. She is crying and saying *no*, and I am standing there watching, knowing he is going to beat her, but this time it will be the worst, or he is going to fuck her and beat her—and there's a word for that, *rape*, but this is the 1980s, and that doesn't happen in marriage. I run to the phone and finally decide to ask someone to *help us*, so I call 911 or the operator, but the lady's voice on the phone says only, *The number you are trying to reach is not in service*, and then I hear the warning-siren busy signal that says, *Hang up the phone, you've done something wrong*, and I realize at last that there is no way out, no one coming to rescue us or to save us or to sit my father down and tell him once and for all that what he's doing is not right.

One summer day before eighth grade started, after I had spent the night with my friend in her double-wide, we went to the local park to watch her brothers at their baseball game. We were sitting on the bleachers when my mom showed up, which she had never done before. My friend's mom walked away with her, and they chatted for a few minutes, then returned to tell me I would be spending another couple of days with them. That suited me just fine, but when it was time to go home, I went to Grandma Wright's instead. I finally found out that Mom had left Dad, and I asked whether we were going back. *Not this time*, she told me.

Unconvinced, I wondered what made this time so different. My brother told me what he had seen, and later, my mom told me the whole story. They had left Junior at home, asleep on the couch, while they went to town for something. Dad got mad at Mom on the way back and began screaming at her while she was driving them to the house, then screamed at her all the way to the front door. She fumbled for her keys as he screamed at her to *open the fucking door*, and when she dropped the keys, he lost it. He began hitting her in the back— always where the bruises would be hidden by her clothes—and kicking her, finally kicking her through the front door, which he broke open, still locked. There on the couch, my brother awoke to see her falling through the doorway and onto the floor and then watched the beating as it continued. When Dad finally stopped, Mom grabbed my brother and drove away as fast as she could, somehow knowing that next time, my father would kill her.

And this time, she didn't go back.

For whatever reason, Grandma softened her stance against helping my mother, and we were allowed to stay there for a week or two, until we moved into a house in town, old and big and drafty. My cousin had lived there throughout a good portion of her childhood, so I always associated it with her and her nice things, her confidence and style. Somehow, she didn't seem scared of life and was full of sass even though she once told me she saw her dad drive her mother's head through their fish tank. That was my father's brother, and it didn't surprise me. I wondered, but never asked, whether the tank was full of water and what happened to the fish and how a woman gets her head out of a broken fish tank and how a daughter pretends everything is okay.

# CHAPTER 11

## *A Long Way from Home*

All my life to that point, I was quick to take out my frustration on Junior, though I always seemed to get in trouble even when I wasn't trying to hurt him. But suddenly, Junior seemed to take a particular delight in tormenting me in our big, strange home. The first year we lived in town, he locked me out of the house over and over while Mom was at work. I would get to the cordless phone through a window and call her, full of anger, but really afraid that I would hurt him if given much of a chance. Sometimes he would pick up the other house phone while I tried to talk to a friend, interrupting us and taunting me, apparently unaware of how much rage I felt and how much I wanted to direct it toward something, someone.

I didn't understand the agony within me, either. I was just a child, twelve years old, reacting to the traumas that continued to haunt me even after we moved out of the holler. The things that tormented me never rested—the kids at school, my brother, my father, the growing discomfort of living in my own body—they all seemed hell bent on reminding me I was worthless. I never felt safe to defend myself or to claim any right to be treated differently. I hated being around the people who were so relentlessly cruel, their jokes and sneers replaying each day like the record skipping over and over in my mind from when my younger self had tried to fall asleep. I felt helpless to respond to the things that made me angry, when anger would have been the healthy response. For years, I shoved it all down as much as I could, but it felt like it took on a life of its own, until it became yet another thing I was afraid of.

After we moved away from the holler, I often jerked awake from nightmares—in them, Mom always went back to Dad, and he was hitting her or raping her again. Sometimes in these dreams, she came out of their bedroom and looked at me, disgusted with me for being so afraid. I was almost always frozen in space, unable to move my own body to run to the door and save her. *What would I have done?*

When I awoke from the nightmares, I would find Mom in the living room, her makeshift bedroom. After we left the holler, we never lived somewhere with enough bedrooms for everyone. She would always assure me she was not going back this time, but I didn't believe her. About a decade later, I started finding myself in makeshift bedrooms of my own.

I had taken all the pain from the holler with me to the drafty house we'd moved to in town, but there was none of the beauty of the forest and streams and phlox to greet me, to reassure me that some good things do persist. I couldn't walk to my granny's or run to the woods. Here, there was lots of pavement and traffic, lights from cars driving in front of my bedroom at night, and memories of the people who had lived in that house before us.

We had to go up to Dad's every other weekend and usually rode the bus there after school. My brother never seemed scared to visit there, but I dreaded being at my father's house. I begged my mother not to make me go, but she said she could not keep me from him. Every time I went, I was afraid I would never be allowed to leave, worried he would force me to stay with him and clean the house and wait on him. I felt that same fear every time I visited him from then on, throughout adulthood.

One night, he left me alone in the house for a few hours. I called my mother and pleaded with her to come get me. She refused, as she refused to even drive on that road ever again once we moved out. She offered to send the police, but I knew there would be hell to pay for that, and nobody ever had to tell me that the police were not coming into our holler to rescue me. So I just cried on the phone and told her that he was crazy, that I was scared of him, and that I hated being there. We hung up when I heard his truck door slam in the driveway, and he went straight to his bedroom without saying anything to me.

I sat in his recliner, prepared to pretend everything was okay until he came out of his bedroom with a tape recorder and told me there was something he wanted me to hear. I did not know what to expect until he pressed a button and I heard myself talking, crying, begging—he replayed my entire conversation with my mother for me, then demanded to know why I had called him crazy. I sat there, trapped, saying as little as possible, wondering how I would make it out of there alive. I should have guessed that my father still tape-recorded phone conversations. It may have even been the same tape recorder that I had been whipped for long ago—with the missing battery cover.

After that night, my mother and I devised a code: if I called and said nothing, but just coughed, it meant she needed to send the police for me. But the one time I coughed my plea to be rescued, she asked whether I was sure until I no longer was, and we never spoke of it again. She hadn't left him until she knew he was going to kill her. She wasn't sure he was going to kill me. Neither was I. And that became my measuring stick for relationships from then on.

My mother had been working for the city for a few years by this point. When we were still living with Dad, he would accuse her of dressing well for someone else, and of being brainwashed. I had wondered what he meant, knowing that no one could possibly convince Mom that Dad was any worse than she already knew.

After school, I usually rode the bus or walked to her office at city hall, and during middle school, I typed a couple of stories on a spare computer there. Dad also liked to accuse whoever was at city hall of brainwashing my brother and me, but we mostly just looked for mini bagels in their break-room freezer and played hide-and-seek in the enormous walk-in safe that protected old cardboard boxes.

Around the time of the summer before my freshman year of high school, Mom moved us to a small trailer in the park that was owned by the city—rent was cheap and utilities were free, in exchange for keeping an eye on the park. The trailer was right next to a hill, and I could walk to a little wooded area next to the picnic shelter or go hiking up the hill behind our house. The city pool was also next to the park, but I was losing interest in the pool by that point. Still, it felt good for a while. Our mother sometimes brought McDonald's home for dinner, and for a time, I had only my own anger to live with.

My brother met some of the boys who lived in the government housing apartments nearby, and sometimes I talked to them, too. One of the boys always had a smile on his round face, and I liked him the best. Another boy always seemed awkward and strangely ready to fight, and my brother let him show off his nunchucks but told me much later that the awkward boy eventually killed someone and put the body in the trunk of his car and drove around with it for days.

After we moved to the trailer, I started thinking that Junior was having a harder time than I was. Boys at school made fun of him—his shoes, his name—and for some reason, I believed it was harder to be an unloved boy than an unloved girl. When it came time to buy school clothes, I asked our mother whether she could buy him some Nikes—I thought that having name-brand shoes would show the other boys he was important after all. She told me she couldn't afford to buy us both nice shoes, so I told her to get him the Nikes, and I would take whatever she could afford after that. By that time, I thought it was useless for me to try to look nice anyhow. Junior got the Nikes, but what really helped him socially happened one day when he rode the bus to our father's house. A boy tripped Junior as he tried to leave the bus, and Junior fell down. When he stood back up, he turned around and hit that boy on the head a few times. After that, everyone liked Junior.

I never did find a way to make friends with the people who picked on me. No simple fistfight could change my relationship with those who had tormented me whether I was nice or cold, whether I tried to interact with them or not. Some part of me always knew that no matter how angry or hurt I was, violence was not an option I could choose. For my brother, fighting back showed the other boys that he wasn't weak, and so they accepted him as one of them. As a girl, there was no way for me to convince the other kids that *I* wasn't weak—I had never seen a girl fight back. Everything I tried just seemed to make it worse, to make me a bigger target. It was better to hope I could disappear.

Dad showed up to our trailer one warm day and asked to borrow Mom's watering hose. Mom never spoke to him and would not exchange pleasantries—sometimes he would ask me during visitation why she wouldn't *speak*, meaning why wouldn't she wave at him when they saw each other out driving somewhere. He made it impossible to ignore him this time, so she told him *no* with fear in her voice.

He kept pushing her to lend him the hose and eventually stepped inside the trailer, though she tried to keep him from coming in, and I felt all the familiar violence follow him. She kept saying *no*, and I watched him grow angrier, until it dawned on me that despite having not hurt her for a long time now, there was nothing inside him that would keep him from doing it again. She had backed up toward the couch as he moved toward her, so I stepped in between them. I told him, *Don't do this. Leave her alone.* And he said something else to her, a few words to let her know that he was still in control, but I did not move, and soon, he turned around and left. Mom called the police so they would patrol the park for a while, and I peeked out the window several times to see whether he would return, perhaps with a gun, but he didn't. To my surprise, he never spoke of that day.

I had a crush on one boy in the fourth and fifth grades, the son of one of our elementary school teachers, though I was never in her class. I adored him and, at the same time, learned to despise him because his family had money, according to my dad. Dad hated rich people, or anyone associated with a wealthy family, and constantly reminded me that they were our enemies, that they were somehow corrupt and thought themselves superior to us. I still had my crush, but by the age of nine, I knew that the little boy would never like me, and I did silly little-girl crush things—lots of staring, giggling, and pining away dramatically with my best friend.

In middle school, there was a different boy—a country boy with light eyes and a set to his jaw. I became obsessed with knowing everything I could about him, but I wouldn't talk to him. I listened and remembered all the little things he said, as if that knowledge would somehow compensate for the closeness we didn't have.

I felt ugly already—hideously, terribly ugly. Sometimes my classmates would tease me for my flat chest and for wearing glasses. My haircuts were always home jobs, and my uneven bangs reflected something unsteady in my mother's scissors-wielding hands. I was rail thin, and god only knows where my mother got my clothes—sometimes the dollar store, sometimes secondhand stores. In my teens and early twenties, I took great pleasure in visiting those stores and wearing the most ironically *uncool* clothes I could find. In middle school, though, there was no irony.

I would go to our middle school dances and spend the entire time crying in the bathroom, being consoled by a friend or two, heartbroken over the boy I liked and by my loneliness, which bore a poverty of its own. It was the perfect distillation of all my fear and confusion, and this unrequited love was a way to finally make some sense of how awful I felt, at least for a while.

Throughout middle school, I took advanced classes rather than leaving for the weekly gifted program as we had done in grade school. I was in those classes with most of the same people I already knew from the fourth and fifth grades. They weren't quite as interested in teasing me as they had been, but I was always waiting for the cruelty. Sometimes it seemed like they treated me as their equal, sometimes I seemed to have a companion who was also at the bottom of the pecking order, but mostly I just felt alone.

We had all our advanced classes in one particular classroom, and as a group, we were the most obnoxious kids a teacher could have. We had a literature and writing teacher in the sixth and seventh grades, and she let me write a longer story for one of our assignments, something I was so excited to write but terrified to read out loud to my classmates, which she insisted on. After I finished reading it, I heard one of them muttering about me just copying the *Odyssey*, but some quiet, defiant part of me knew that my teacher's opinion was more important.

One other teacher was responsible for our other subjects—advanced science in sixth grade, math, and maybe something else all the way through eighth grade. That teacher was an older woman, overweight with iron-gray hair and thick calves, always clad in an old-fashioned floral dress. For some reason, we decided to give her hell all the time.

She would walk into the classroom to find that we had turned every piece of furniture upside down, including all the long tables we sat at. We couldn't turn her desk upside down, so we carefully turned over each object that sat on it. On another day, she could walk in to find that we had the lights turned off and were all hiding—in cabinets, behind bookshelves, and even under her desk. I was under her desk once, hiding with a boy, when she sat down, apparently too unmotivated to cajole us out of our hiding places. We stayed there, studying her pantyhose and laughing silently, until she finally moved, and we scrambled out.

Sometimes we would sit on our tables and pretend to meditate, ignoring her pleas to sit in our chairs; other times, we would pretend we were asleep, and no matter how much she threatened us, no one would move or give up our positions unless she started talking about getting the principal. We often convinced her to take us to the break room during class, where we would get chips and pop and candy, which I'm sure greatly improved our classroom behavior. We had pizza parties more often than the *regular* students. At least once, we made her cry with our obstinance. We were quite horrible to her, yet she was terribly patient with us. I don't know whether it was because she thought we truly were gifted children, or she thought we were acting out and needed to express ourselves, or she just didn't know how to deal with a room full of bratty kids who didn't appreciate how lucky they were to be in an accelerated learning environment. Whatever it was, that was a highlight of my middle school experience.

For a while, the lowlight of middle school was my obsessive crush. I thought constantly about how he did not like me, and sometimes I would fret over working up the courage to call him. Once, I phoned him and asked him why he didn't like me. He was probably quite taken aback and assured me that he did like me as a friend, that he would talk with me at school, and so on. I asked him the most uncomfortable questions, desperately wanting to figure out what made me so repulsive. He gave me kind answers, and eventually, in high school, we occasionally spoke to each other like friendly peers. In retrospect, I am sure that any number of our middle school classmates would have told him how obsessed I was, and he probably had no idea how to interact with me, knowing I idolized him.

I outgrew the crush by the time I entered ninth grade, and it is a good thing, too. He had an older brother who somehow met my father. By that time, with no woman in the house, Dad had a strange array of friends who would visit him on a regular basis. There were lots of college girls who came up, and it seems now that they were probably doing pills and getting weed from my dad. There was one, though, that my dad seemed to particularly admire. He said she was studying psychology at the university and wanted to be around him so she could try to figure him out. I wondered at her curiosity, but my dad seemed to think it was funny and would talk about being crazy or being able to convince people he was or wasn't, depending on his goal. That was one of the things that frightened me most about him—I never knew whether he meant to be crazy, whether he truly was, or whether he really just had control over everything, over everyone.

When I was thirteen or so, I went to my father's house and met that older brother once. He was even more good looking than his younger counterpart. My dad made me do his laundry sometimes, and I would find myself folding that young man's underwear, unsure how that fit into the larger story of my old feelings for his younger brother, and even more unsure how my dad could approve of me folding another man's underwear.

Unfortunately for him, that young man shared my father's taste for painkillers and went into Dad's bedroom one day, thinking my dad was either gone or safely occupied elsewhere. According to my father's telling, he came into the house to find the boy in his room, looking through the junky mess on his dresser and stealing pills. He forced the young man out into the yard and called my uncle, who drove to his house and held the boy while my dad beat him senseless. Later, I found out that the boy's mother—the mother of the boy I had adored—accused my father of beating her son with a shovel. My dad laughed that off and held up his broken hand, wrapped in a white cast—he had broken it by hitting the nineteen-year-old repeatedly.

# CHAPTER 12

## *Out Loud*

While I was still in middle school and for a short time in high school, I attended the youth-group meetings at our church every Wednesday night. Granny would be upstairs, having Bible study, singing and praying, while I was downstairs with a room full of kids and an adult or two. Christianity was falling apart for me, and everything else was also falling apart as I grew a little less flat chested.

I asked questions that fully irritated the youth-group leaders, a married couple who looked like they probably had never fought it out on a gravel road. I asked them how the earth was populated by just Adam and Eve, when that meant someone would have had to commit incest pretty early on. They said that obviously God had made other people along the way, and I asked what other parts of the Bible were not literal or what had been left out. I asked how I could believe any of it, why I should take any of it literally, when there were important things left unsaid?

I wanted them to make it make sense, but I was too cheeky about it, and they told me to stop asking questions or stop coming to youth group. Part of me was triumphant—I knew that I was right, that things didn't make sense, and that they didn't have any good answers. But the comfort I had held on to for so long was gone, and I didn't know how to tell the youth-group teacher that if he couldn't give me that back, I wouldn't have anything else to assure me that somewhere things made sense, that there was a reason for my dad and his world, and that even though I felt so terribly lost, I would someday be safe and loved, and everything would be okay.

Eventually I ended up praying in my own way, saying things like, *God, if you're anything like what I imagined for the first ten years of my life, you know what I'm up to, and you know that I'm trying. Just let me know if I need to do something differently.* And I heard his holy response, *You're gonna be all right, girl. You'll be okay.*

The summer I turned thirteen, I started my period while with my granny, who was visiting another older lady in a clean-looking trailer park. I lay on her friend's carpeted floor, holding my belly in pain, wondering what new hell I was in.

Around that time, my dad started a relationship with a new woman who had three kids of her own and was kind to me. She and my father had a history, but I didn't know exactly what it was and didn't ask. I started going to his house more often, even though my old room was taken by one of the girls, and my new room in the addition he mostly finished never felt like mine at all. I almost always enjoyed the company of the other children and the sound of laughter, even the disagreements. It felt like we were a family. We even called each other family—Dad's girlfriend was my *stepmom*, and her children were my *stepbrother* and *stepsisters*.

My mother had dated very little, that I knew of. I woke up one night to hear her crying in our living room. Since there were only two bedrooms in the trailer, she slept in the living room. I was at the end of the trailer, but the walls were paper thin. I lay there, scared to move, not knowing who she was talking to. I listened to her sobs, and because the person she was talking to was not yelling, I eventually felt it was safe enough to go back to sleep. In the morning, I asked, *Did he hit you?*

She told me no, but she was still so traumatized by what my father had done to her, she was uncomfortable around men.

Still, not too long after that, she ended up going to Las Vegas to visit a man she had met through a mail dating service—they had written letters back and forth. She came home with a ring on her finger and announced that our new stepfather would be there in two weeks.

When Frank arrived, he immediately set out to establish the rules. We were to respect and obey him without question. It seemed like he criticized everything we did, everything our mother did. Frank implemented new rules all the time and announced them to us as if he were the emperor of the two-bedroom trailer we were suddenly crowded into together. Our mother went along with everything he said, and it felt like she forgot that we children were there, that we had enjoyed a brief respite from having a tyrant in our home. Maybe she was just relieved he didn't hit her.

It wasn't long before Junior moved back into our father's house, unable to stand living with Frank. In every other situation, I had always been the more argumentative one of us, but somehow, I managed to hold my tongue enough to live with this new man who immediately expected us to respect him, obey him, and call him *Pops*. We called him by his first name.

Throughout the summer, my father and his girlfriend took us swimming at a lake in Bath County, which always seemed poorer than our county as a whole. A concrete pad sat maybe a hundred feet away from the shore. We were able to duck our heads underneath the edge and bob back up into the roomy pocket of air. When the water was high, it would drain into a deep, empty tunnel that we could look down into. I grew to love that place and taught myself how to dive from the top of the concrete pad. I would climb back up the ladder, over and over, to perfect the arc and to make sure I kept my legs straight and together.

There were often a handful of unemployed men who fished or drank on the bank in the afternoons. One day, one of the old men told my father that he must be proud of me, with my nice little body. I did not know why we left so early that day, but I found out soon that I had done something wrong to solicit that attention. The whole ride home, I sat in the back of the truck with my brother and the other kids as a weight grew heavier in my stomach. We all knew that Dad was mad, and he had only said a couple of things to let me know it was something I had done. *I bet you're happy with yourself, aren't you. You just love getting attention.* I hadn't thought about other people watching me, but I burned with shame, and my father's girlfriend did not look at me.

When we got home, he made it clear—my careful falling, the only moment in which I felt graceful and perhaps even talented, could serve no end other than to seduce the drunk grandfather at the lake, so it had to stop. Wearing a bikini was suddenly a disgrace, and I was trying to show off like some whore. I couldn't tell him, *No, no, I just love the way it feels to swim and dive and feel so free and maybe be good at something. I didn't hear that man, and that's not my fault, and what kind of old man compliments another man on his daughter's body?* I couldn't say anything. I stopped my lovely falling. I tried to hide myself better, knowing that Dad would be watching from then on and that my summer days at the lake were no longer for me to enjoy.

For a short time, I had a friend who lived in that same county. I met her through my dad's girlfriend, somehow, and loved her instantly. She was pretty and funny and seemed to like me despite me not being as pretty or quick to laugh as she was. I went to her home only once, and we hung out in the woods behind her house, running around with a happiness that I had never felt before. We found a patch of mayapples and I ate the fruits, not knowing I should make sure they were ripe, but someone was watching out for me and I did not get sick.

When she felt like it was close to time for her mom to get home, we made our way back to her house, and her stepdad got there soon after. For some reason, he was instantly angry at her and began yelling. To my surprise, she yelled right back and didn't show fear even when he yanked his belt off and began hitting her with it. She backed into her bedroom and shrunk into the corner while he hit her. I watched from the doorway, not knowing what to do. She didn't cry, but screamed and glared at him with disgust until he finally stopped.

I stood there and stared, knowing I should help her and wishing I could protect her, but I was unwilling to take that whipping myself. Unsure how far he would go, what would happen next. I knew afterward I had failed her. There was no one else who could have stepped in, but my helplessness showed me once again how little I could do for the girls and women I loved. How little I could do for myself.

When she was able to stand up, we left the house and ran back into the woods. She decided she was going to run away, and I decided I would go with her, believing we could understand each other's suffering. As it grew darker, though, I started wondering where we would go and how we would survive. I voiced my doubts, and she insisted she wasn't going back, though I was free to go without her. I mentioned her mom and how scared she would be. My friend didn't care but slowly softened as the sun set. We made it back to her house to find her mom talking to her stepdad, and they decided I wouldn't be spending the night after all. My dad picked me up a while later, and I told her goodbye, still happy I had a friend who wanted to run through the woods with me, who had her own wildness, and we could run free and wild together in the sacred forest. I called her a couple of times after that, and sent her a letter, but never heard from her again.

I think of her now and wish I knew her last name. But I know if I found her, I would ask: *Did you hide your wildness away, keep it safe until no one else could control you?* And I know the likely answer.

That fall, I spent one night with a friend I considered family, who was a year or two younger than me but already had the body of a woman. She lived in Elliott County, in a small, grimy trailer in a small, rundown trailer park. Most of the time when I was there, the adults were pretty much gone, or we were out walking around the tiny town.

She had an older cousin who showed up at their trailer that night, someone who had been or was related to her through marriage or a former marriage—it seemed like a murky relationship. Even though he was really cute and six years older than I was, he appeared to like me. He put his head on my lap and said things that made me think maybe he wanted to be my boyfriend, even though it seemed like my friend was jealous and might want him for herself, cousin or not.

Her mom's boyfriend, Louis, and a friend of his walked in at some point, and it was clear that the cousin's company wasn't completely welcome. I had spent time with my friend, her mom, and Louis during the summer before, and Louis was always particularly nice to me. Once that summer, he had driven to Morehead and saw me and a friend walking from the movie theater. He called out, *Hey, honey!* to me, and when I recognized him, I was surprised at his friendliness and said it back to him. I thought of him and his girlfriend as new parent figures, and I would write her letters, though she never wrote back. They seemed to have a lightheartedness that extended to me when I was around, and it was a relief to feel likable.

That particular evening, Louis wasn't as friendly as usual. He sat on the love seat in the living room, asking pointed questions of the cousin, whose head was still on my lap. Louis's friend sat on the couch across the room from Louis, mostly watching the television that droned on in the background. Eventually, Louis told me to get up and come sit next to him. I didn't want to leave the sweetness of sitting with the older boy but was afraid to say no, so I reluctantly sat on the love seat, next to him.

He took my hand in his and interlaced his fingers with mine, the entire time talking in an oddly threatening manner that seemed to come from nowhere. I tried to pull my hand away, and he held on tight, so I dug my nails into his hand, hoping he wouldn't react too harshly if I kept my tone light. He acted like his feelings were hurt and asked why I wouldn't hold his hand. I told him he was too old for me, and he said he was only thirty, definitely not too old. He eventually pulled out his wallet and handed me his license, which showed he was thirty-two. I stared at the picture of him, with his light-blond hair and dark eyes, wondering what I could do to get out of the situation. He kept grabbing my hand, and I kept pulling it away, defying him with as much humor as I could muster, though it seemed like even the air around me was changing.

He grabbed my hand once more and finally held on to it tightly enough that I couldn't pull away, turned it over, and began rubbing the back of my hand against his bulging crotch. I didn't know what to do. His friend was looking at us with a smirk. I glanced at my friend, and she was glaring at us both. So I looked away, toward the floor, ashamed and embarrassed and afraid to move. He told the nineteen-year-old cousin it was time for him to go home, and Louis's friend got up to drive him there. When they left, my friend stood up and said she was going to bed, the anger in her voice apparent. I sat there for a moment and realized that I could go to bed, too, so I jumped up and said I was sleepy.

I made it to the hallway, and he told me to come back, to sit beside him. I looked at him, not sure what kind of crossroads we were at, but knowing I would have only myself to blame for whatever happened if I returned. I told him no, I was tired and needed to go to sleep. With a serious edge to his voice, he told me again to come back and sit down beside him. Once again, I told him I was going to bed, and I quickly walked into my friend's bedroom just a couple of steps down the hallway.

She was mad at me when I came into her room. When I asked why, she said she didn't know why he and I had to act like that, and I tried to explain to her that I didn't know what to do. She told me Louis had a peephole in the bathroom and would watch her taking showers, but she had found the peephole and stuffed toilet paper into it. Then, one day while she was showering, she saw it moving as someone tried to push it out of the hole, and she put her finger there to make sure it wouldn't come out.

The next morning, the house phone rang and I answered it, but there was an immediate click as the caller hung up. It happened again, and I told my friend. *It's him,* she said. *He's dialing our number and letting it ring, and when you pick up, he's hanging up.* Though she didn't seem alarmed and drifted back to sleep, I didn't know what to think when the phone rang another ten or more times that morning, apparently as Louis waited for one of us to pick up again while he called from the bedroom at the end of the hall.

Her mother finally came home late in the morning, and as she drove me to my dad's, she crowed over the man she had been with the night before, telling us how they danced all night long and that she was leaving Louis. Since she was leaving him, I thought I might as well let her know what he had done, so she would realize she was making the right choice. My friend was angry—she didn't want me to say anything.

*You don't think I should say anything?*

*Well, it's too late now. Now you have to tell her.*

*Tell me what?* her mom asked. So I told her, and not a lot was said after that.

Later that week, I came home from school and found a state trooper waiting for me in the living room of our trailer. He asked me careful questions as my mother and stepfather sat there, listening. After he left, my mother asked her own questions, and I quickly learned some important things. I should have called someone to come get me. I should not have been wearing shorts. I should not have even been awake.

By the following summer, the situation had evolved dramatically. At first, all the adults insisted that I testify in court, that I prevent anything from happening to another girl at his hands. Then, as my mother's questions amplified, dissent crept in from everyone I loved: *Why was she awake? What was she wearing? She wanted the attention anyway . . .* Finally, my friend's mother decided that she wasn't leaving her man and that he hadn't done anything wrong. My father's girlfriend—my *stepmother*—didn't want to talk about any of it and said she wasn't picking a side. My friend even seemed to forget about the little peephole into the bathroom that was apparently made especially for her.

As my dad drove me to court on my fourteenth birthday, he told me everything I needed to know. That I had humiliated my father. That he was going to kill that man. He would kill that man, and what the fuck was wrong with me anyway? Did I want to spend all my life acting like a goddamn whore in a goddamn trailer?

I had never kissed a boy.

Soon, I sat in the full courtroom not far from the man. Other people sat in the back of the room—his relatives? His friends? They were not my relatives, not my friends. The prosecutor asked me whether I was ready, and I calmly told him: *I have nothing to say.* Within minutes, I sat in the judge's chambers, surrounded by men asking questions and making declarations: *Has someone threatened you? You can't do this— think of the other girls he might hurt. Everyone's waiting for you, you have to talk.*

For the first time in my life, I refused. I told them again: *I have nothing to say.* And then, I said nothing.

I knew by that point that it didn't matter what I said anyway. Someone was going to use my words against me—both in that *court of law* and at home. I felt powerful, for a brief moment, when I refused to speak, when I realized that I *could* refuse to speak. I could withhold my truth and protect myself from the betrayal I knew would follow if I made myself vulnerable to them. But after fourteen years of speaking and being punished, there was a dark lesson taking shape within my mind. I realized that the people who were supposed to love me, who were supposed to protect me, would actually sacrifice me and send me to a witness chair to be cross-examined by a man who didn't know me and whose job was to reveal me as a liar. The people I loved sent me to that courtroom with my father—my mother didn't come, my *stepmother* didn't come.

Before I got to that courtroom, I knew they no longer cared what had happened—they didn't doubt it *had* happened but were sure I had wanted whatever he had done, no matter what I said. And if my own family felt that way, I knew everyone else would, too. I knew that the truth no longer mattered, especially my truth. That there was more risk in speaking than in keeping it secret.

# CHAPTER 13

## *Hunger*

On the ride home from court, my father told me again how I had humiliated him. How I was just like my mother. How he would kill that man. And he drove to a fast-food restaurant, but I wasn't hungry as I sat next to him in the drive-through, every bit of myself knotted up inside, afraid he would annihilate me with his rage, controlling my face so that I showed no fear, no anger, no despair.

I had to go to counseling for a while, in a building on Main Street, where I sometimes saw too-thin adults sitting on the steps. In court, the judge sentenced the man to probation, without me saying a word. *Why?* I often wondered afterward. The cousin was subpoenaed to testify, but *he had to work*, so everyone understood he wouldn't be showing up. Maybe the judge already knew this man in front of him. Maybe he knew what it was I couldn't say.

I couldn't have told the judge that I realized it wasn't the worst thing—he hadn't raped me and had hardly touched me. Even though shame and fear were still there, even though I still wonder what would have happened if I had gone back to sit next to him, it was not the worst thing. I couldn't have made the judge understand that I only ever said anything because I wanted to help this woman who I thought might be like a mother to me, even though she made the worst gravy and biscuits

I ever ate, and I had not wanted the grown man to want me, but I had lapped up that family's attention like a starved dog.

Did I deserve what he had done? Had I asked for it? We were living in two different worlds, he and I. I hadn't been afraid of him and didn't recognize him as a threat. He made holes through cheap paneling and flirted with girls who hadn't kissed anyone.

I told my counselor a little about what had happened and a little about how I was afraid of my dad. She told me she was addicted to nose spray and not to tell anyone. There was a painting in the waiting room, and I studied it endlessly. Impressionism—I had the slightest understanding of that painting style. It was always one of my least favorites, maybe just a little better than abstract art. Everything was so blurry, so undefined. The world melting into itself. The faces unreadable.

The last whipping I got came when I was fourteen years old. My father's girlfriend and her three children still lived with him. Her daughters were both younger, maybe nine and eleven, but the son was a year older than me. On a summer afternoon, I sat on his lap as he rested in a dilapidated rocking chair. When the chair gave way beneath us, he threw his Mountain Dew can across the room in anger, though at what, I am not sure. His sisters were quick to tell my father and their mother when they returned, since their brother had made a mess in the house. My dad whipped him, I remember, and I'm sure his mother was never able to control him after that. He was livid that this man was able to strike him—not his father, not even really a stepfather. The man who slept with his mother.

I didn't expect it, but I got whipped, too. I had no idea I had done anything wrong. Sitting on a boy's lap, however, was unacceptable. Though we slept in the same house, sometimes in the same room, and ate together and called each other's parents our own, this was a boy I was not to sit so close to. I knew without anyone telling me that the reason was the closeness with a boy, the good feeling I had when he was nice to me, when he didn't seem to think I was repulsive. I wasn't allowed to have that good feeling and was likely a whore for wanting it in the first place.

That was around the same time my dad rested his hand on my shoulder for the first time, as we walked toward the house together. We were coming from the driveway and talking and laughing about something. He put his left hand on my right shoulder as we walked, and I was surprised—he never reached out like that, and for a second, I thought I had finally done it, I had finally won his love.

But his grip tightened, and I looked at him in confusion, trying to understand. He had a smile on his face—the same smile I had seen so many times. He squeezed my shoulder so hard that I could no longer walk and buckled from the pain, collapsing there in the yard next to him.

*Dad, you're hurting me, please.*

He looked at me and said nothing, then let up and walked back into the house, our conversation forgotten.

After she and my father argued one day, my *stepmother* told me she noticed that I complained about my stomach hurting every time they had a disagreement. She asked me why, and I asked her, *What if he hits you?* She assured me he wouldn't, and I hoped she was so confident because she knew something about him that I did not. When he did hit her, it was beyond whatever I had imagined. He hit her son first, and when she tried to stop my father, she found herself thrown onto their bed as he choked her. She moved out soon after. They reconciled to some degree for a while, but eventually, it ended. It was the last time his house was clean, or full of laughing children. It was the last time I ever thought he might be okay.

I entered high school just a couple of months after having refused to testify in the courtroom. I was angry at the world, and high school did nothing to change that. I had always been an A and B student, always capable of earning As but rarely really trying. In ninth-grade gym, I earned a C one quarter and then for the entire class. I also earned a C in geometry, of all things. In gym, I hated running around, doing laps and dancing to "The Lion Sleeps Tonight," trying to learn our overweight gym teacher's choreography. I hated being graded in volleyball, where I was scared the ball would hit me in the face, or someone's elbow would catch my glasses and they would get broken. When I was younger, I always got whipped if my glasses were broken, no matter what the situation was or who was responsible. According to my dad, I was responsible for them no matter what, and I took that responsibility seriously.

In geometry class, though, I spent most of my time thinking about ways to kill myself and how much I hated my classmates, many of whom had been my tormentors from the gifted program. We had an interior brick wall near the lunchroom, and sometimes I would drag my knuckles across it, tearing off as much skin as possible in one rough slide. I tried to make myself vomit into the school toilet but couldn't figure out how to gag myself. I tried not to eat but was no good at starving.

Each day, I walked into the lunchroom in a haze of confusion that was periodically interrupted by terror at being in the wrong place, saying the wrong thing, doing everything wrong in general, always. My mind felt alien, hostile.

At home, I kept a razor blade in my bedroom, and I showed it to a girl who came over once. She warned me to be careful with it, and I said, *Oh, don't worry, it doesn't hurt.* To prove it, I stuck the point of the blade as far into my leg as I could jab it and pulled hard upward for about an inch. *See? It doesn't hurt.*

She recoiled in horror, and something about that surprised me. Weren't all girls like us feeling this way? I could sense it, but it seemed so inconsequential at the time—I did not think of it as real pain. Feeling physical pain seemed to ease the anguish that burned inside me. I walked through our small trailer, past my mother and stepfather as they watched television, with a line of blood rolling down my leg. I stuck a bandage on it and went back to my room, unnoticed. The scar is much wider now than it seems it should be, considering how fine a line the razor drew.

Thoughts of suicide were nothing new to me, but I was not always interested in killing myself when I wanted to hurt myself. The first time I pretended to cut myself, I was about five years old and found a tube of Halloween vampire blood in my brother's bedroom. I squeezed a line of it across my wrist—how I knew that was the right spot, I have no idea—and ran into the kitchen, clutching my arm and dragging my leg a little, for effect. My mom was distracted, but when she saw my wrist, she started screaming and rushed me into the bathroom, thrust my wrist into the sink, and began running cold water over it. Concerned by how upset she seemed, I told her, *Mom, it's not real. It's fake.* She fairly exploded because I had fooled her in such a way, and that began a new favorite pastime for me that lasted through my teen years, though I never went quite that far with it again.

As a fourteen-year-old, when I was thinking about death, I was seriously contemplating the repercussions of various approaches. My favorite fantasy was one in which I would somehow procure a handgun, bring it to school, and make a small speech before shooting myself in front of my geometry class. Some very publicized school shootings occurred around that time, and it was the first time I saw the video for Pearl Jam's *Jeremy*, in which a young boy does much the same as I imagined doing. But whenever I asked myself whether I wanted vengeance, I quickly realized that I did not wish my classmates any harm, other than to know my pain for one moment.

By that point, I was overwhelmed by their ridicule, which had gone on for more than five years. It was hardly anything by the time I was a freshman in high school, but the looks on their faces said everything to me. I had stopped trying to perform well on the Speech and Drama team—during middle school, I had occasionally won awards, but when I did, the popular guys on the team would ask with disdain, *You won something?*

My father took me shopping at a clothing store in eighth grade—he somehow had plenty of money on hand, so he insisted on taking me to a real clothing store and told me to get whatever I wanted. I was so excited to have a silk shirt before they went out of style, and I wore it to one of the Speech and Drama competitions. When we were getting on the bus, one of the kids asked me where I got it, and I think they complimented me on it. For some reason—whether they asked or I volunteered the information, I don't remember—I told them how much it cost. Soon after, someone else told me it was a nice shirt and asked how much it cost. Then another, and another, and another.

I realized they were mocking me, and I finally wished that I wasn't wearing my new silk shirt and that I had never gotten it at all. I was afraid to wear it to school after that, thinking they might pour their derision on me without mercy, but it was the most expensive thing I had ever owned, and I felt obligated to wear it, although I assumed my father had probably stolen the money or sold drugs to get it.

I had sat with some of the popular girls in one class in eighth grade, but another kid brought me down a peg when I joined the other girls in making fun of him. *You're just their errand monkey,* he said with contempt. He was right—when everyone finished their papers, I would take them to the teacher's desk at the front of the room, happy to be so visibly part of their group, pushing away the nagging thought that I, in fact, did not belong.

I just wanted to tell them what my life at home had been like that whole time. Distraught over the nasty words and looks they seemed to take such pleasure in, I did not know how to stand up for myself. I could not understand what I had done to deserve it, but most of the time, I believed it was my fault—after all, I did not look like them, I did not own the things they owned. I realized I did not know how it felt to *be* them. In my isolation, I wanted them to have to listen to me, and I wanted them to wonder how it felt to be *me*, trying to bear their cruelty while I was trying so hard to survive my home, to endure being in my body.

But I said nothing, did nothing.

When I look back on those years, I try to make sense of how I kept going. All the things that had felt possibly *safe* and *good* were suddenly gone—church, my mother, my stepmother. The scraps of approval and affection were no longer, and I was further away from everything, and everyone, than I had ever been before.

# CHAPTER 14

## *Happy Now*

The summer after my freshman year, I ended up going to a movie with an older boy from school. Shawn flirted with me a lot wherever I had run into him—at the city pool, perhaps, but he was a rougher sort and not the kind of teenage boy who spent his time by the pool. Since Mom worked for the city, we got discounted passes. Shawn was the type who started smoking cigarettes when he was fourteen or fifteen, and he went on to join a motorcycle gang, though what that meant in our little town, I was never sure.

Shawn told me to meet him at a movie, and I was excited to go on my first date—it seemed like this was what normal people did. I didn't have to wonder for long whether he would make a move—he spent most of the time kissing me too hard, to the point where my lips were bruised a light purple the next day. He also put his hand down the front of my pants and into my vagina. A few minutes after that, he pulled his hand out and looked at it in the light of the movie, then laughed a little and wiped it on my jeans. I saw later that it was blood he wiped on me, and he left my breasts sore from squeezing them so hard. I was just happy that someone finally liked me, and it didn't occur to me it was a problem that nothing he did felt good. I was excited afterward at the thought he was interested in me, but he didn't call me or otherwise show any inclination toward seeing me again. We may have talked again at some point, but I had no idea what to expect and so expected nothing.

James, a boy from health class, called me a couple of weeks later and came over to go for a walk together. I told him I had gone to the movies with Shawn and wondered whether I should date him—as if I was asking for advice, since the two boys knew each other. As if Shawn wanted to date me and I had a choice in the matter. After a minute of silence, he responded that he didn't think I should date Shawn, but he thought I should date him instead. I was shocked he asked me to date him like that—it was the very first time a boy ever asked me to be his girlfriend, and he became my very first boyfriend. He met my mom and stepfather, who weren't impressed, but I guess they didn't think it would last long enough to be of any consequence.

That summer, James decided he wanted to be a hippie, and he asked me whether I wanted to be a hippie with him. I turned fifteen, and he was sixteen; he would turn seventeen in the winter. All I knew of hippies came from listening to my mother's one Janis Joplin album while we were still in the holler and from having a vague notion of what Woodstock was. James listened to the Grateful Dead and made me a mixtape of their songs, which to this day is the best mixtape I have ever heard. After giving up on pop music, I had turned to Chuck Berry and Sam Cooke, along with the Johnny Horton tape that my stepfather brought with him from Nevada—I had the least relatable music taste of anyone I knew. I was happy to give up on pop culture altogether, and James introduced me to another culture that made much more sense at the time—a *counterculture* that itself rejected the entire world I felt so rejected and battered by.

James also wanted to become a vegetarian that summer. At first, we went on a lot of hikes and took turkey sandwiches and apples from his mother's house, but then we began eschewing the meat for grilled cheese sandwiches. His mother had salad all the time, and whole wheat bread—stuff that tasted and felt good to me but that my mom and stepdad didn't buy. When he asked me whether I wanted to be a vegetarian, too, I said yes right away and ate whatever I could that didn't clearly involve meat. How nice it was to have someone to be *something* with.

My mother refused to support my new diet and wouldn't make any dish meat-free, or even a portion of the dish. Since she and my stepdad ate meat at every meal, I learned to cook fifteen-bean soup and potato soup. I taught myself to make bread so I could have whole wheat bread. She didn't want to buy me soy milk, which I wanted to try, so I spent my own money to buy all the health foods I had never heard of until then. I didn't get an allowance, though, so I ended up mostly eating the nonmeat side dishes they cooked—mashed potatoes, canned green beans, and the like.

That same summer, I had my first job, working for the United States Forest Service. They had an office right outside Morehead, by Cave Run Lake. I earned minimum wage—something close to five dollars an hour—and spent forty hours each week doing some sort of work with another girl from school who had also signed up for the employment program for high school sophomores.

By that time, James had reintroduced me to smoking weed. I had smoked with my father when I was thirteen or so, camping for the last time with our cousins from Tennessee. The weed had made me feel irritable, but not too long after, I asked my dad to teach me to roll a joint, hoping it would make me feel good that time. He did, but I still didn't feel a high. I persisted with James, though, and finally developed a liking for it. After a few more tries, I was thoroughly enjoying it. I had intense hallucinations just riding in James's mother's car, listening to Jefferson Airplane or Pink Floyd. Sometimes I would ask my dad to get us weed, and sometimes he bought it from my boyfriend.

I lost my virginity that year. Didn't lose it, really—I set it aside quite willingly.

Some of the older men at the Forest Service knew my dad, and some of them liked to smoke weed, so they would buy it from me, too. One guy took Mini Thin pills all day long *for his asthma*. I did other things out in the woods as we spread lime and seeds and fertilizer and straw to build ponds. I took off my shirt one day, wearing no bra, since it was as hot as hell and the older boy I was working with had his shirt off. I asked him whether he minded, and he said no—that seemed good enough for me. I didn't think of myself as a girl in this boy's eyes—just as a flat-chested, unattractive female he wouldn't want to see anyway. Later it would occur to me that boys like to tell stories about such things and that I just didn't have a good sense of what people expected of me or how much they could really accept. Much later, I realized that when it comes to taking off shirts, most boys his age do not differentiate between girls like me and other girls.

James spent most of that summer with his grandparents in Ashland. My mother wouldn't let me call him from our house, even if I paid her back for the long-distance charges. That summer, I put almost all the money I earned toward phone cards and walked to a pay phone in town to call him, though occasionally I would try calling from our house if my mother and stepfather were in bed but I thought maybe I wouldn't wake up his grandparents. Phone cards were terribly expensive at the time, and I managed to blow my entire salary on calling him and buying a few CDs.

When he came back and school started once again, we spent a lot of time at his mother's house after school. Frank and my mother decided to crack down on that, so they had me come straight home after school to do chores—namely, loading the dishwasher and washing all the dirty pots and pans by hand. I would then walk to meet James, and we either went to his mother's house until shortly before she would come home, or we went up into the woods behind the university's radio station tower, where we had stashed a gravity bong for smoking weed.

We would often smoke a little and then go down to the university library and into the basement, where they kept the bound periodicals. We did our homework completely stoned, and one night, after doing a lot of Algebra II homework, I ended up hallucinating the quadratic formula. We would also have sex in the basement, in the woods, in his mother's house, and wherever else we thought we could get away with it. I knew how pregnancy worked but never thought about condoms or birth control.

I loved the sex, but I also learned that I shouldn't enjoy it to the fullest—I had to rein myself in a bit and not enjoy it *too much*. He didn't like it when I orgasmed, so I learned to hold my orgasms back. I wanted to have sex all the time, and he called me a *nympho*. One time, he didn't want to have sex at all, and I rubbed myself lying next to him in bed. When I was finished, he looked at me and asked with disdain, *Happy now?*

Even as a very young girl, I somehow knew that sex was a problem all around me. It was when my father rubbed calamine lotion on my poison ivy–covered legs and said, *You know I'm not doing anything wrong, don't you?* and when I was five and slept in the bed close to him one night and tried to put my foot on his leg, and he moved away. I didn't understand why he didn't want his daughter's affection. It was every moment in which an older man looked into my eyes and smiled knowingly, the moments in which my father would lose it and call me a whore or a slut or whatever else. It was like I wore a flashing sign that said, *Take what you want!* and it took many years for me to remember who the first really was, who really took my virginity, to whom I *lost* something. But we never really forget—we just tuck things away, and they quietly creep into each of our actions, our thoughts, our words, our principles, and our fears.

I learned so much the year I was fifteen. I lied to my mother and told her I was spending the week with my father so I could go to my first rock concert—all the way to Providence, Rhode Island. There, I took

LSD for the first time—not a large dose, just enough to feel something different happening with my senses. Over the next two years, I tried opium, mushrooms, a few more doses of LSD (with a little more *oomph* to them), and DMT. It was a mother's nightmare. I stopped wearing deodorant and smeared patchouli oil on my armpits instead. I smelled like body odor all the time and did not care. I wore bell-bottoms that had actually been around since the 1970s and huge tie-dye shirts with Grateful Dead logos or mushrooms on them.

Although James and his older friends helped me feel like I finally belonged somewhere, I was still angry with the world, and now I had a language to help me articulate that feeling, however imprecise. I didn't think I was rebelling against my parents—I still came home after school to do my chores, and I was never more than a couple of minutes late for curfew, which was whenever the sun set, regardless of how early that could be in the winter. Thinking that I was rejecting some system or broken culture allowed me to say, *I can't do this anymore,* and *I do not belong here.* I found a reason for my not feeling *okay* that made my environment, my society, the problem—not me, not something inside me.

And that helped. It helped me to say there was something wrong with hierarchy, something wrong with societal norms, something dreadfully wrong with our culture of exploitation. It let me practice saying, *I don't belong here,* before I had to face the family and community who still claimed me. I learned to say, *I can't be a part of this,* to an audience that wasn't listening, and that experience helped me eventually say it when it counted.

While I was finally excited about my not belonging, I still felt compelled to achieve academically, though it felt a bit like a game at that point. I didn't take my classes seriously, and I didn't take my teachers seriously, but I enjoyed having mastery over the work they assigned me. I was a smart-ass in class and often still stoned from the weed we smoked in a cemetery on our way to the bus stop. Still, several of my teachers managed to have an impact on my thinking, whether they knew it or not.

In my sophomore Algebra II class, my teacher one day suggested that we take a practice test at home to prepare for an upcoming test. I raised my hand and asked him whether we would receive points for the practice test, and he said no. In typical fifteen-year-old fashion, I asked with a smirk, *Why would I do it, then?* He stopped in his tracks and stared straight at me to respond, *To learn.*

That was the first time a teacher had ever really made me think there was an intrinsic value to my learning. I had always thought of my good grades in school as being for others—to please my teachers, to please my parents. It was one of the few ways I received positive attention, when I did: *She's a smart little thing.*

I went home and took the practice test that night, then checked my answers and made sure I knew how to do all the problems. I scored higher than anyone in the class for the rest of the year, and since I earned almost every single bonus point our teacher offered, I ended the semester with a grade of 105 percent. The other *smart kids* who were in the accelerated classes with me wanted to pair up anytime we got to work together. They wanted something *I* had at that time, and though I did not like them, I would partner up with them and proceed to do most of the work.

The best part about dating an older boy and smoking lots of weed with him was that I found myself once again in the woods much of the time—smoking at our hidden spot or hiking the trails behind the university lake, walking in the woods around my house, or climbing the cliffs that sat above my granny's house and marked the border between her property and the Daniel Boone National Forest, along the ridgeline of the hills that cradled her fields and garden and home. We would often smoke and sit quietly, or my boyfriend would talk to a friend while I watched the leaves and noticed their perfect arrangement along the branches. I discovered that flocks of birds flew in perfect synchrony with one another and in time with heartbeats. That the wind loved the trees and that the forest floor loved the leaves, that the heat and the cold and the sun and its setting were all singing a love song. That the wordless joy of the forest was not lost in my past.

And I felt hope.

# CHAPTER 15

## *Love and Marriage*

I cheated on James shortly after we started dating. It wasn't that I particularly wanted to cheat on him—it was just that one of his friends made advances, and it didn't occur to me that I should say no, that I could say no. I told James but wouldn't tell him who it was. He broke up with me but decided to forgive me not too long afterward. There was a lot of forgiving yet to come, between the two of us.

James started college at the university in Morehead the same semester I started my junior year of high school. He made new friends, older college students who lived in houses they rented and had parties in. James moved in with them for a portion of the semester. I was part of his night life sometimes, on the rare occasion I was allowed to stay out past dark.

My stepdad went through my purse around that time and found the clay pipe I had made in art class—a ceramics project I had hidden in a bigger clay pot and fired in the kiln. I was grounded for a while, and then my mom sat me down at a fast-food restaurant and laid out some new ground rules: I would start shaving my legs. I would start eating meat. I would stop smoking pot. These things I was doing, they made her look bad. Everyone knew about it.

I quickly told her I would stop smoking pot, since it was illegal and I was living in her house. I thought that was fair. But I figured what I shaved and what I ate didn't really affect anyone but me. When I did find myself around someone telling me, *It's okay to smoke a little—she'll never know,* I just said, *No, I gave her my word.* Somehow, that still meant something.

Sometimes, when I couldn't go where James was going, I asked him to stay with me, to skip the party. He didn't, though, and I had a nagging sense that something was changing, that he was further away from me than it seemed. I was scared of losing the one person I thought would ever love me, so I just quietly worried and waited to feel good again.

One of his older friends decided to tell me one day that James was spending an awful lot of time with one of the college girls who sometimes came to their parties. I didn't believe he would cheat on me, but I was filled with jealousy and a new kind of anxiety I had never felt before. Each time I came to their house, I scanned the room for the blond girl whom I never really met, whose name made my stomach hurt.

Then James failed out of the university. After Christmas break, he transferred to Eastern Kentucky University, all the way in Richmond. I was working at Arby's, and once again, I spent all the money I made on phone cards to call his dorm room. Sometimes I left messages with his roommate. Mostly, the phone just rang. I would stand at the pay phone closest to my house and listen to the endless ringing, another taunt I could not fit into my mind. I wrote him letters and waited for his responses. My intuition told me something was wrong, but I desperately wanted everything to be okay, so instead I hoped that *I* was wrong, that my gut was wrong, that there was just something wrong with me.

There seemed to be an impenetrable wall between me and whoever was near. Then I fell in love with a friend's younger brother. We shared one kiss—in my excitement at finding him and his wit, his mind, and his love for music that I had never heard and that became the soundtrack for those months of my life, I kissed him lightly in one of the sweet groves of trees near my trailer, though he was not enthusiastic in the way I thought he would be. His face seemed to be made like a painting, eyes that narrowed just a bit, lips always on the verge of a smile.

He wanted me to break up with James, who was so far away by now, but I wouldn't. And yet, I couldn't pretend I wasn't in love with the younger boy, in love with his whole family. On school mornings, I walked to their house just to be around their laughter and their apparent understanding of one another, which seemed to extend even to me. I visited the sister after school sometimes—she was a year older and mostly seemed to tolerate me. She wrote me a letter one day, telling me to choose between her and her brother, as I couldn't be friends with both of them. I chose him, the one who had not given me an ultimatum.

I thought she would understand, just as I expected him to understand why I couldn't choose him over James. I showed up with a loaf of homemade bread once, and only the parents spoke to me, the kids all busy in their rooms, and it slowly dawned on me that something had changed. I'd walk to the bus stop near their house for a while longer, but there would be no laughter for me, no belonging with their family, and finally, I caught on.

James returned from school just as I ran out of other people to love me, and he hadn't made good-enough grades to go back the next semester. I had just turned seventeen that summer, and my mother and stepfather told me we were moving to Elliott County, which offered even less to entertain a teenager than where we were living. They said I could finish my senior year at my current high school and continue working at Long John Silver's—Arby's didn't last all that long—but I would have to drive straight home every day unless I was working, and no socializing. I knew what that meant—no more seeing James unless he could find a way to drive the thirty minutes to our new house, which would sit along a high ridge near the narrow, winding road that he and I often drove to our pot dealer's house as we meandered along the country roads, listening to Pink Floyd and Led Zeppelin and the Grateful Dead, me sometimes writing poetry. I was devastated. I didn't have a lot of friends, but this move would mean that I only experienced the worst of school and work, and none of the good things—hikes with James, going to his friends' houses, trying to be friends with the few people who still talked to me.

When I told him, James and I decided we should try to live together. I knew that my mom and stepdad wouldn't let me see him if they managed to take me to Elliott County, and I was certain I would lose him. I was sure he was the only man who would ever love me, and I clung to what we had, no matter how unhealthy or unhappy I sometimes knew it to be.

James didn't have a job but could probably come up with something, and I could finish my senior year living in town, closer to school. I thought it was a pretty reasonable idea with clear benefits that my mother would appreciate—less driving, saving gas money, and . . . probably some other things, too. But as soon as I started talking, she blew up and yelled that I wasn't going to embarrass her by living with a boyfriend when I wasn't married. I didn't understand her old-fashioned morals in the context of our history—they didn't fit.

She yelled herself into a frenzy, though James and I were sitting there quietly, and I was fully unprepared for her to respond with anger. Finally, she said, *You want to live with him? You marry him. I'll sign the papers today if you want to marry him. If you really want to live with him so bad, you do that!* James and I left a short time later and sat in his mother's car. *What do you think?* I asked. He paused, then said, *I think we should do it.*

*Do what?*

*Get married.*

And so we did. We went back inside and told my mother, who immediately started crying and asking me whether I was sure I wanted to. My stepfather just said that now she had to let me, since she had offered to sign the papers. I didn't know what to say except yes, I was sure, we were sure.

I don't know that she wanted me to get married. Historically, it is an easy way to be rid of a daughter, and I was probably giving her some gray hairs by that point, with my refusal to shave my legs or eat meat. Even though she didn't go to church, my mother would occasionally refer to God as if that was something she believed in, so I thought she might have been concerned about me *living in sin*. Or maybe with what everyone else would think about me living in sin. At the time, I didn't understand how she might have struggled to raise a girl. I couldn't fathom the difficulty of mothering a girl, with so much unhealed trauma around the experience of being a woman.

Two days later, we managed to get a preacher we had never met to marry us in a church we had never attended. I could only think, *This isn't right.* I briefly considered saying no, that I didn't want to, that I had just turned seventeen and didn't know the first damn thing about being somebody's wife, and if I were the betting kind, I would bet I was going to have a hard time figuring it out. But like everything else I had ever identified as *not right* in my life, I decided that what I thought didn't really matter. And anyway, wasn't James the only man who would ever love me? I thought it was my one chance to get married. One of my only friends at school soon told me, *You've clipped your wings,* and it took me twenty years to figure out what he meant.

Just like that, I joined a demographic I knew nothing about. Technically, I was a child bride, though I would have told you it was my choice and I knew what I was doing. I wasn't marrying my rapist. I wasn't marrying a man decades older—James was just a couple of years older than I was. Compared to my mom, who had run off to Jellico,

Tennessee, to marry my father when she was still seventeen, I was doing pretty good.

I didn't know how difficult it would be to finish high school, to heat our house, to keep my sense of hope alive. I didn't expect that I would lose all respect for my new husband, that our life together would never feel light or exciting or free. Having no preparation for adulthood, still reeling from all the nightmares of childhood and praying for the return of the indescribable magic I had found in nature, I took on the responsibility of caring for myself, thinking the work of raising me was already done. Many people could have told me—though none did—things were going to get worse before they could possibly get better. I wouldn't have listened anyway. I wouldn't have believed them.

# CHAPTER 16

## *A Pretty Smile*

We moved into the same house that James's college friends had rented, and each day I walked into the same entryway where his friend had told me James was probably sleeping with one of the college girls who was always around. At first, James got a job with the sawmill where Dry Branch Road met the highway. The highway was KY 519, just a two-lane road. My old church sits right off the road—the church where I learned about Jesus and was molested, saved, baptized, and finally told to leave.

James didn't work at that job for long but got another job at the sawmill a little farther down 519, closer to the road that would take you out to Amburgy Rocks, those five cliffs that sat partially on my granny's land and just a bit on United States Forest Service property. I didn't understand what happened to keep that job from lasting long, but next he got a job at a sawmill in Carter County, which took about forty-five minutes to get to each day.

I started my senior year in high school a couple of weeks after we got married, and everyone was surprised when I told them no, I wasn't pregnant, which filled me with a certain pride, though I knew I hadn't been careful enough in avoiding pregnancy to really be all that proud. We had one car, the 1986 Dodge Aries that Mom and Frank bought me for $600 after I turned sixteen. In their wisdom, they told me I could have a car or braces for my teeth, and in my wisdom, I chose the car.

Why was that the one time I was allowed to make a choice for myself? I didn't have the experience or insight to understand the relative value of braces at that time. I had no idea that it would just get harder and more expensive to fix my teeth, that there would be times I would resolve to do it, and other, more important things would come up that I would have to spend the money on instead. I couldn't predict the amount of shame I would endure as I looked in the mirror or how I would try to hide my teeth every time someone insisted I *smile for the camera*. The one time I was given control of my own body was the time I needed an adult to make the best decision for me.

James had to be at work at six in the morning, so I got up at four thirty to cook his breakfast and lunch, drive him to the sawmill, and then drive myself to school. Thankfully, the job didn't last that long.

We had roommates, God bless them—another couple. Now that I was no longer under my mother's roof, I saw no reason not to smoke all the weed I could, though I found that it was no longer an adventure but that I felt confined and anxious getting stoned in our house. There was always a party there, whether the living room was crowded or there were just two of us up all night, fully immersed in a chess game with a level of concentration made possible by the potent acid I generally had on hand. Since James couldn't hold a job and my paycheck from Long John Silver's didn't go far, we started buying sheets of acid to resell.

I don't know how the bills got paid, if they got paid. I may have met our landlord once. He was the father of a girl I went to school with, a girl who seemed poor and somehow more sexually advanced than the rest of us by middle school. She had a cute boyfriend from middle school onward, and last I heard, she married him and they moved into that house next to her father's several years after our heyday had ended.

The people at our house were almost always smoking weed or tripping on psychedelics. For the longest time, it seemed like a continuation of the scene that had unfolded when James's college friend and his roommates lived there. Back then, the house had felt light and comforting, airy and peaceful. I don't know whether it happened slowly or quickly, but somehow the feeling inside the house changed, and everything began feeling dark and dirty. Strange people eventually started coming around, and things were stolen off our porch when we left them overnight for a yard sale. Things were stolen from inside the house, too, and I couldn't begin to guess whether it was someone we counted as a friend who had done that.

Since I always had it on hand, I began taking LSD pretty regularly, though I found it had no effect the day after I had just taken it. For a while, I took it every other day, which gave my system just enough time to reestablish sensitivity to it. I loved nothing more than to play chess with a couple of different people while I was high on LSD, and we watched the Woodstock movie over and over that year. Since staying up all night and tripping had become habitual, I often missed entire days of school, showing up as soon as I could drive myself there safely. Now, I could laugh—or cry—thinking about my ability to judge what was safe back then. The truancy officer finally called me in and asked for directions to my house. I asked her what she needed that for, and when she told me, I understood I had to have a doctor's note to miss any more school. From then on, I went to the health department constantly, getting an excuse for whatever malady seemed to sound best at the time.

When I did make it to school, I was a sight to behold, with my unwashed and tangled hair, bathing once a week or so, pupils as big as dimes. We had a couple of pot plants growing in a closet, and James insisted we couldn't turn on the closet light to look at them—it would mess with their growing cycle or something like that. I didn't understand much of what he said about what we should and shouldn't do. It made me feel like a child again, struggling to comprehend what my father's rules were and what I had to do to keep him happy. I tried to just memorize everything and obey.

One afternoon, I lit a candle to carry into the closet with me—candlelight not being strong enough to disrupt our delicate plants and their growth hormones—and looked at the plants to see whether I saw anything of interest. I peered over the candle with my long, unwashed hair hanging above it, and soon my hair was on fire. I ran out of the closet to James, not knowing what to say, but he quickly grabbed a pillow or blanket and smothered the fire. My hair was singed all over on one side, but when I brushed it, the burnt pieces fell out, and I had no gaping bald spots, *praise the Lord*. The next day, when I walked into the school atrium, a girl greeted me by telling me that my hair looked good.

*She brushed it,* another girl pointed out, rolling her eyes. She was right—otherwise, I couldn't tell you how many times I brushed my hair that year. But you could get the number by counting on one hand.

My senior year, I had an English teacher who had us read *The Catcher in the Rye* and *Lord of the Flies*. While a lot of our rooms in the school were too cold during the warm months, hers was always mercifully comfortable because she stuffed the air-conditioning vent with paper towels to block the air. I sat right below the vent, and one day, I noticed I was terribly cold and someone had removed the paper towels. Several days later, I asked her after class why she had done that, and she hardly tried to suppress her laughter as she explained that other students were complaining of a particular student's body odor, so she removed the paper towels to combat the unpleasant smell. I found something about her explanation discomforting, and it took me a while to fully realize that the student with the offensive odor was most assuredly me.

Still, one day this teacher handed back a paper we had written, a personal narrative, which I had turned in but then requested that she let me revise, even though I had gotten an A, just to get it right. On my final draft she wrote, "Very beautiful. Your revision turned this into a jewel." She took me into the hallway to tell me that I shouldn't be hanging out with the people I was associating with, that they were bad news and would drag me down. She said that I was able to do something my peers could not do, that my writing was not at all average but beyond that. *Do you understand that?* she demanded to know.

Did I understand? I understood writing was the only thing that felt natural to me, the only time I felt I could make sense of the world around me. I understood I couldn't play the guitar or be confident like James, and I wasn't pretty enough to be a contender for the prom queen, and I apparently stank to high heaven. I understood that the only way I could stop hating myself and my life and everyone around me was to be a different person—not the girl who lived in the holler and who was afraid of the world, but maybe this girl who smoked a lot of weed and wore tie-dyes and had older friends anyway, so I didn't need the kids around me to like me. That I could have a husband—one person in the world who liked me as I was, or at least thought I was good enough for now. All I really understood was that I needed to survive, but I had no idea how to. I didn't understand that this wasn't what life should look like.

So I told her that I loved to write, that I wanted to write, and in her characteristic exasperated way, she told me that I should, that I had to do something with it, and *Don't just screw around.* But of course I did, until I didn't.

I also had a sociology class that year, and the teacher was funny and comfortable with all the students, for whom I had utter contempt at that point. I missed class so much that, one day, he told me I would come out of there with a C. I argued with him: *You know I have learned more than anyone else here. You know I understand more than anyone else here. You know that my work is A work, that when I have been here, I earned an A.* And *Yes,* he said, *all those things are true. But you weren't here. So you get a C.* After pleading my case for a few more minutes, he offered me a deal: if I read *Night Comes to the Cumberlands* and wrote him a paper on it, he would give me an A in the class.

I got the book immediately and started reading, wondering what it was about it that made him think it was worth me reading in exchange for the grade I wanted. Soon, it began to make sense as I read Harry Caudill's account of the history of Appalachia. I read as little as it took to complete my assignment and wouldn't learn until years later how and why that book was incomplete and, to many, an insulting perspective. But for me, reading it at the age of seventeen was a turning point, a moment of self-realization.

As the book unfolded, it seemed to illuminate the history of the region, the history of my people, in such a way as to account for the desperation that pervaded the water we drank, the air we polluted, the mountains we plundered, the love we longed for and withheld from one another. It made me see my father, for the first time, not just as my father, but as a descendant of sharecroppers, of thieves, of Irishmen, of desperate immigrants, of settlers who could not read or write and had never seen gold and so traded vast swaths of land for single, shiny gold dollars. The heartbreaking history my father told me through his stories, bits and pieces both recent and distant, now had a context—we suddenly fit into a narrative, and that brought us a little closer to making sense. For the first time, I saw myself as a great-granddaughter, a descendant—not just a *self*. But it made my self more complicated than I ever had conceived of it being.

How do we define a *self*? As the differentiator: *I can't understand you people.* As the reference point: *I didn't see anything.* The victim: *Why did this happen to me?* The perpetrator: *I didn't mean to . . .* The self, of course, is the main character of each of our stories—the hero, the martyr, the one whose suffering really matters and whose goodness is remarkable, whose shortcomings are both comprehensible and forgivable. The Bible tells us that the body is a temple, a sanctuary for the soul, a home for the *I* of every thought.

In my house, there are many mansions.

# CHAPTER 17

## The Walking Wounded

Granny was terribly worried about my health from the moment I told her I was a vegetarian. She could not fathom that a person could be healthy without hamburgers, sausage, bacon, and Christmas hams. My entire life, she had fed me in a way only a hardworking country grandmother could do, making biscuits from scratch and gathering the eggs herself, growing and canning tomatoes and green beans all summer long, peeling potatoes with a paring knife that she stopped with her bare thumb as I watched, amazed she did not cut herself.

Granny's religious views seemed to complicate her morals in response to my meat-free diet. On one hand, she told me it was the Lord's will that we eat animals because the Bible said we had dominion over them. On the other hand, she had no qualms about slipping some ground beef into the vegetable soup she brought me in quart Mason jars, the soup she cooked up and canned for those cold winters. She promised there was no meat in the soup but seemed flustered at the question. Of course I could see the little clumps of fried hamburger, but even as an arguably book-smart teenager, I thought there had to be some kind of explanation beyond my comprehension—maybe it was a flavoring I knew nothing about, or a mystery vegetable.

I used to ask her to lie—*pretend*—that I hadn't called or wasn't visiting so my father wouldn't know I was close by when I saw her, but she would never agree to that dishonesty. And yet, she felt justified in her ground-beef deception because she was convinced that feeding me meat was part of her maternal duty, directed by the will of God himself. I could not make sense of it when I was a teenager, and I didn't want to make her feel bad, so we both ended up pretending that the ground beef in her soup was a vegetable.

She offered to give me her camper if I would eat meat, and another time, she offered me $300. With a sense of valiance, I declined both. I had stayed in that camper often as a child, "camping" in her backyard, next to the henhouse. My brother and our various cousins and I would listen to the country station whose signal somehow found its way into our holler. We would play cards and games for hours, laughing and enjoying the time that could be uncomplicated by the adults in our lives.

Though I refused Granny's offer at the time, I soon ended up living in that camper. At some point, my husband and I decided we could no longer afford to pay half the rent for the house we were living in, and we gave our roommates unceremonious notice before moving out. We decided to live in Granny's camper, which was then parked in her cow field, closer to my father's house than hers. My father ran a simple wire to it so we had enough electricity for a light at night and perhaps a radio. There was no water to connect to, so I brought it from the creek in a bucket to wash dishes, and we went to my father's to use the bathroom and shower.

It almost seemed like it would work for a while, though my dad often pressured us to come to his house. My husband was intimidated by him and, as my first boyfriend, had caught the full force of my father's threatening, domineering attempt to be protective.

On the other hand, before we were married, we were always allowed to spend the night at my father's house and sleep in the same room—sometimes on the floor, sometimes in the bed, according to my father's whims. He told me, *You better not be having sex in there,* and I said, *Oh no, of course not.* And he gave us weed sometimes, let us smoke our own anytime. Once, he went clambering up one of the hills near the house, searching for a pot plant that he had neglected for a while. He brought it back to us, all purple-green and strong smelling, but lacking any real substance, once you got down to it.

One night, my father beckoned us out of the camper. He *needed* my husband to go somewhere with him, he said. They would be back soon, he said. I was grouchy. I do not remember any particular frustration, other than the fact that my dad was taking my companion away to go on some dubious mission, and neither my husband nor I seemed able to deny my father. So they left, and I sat in his house while his new wife and children slept—he hadn't stayed single for long after his previous girlfriend moved out and finally broke it off for good. As the hours passed, I grew more and more irritated. I knew I couldn't express any anger toward my father, so when they finally returned, I tried to blame my husband for staying out so late.

He didn't want to talk until we returned to our camper. When we got there, he told me where they had gone—to a friend of my father's. That friend had light-blue eyes and made knives as a hobby. He had a little workshop filled with handles and blades that he fitted and sharpened to sell or trade. At least, that's what my father told me. I was always left to sit in the cab of his truck while my father went into the workshop. There could have been anything in there.

Earlier in the year, before we moved into the camper, a college student with a funny nickname, who came to our house a lot, had mentioned the mushroom mines in Carter County. In the 1920s and '30s, a 186-acre mountain was turned into an underground limestone mine, with 2.6 million square feet of tunnels honeycombed deep into the rock. From the mid-'50s to the late '70s or early '80s, a commercial mushroom business began operations, went under, tried again, and finally closed.

In 1995, before James and I married, my father told me that his friend the knife maker owned the mines. He urged me to go there with James and Junior, so we could camp while my dad's friend slept in the cab of his semi, which was parked just inside the mines. The entrance to the mines was littered with broken bottles, and the walls were covered in graffiti. A few years later, a young man and his girlfriend killed his parents and brought their bodies there. There were stories of satanic rituals, occult worship, drug deals, and ghosts in the mines—but we did not know that yet.

Why my dad had encouraged us to go there, I did not know. The entrance was framed with thick walls, and some sort of metal skeleton of a roof loomed above us. It was a chilly day, but the sun glinted off the shards of glass that lay everywhere. My brother and boyfriend walked around, exploring the outside of the cave. I stood in the abandoned entrance, wondering why my dad's friend always looked into my eyes so deeply, why he always smiled at me, why it felt like he knew a secret about me.

The cave was fairly warm, and we slept close to the entrance. Still, the stagnant air made us sick, and in the morning, I woke up feeling suffocated. A year later, when the college boy with a funny nickname mentioned the mines, he told us he had heard that someone burned the semi cab that was in there. We mentioned that to my father, and he and his friend wanted to know who did it.

So when my father took my young husband to his friend's house, it was because he and his friend wanted to question him. They took him into the workshop and showed him the knives, asking him questions about our acquaintance and the story we had heard. Finally, one of those two middle-aged men said he would love to get ahold of whoever had burned that semi—*Wouldn't you love to get ahold of him?*—with one of those sharp knives in hand. He held the knife to my husband's throat—*Just like this. Feel how sharp that is? It would cut right through somebody.*

And after my husband stood there with a knife held to his throat by two crazy, drugged men and somehow convinced my father and his friend he could be of no further use to them, after he told me what had happened and how those men did not believe that we did not have the information they wanted, that *he* did not have the information they wanted, and after he said he couldn't live next to my dad's house anymore, we packed our few belongings and drove off in the middle of the night.

I don't know what people thought when I went back to high school for my senior year, married and clearly high most of the time. Even when I was there, I wasn't there. It was the perfect ending to all those years of feeling completely, painfully alienated from my peers. If it takes a village to raise a child, I was the warning sign that our village had failed, or that there was no village after all.

I didn't talk to James about how I felt, and how I suspected he felt, regarding our attempt at a relationship. I had learned to listen and be quiet, to not make any noise. I never responded to people who were cruel or condescending, but I wrote words down. My voice became adept at self-protection, as I said one thing and meant another, as I remained silent and thought everything. My silence had at once kept me safe and made me vulnerable in childhood. That silence was a large part of my self-sabotage as an adult.

So many people who endure poverty as children end up making unhealthy choices or accepting their lots. Those around us don't realize that some of us never feel like we have a choice, never know we have a voice or a right to speak. Some children are taught they deserve and have such power, but for those of us who weren't given the privilege of that knowledge, we go on doing the things we saw adults around us do, we subconsciously choose the lives that were modeled for us. For most of us, there is no flash of understanding when we turn eighteen, no sudden self-awareness that transforms our child selves into responsible, world-savvy adults. We fight the demons that embedded themselves into the fabric of our consciousness, not knowing why we always feel like we're in a fight. We walk through the world as if we are part of it, but our anguish constantly reminds us that the world neither loves nor wants things that are broken.

# CHAPTER 18

## *Holding On*

In the spring of my senior year, James and I went to a music festival in Berea, the home of a college my art teacher had recommended I attend, and we decided we would move there after I graduated high school. A lot of the people around us were tripping on acid at the festival, though I was sober at the time. It took place in the forest that I didn't yet know belonged to the college. There was a Grateful Dead cover band, and young college students gave talks about being vegan and saving the world by recycling.

I fell in love with this new forest, which looked like the one I had grown up in. But instead of men like my father and the darkness that seemed to grow around him, the young men wore tie-dyes and played instruments or danced without fear. Young women stood onstage at the amphitheater and made impassioned speeches. I thought it was the perfect place for me—the best of where I had come from, with plenty of room for a culture I believed in.

We went back a couple of weeks later and found an apartment for rent and put our deposit down with the money I had received as graduation gifts. One day, my mother gave me a message that I needed to contact the college—they had called her phone since I didn't have one. I reached them from a pay phone, and they said they had six spots left and one of them was mine if I wanted it. They asked whether I was serious about coming there. Standing in the Save-A-Lot parking lot, I told the admissions officer yes, I was moving there next week, one way or another.

When we got there, James spent a bit of time submitting applications and working here and there. For a while, he worked at a factory, putting in long hours. We hardly had any food or money. I cooked soups and spread the ingredients as far as I could, sometimes eating one meal a day, figuring that since my husband was working, he needed to eat more than I did—I was always giving away what I needed. I spent a lot of time reading, going to the library and picking out anything I could find to stave off the boredom and loneliness while he was gone. At that time, I had never been alone for very long and was afraid of what being by myself meant. I probably feared I would be left alone forever, and in my mind, losing the *possibility* of being loved by a man had to be worse than all the suffering that comes with a relationship not truly defined by love.

After a few weeks, he came home early one night, and my immediate happiness to see him quickly gave way to dread. He had walked out of the factory over something his supervisor said, and that was the end of that job.

Soon, I started working in a Laundromat. The old man who ran it showed me around and put me to work cleaning the machines, sweeping, mopping, and doing laundry. I would call James during my lunch break, and sometimes he was home, sometimes not. The old man liked to sit in a plastic chair between the rows of washing machines and watch me while I mopped, and soon I decided I could no longer take that for just over five dollars an hour.

I called the college and asked whether there was any way I could work for them. Since I hadn't officially begun my first semester, I wasn't considered a student yet and wasn't eligible to work as such. Someone pulled some strings, though, and soon I was on the housekeeping crew at the college. It was long, hot work. Once, we cleaned out maggot-infested trash that had sat in an empty dorm kitchen for months, but I had people my age to talk to, and a steady paycheck.

One day, I came home and James said he hoped I didn't mind, but he had run into some traveling hippies in town, and they asked for spare change. The alarm on my face must have been clear, because he reassured me he didn't give them any change but instead had invited them to eat a homemade vegan dinner with us. We had no money to spare and often dug around for loose change to buy gas—once, I bought thirty-seven cents' worth at the gas station down the street from us. But I felt comfortable with feeding people, and I was sure we could do something kind through food.

A black guy and a white girl showed up at our apartment that night—they were probably my age or close to it. They were traveling with a Rainbow tribe—young, wandering hippies—and they stayed with us for a few weeks, and then the young man ended up staying with us for several months at different times over the next couple of years. He was a lanky thing, over six feet tall, and his body was so stiff, he couldn't get cross-legged when he sat on the floor. Sit on my floor he did, though, and it seemed like he took up most of the room when he sat there beating on a drum, often while I was trying to read Plato or Aristotle for my freshman philosophy class.

During my senior year of high school, I had tried to teach myself yoga from a book, but I have never been good at learning physical skills by reading about them. I gave that yoga book to the young hippie, hoping he would gain enough flexibility so he could cross his legs. He started doing yoga from the book and became interested in Eastern philosophies, meditation, Buddhism, and so forth, to the point where he soon went to the same college I was attending and then moved to India to teach English and study Buddhism and Buddhist dialectics.

My freshman year of college was, in some ways, an extension of high school, though I was thrilled to find that I could reinvent myself and that no one knew me from before. No one I met had ever known me to cry or be humiliated by my peers, and there were far more liberal, hippie types at the college than there had been in high school. I almost felt like I belonged.

After the philosophy class I took as an elective my first semester, I felt my mind changing, expanding as I struggled with the logic exercises and analytical reading. I loved it. I would go to my professor's office and ask him questions after class, which he urged me to ask during class, but I was too self-conscious, at least at first.

I also took a course on argumentation and debate, and James started complaining that I liked to argue too much because of it, and picked apart every little discussion. I almost felt bad about it, but he spent most of his days playing guitar and smoking weed with my college friends, so I think it evened out, our ways of frustrating one another.

During the spring leading up to the first break in our marriage, I worked at a Denny's, waitressing in the small college town with the women and young girls who were not college students, not vegetarians or vegans, and who tried to convince me to let them put makeup on me and fix my hair. James protested me getting a job at first, not because I was also a full-time student or because the college required me to work ten hours on campus as well, but because he said I would complain about him not working. Desperate to pay our bills, I assured him I would not complain, and I didn't.

While I was working or doing homework one night, James went to a party at a friend's house and came home with crystal meth. He had tried it in the bathroom at our friend's house and thought I would like it, he explained. By the time summer began, I was snorting crystal meth almost daily, and I somehow became a relatively successful waitress, making more in tips than any of the other women, but my body rebelled constantly, hardly able to take in food. When I did try to eat, my body reminded me it did not want any food at that time. By the end of the school year, my professors had started telling me I wasn't looking well.

There was a guy at work, though, who thought I looked well enough to flirt with. He was cute and had a great smile, though he was a lazy waiter. He talked to me a lot, and outside one night, during a smoke break, he told me his girlfriend didn't mind him being with other people. He pulled me to him at some point, and it was more than I could stand. I told James that night, lying in bed, that I wanted to have an open relationship. He didn't say much. I asked him whether he wanted to talk about it, and he said no, he would say something he regretted. So we didn't talk about it.

A few days later, I made my way to the party house affectionately known as *the crack house*, where this coworker was hanging out with some of my sort-of friends. The cute, young flirt had actually gotten fired or quit his job, so I had gone out of my way to stop by the crack house a couple of times, hoping to see him there. When I finally did, there was no fire, no spark. I knew right away that my excitement over being flirted with, being wanted by such an attractive guy, was indeed not going to have any long-term benefit. I felt dirty and ashamed before we even started. After a few minutes of chatter around the other friends, he led me into someone's bedroom and sat me on the edge of the bed, where I waited for him to do what he wanted and be done. It was only then that I wondered about his girlfriend and realized I had most likely fallen for a trick, and I probably wasn't the only one.

The worst part was knowing I had gone out of my way to see him. I never went to that house to party, and it had a feeling about it that made me uncomfortable, like the darkness I had left behind in Morehead. That boy knew how to use his smile to make a girl feel special, and as I followed him into the bedroom, I tried to ignore the dawning realization that I was anything but special. My shame at wanting to feel pretty and wanted and worthy of his lovely face and lovely smile was endlessly multiplied as I saw the truth of myself, how I had come to him like a starved animal. A married woman pretending this fit into my relationship or my own map of desire. Knowing it was a lie that his girlfriend was okay with this. Having my friends-acquaintances watch me walk into the bedroom, come back out, and leave shortly thereafter because I had no other reason to be there. Because I wanted that scrap of affection, there was no lie that was too big to tell myself. And though I forgot his name not too long after that happened, I still can't forget any other detail.

# CHAPTER 19

## *Letting Go*

My college classes, though, were incredible. The college itself was the first interracial college in the South, as well as the first to educate men and women together. The most important aspect of it for me was that it was completely free, and I could therefore afford it without going into debt—a rarity I didn't appreciate at the time. But I also didn't understand then that I could have gotten scholarships and taken out loans to attend other schools. When I took the ACT test, the paper forms we filled out already had Morehead State University listed as a college that would receive our scores. I added Berea College to that list because of what my art teacher had said. Despite my constant defiance of teachers and school rules, I was still listening.

I went to college because I wasn't sure what else I could do. I didn't have sense enough to understand what college meant or to understand student loans and terms. I knew that the little college town had people who seemed like me—they liked to take LSD and kick a Hacky Sack and listen to the Grateful Dead. College seemed a safe way forward as I moved toward an uncertain future. There had been so many times I wanted to die, to finally be done with the difficulty of surviving. But dying never seemed to be an option. Maybe I never lost my childhood fear that if I couldn't figure out how to survive my life, someone else would have to be me. School was the only thing that had come easy for me growing up, which set me apart from the majority of people who grew up as I did. Unlike them, when I didn't know what to do with myself, my ability and desire to perform well at school could easily serve me. It was probably the only aspect of my unconscious thinking that did so.

I had signed up for a philosophy class as an elective but thought I would be an English major. I found myself surrounded by people who knew words I did not know, which I wrote down and looked up in a dictionary after class, so I would never be in the dark about that particular word again. My professors didn't mind my questions, and I never ran out of them. Finally, I felt free to ask questions, to argue, to say what I thought. Finally, I was allowed to have a voice.

I ended up with what I thought was a large group of friends. For the first time, a lot of people knew me and seemed to like me. I had a best friend who looked similar to me—long hair, unshaved, and we were both vegan by that time. Many of my friends were hippies and looked it, to varying degrees. I smoked weed, but I usually just did that when I was also going to take psychedelics—otherwise, by the time I was eighteen, smoking weed brought that familiar anxiety rushing back. I drank a little more than I had before—though not much, still. My best friend didn't mind doing just about anything, like me. When I offered her crystal meth, she snorted it with me, though I was the one who always went just a little *too far*, who wanted more than anyone around me wanted, whether it was LSD or meth or the conversations my professors offered, which I sought at every turn. All that childhood hunger had left me insatiable.

On one of the last few days before school ended for the year, a friend had a keg party, and I decided to go. I didn't take James because I liked talking to this friend so much, an older guy who I thought was the smartest person I had ever met. I may have had a small crush on him. I would ask him his thoughts about various topics or get his opinions on James's ideas. The more I did that, the less confident I felt that James was as smart as I had once thought he was. The more I talked to my guy friend, the more I felt that my own beliefs had been naïve and not entirely logical. I didn't know it at the time, but he often told his girlfriend that he didn't know why I was with James, that I was so much smarter than my husband.

At the party, I started drinking right away, and while I wasn't keeping track of time, I'm pretty sure it didn't take long for me to feel the effects. A girl I knew from school started drinking with me, while a cute boy who was clearly hoping to win her over drank a little with us. Julie and I rummaged around our friend's house until we found a bottle of vodka and some orange juice, which we claimed all for ourselves. Soon, she and I started making out in the kitchen, standing in the middle of the floor. I forgot about the party that was still going on until our host cleared his throat loudly and said with a grin, *I hope you all brought enough for everyone.* We hadn't, so we went outside and continued our make-out session sitting on the grass.

Eventually, my friend Iris asked whether I wanted her to drive me home, which sounded like a terrible idea. It was clear, though, that the make-out session could continue in the back seat of my car, so Iris drove, with the long-legged, dreadlocked hippie who sometimes lived with me in front, Julie and I in the back. We took Julie to campus to drop her off at her dorm, but at the last traffic light, Iris—who had only had one cup of beer hours earlier—turned left even though the arrow was red. Red-and-blue lights flashed immediately, and she pulled over on campus property.

The police officer asked some questions about where we were coming from and whether my friend had been drinking, which Iris answered truthfully. The police officer asked whether he could search the car, and Iris told him it wasn't hers. When he asked whose it was, I leaned forward with a drunk, happy grin and said it was mine, and I would prefer he didn't. He asked our ages—none of us were twenty-one—then looked at the other officer with a smile and said, *Well, since this is a zero-tolerance state, we'll arrest them all and then search the car.*

That was also when I found out Julie was seventeen. *You're seventeen?* I asked, shocked. I felt as if kissing an underage girl was the most immoral part of my evening. He sent her to her dorm, and Iris and I went into one cruiser, my dreadlocked friend into another.

At the station where we were booked, I was still drunk enough to give the female officer a grin when she patted me down. She asked whether I had anything in my pockets, and I told her I had a Mini Thin, which she pulled out and told me wasn't good for me. We had to be driven to the county jail for holding, which was in Richmond, where Eastern Kentucky University had been designated the third-ranked party school in the nation around that time—the same university James had failed out of. There were two mattresses on the floor, and Iris was the only person in there with me. Wearing nothing but my jail jumpsuit and still too drunk to care, I quickly fell asleep.

The next morning, they gave me my phone call, and I called my house phone number. Nobody answered, which seemed strange, so I left a message. I was released on my own recognizance, and they sent me out the back of the jail, where my dreadlocked friend was waiting.

We scrounged some change for a nearby pay phone, and I called a couple's house whose number I had memorized, explained where I was and how I couldn't get ahold of James. They came to pick us up a while later, and I finally got home.

I walked into my unlocked living room with nothing on me except what I had taken to the party, no doubt looking like I had spent the night in jail on a dirty mattress. My mother-in-law, sister-in-law, and James's grandparents were sitting inside.

*Where's James?* they asked, clearly irritated.

I told them I didn't know and had spent the night at a friend's house.

*He knew we were coming. I can't believe he did this to us. We have been waiting here for two hours.*

They got tired of waiting and eventually left. They were angry at him, and like everything else, I was sure it was somehow my fault. I made a couple of calls, but no one had seen James. I walked up to campus, to the dining area, where I was relieved to find him sitting at a table alone, not eating. I thought he would be relieved to see me, or maybe upset because I had stayed out all night. He was neither. Instead, he told me he wanted a divorce. I begged him to reconsider and told him I no longer wanted an open relationship and we could go to counseling, but his mind was made up.

Since I was still working, and paying for the apartment, we decided I would be the one to keep it. Since he wasn't working or paying for anything, we decided he would continue to sleep and eat there for as long as he needed to. We would have an amicable breakup, mature and conscious of our underlying friendship.

I asked him once to hold me at night as he slept beside me. *No,* he told me, *you make me feel dirty.*

Another time, I asked him whether we could spend some time together before he moved out—work on our friendship. *Sure,* he said.

*Tonight?*

*Sure.* But when I got home, he wasn't there. He wasn't there a couple of hours later, either, so I called a friend's house, and he was there, enjoying an impromptu party. It was raining a little, so I asked whether he needed a ride, but he didn't. I wondered when he would be getting home to spend that time with me, but he didn't know.

It dawned on me that he didn't care about *our friendship* and that, in fact, he was done with me and I had been a fool. I was angry then. Angry at him, angry at myself. I found a razor blade—it wasn't hiding, I always knew where they were—and dragged it upward along my right thigh six or seven times, moving through the flat moles on my leg without notice. I pulled the blade along my left arm but realized it would be too visible—*always put the marks where no one will see.* It suddenly occurred to me that there could be *too much* blood, that I could go *too far*, so I took a cold shower to encourage the wounds to close, quietly begging my skin to knit itself back together. James saw them a day or two later and snorted his disgust before turning away.

But something had changed as I watched the blood stream down my legs and wash away into the shower drain. I whispered a promise and a prayer, asking God to *Please make it stop, and I will never cut myself again.* I knew I didn't want to die this way, in my efficiency apartment or even at the hospital, covered in gashes that no one could sew or couldn't sew quickly enough. I also knew I wasn't sure where that fine line was set, where all the most important veins and arteries lay pulsing beneath my skin. And I suddenly understood that there were enough other people in the world who were willing to do me harm and that I couldn't do this to myself anymore. It wasn't exactly self-love, and I didn't turn my life around and stop doing things that filled me with shame or go out and choose better relationships. I just promised not to cut myself anymore, and so I didn't.

I wore long shorts in the summer heat, and pants if I wanted to be sure no one would see the cuts. But their starting points stuck out below my shorts, and my father saw them once. He demanded to know where they came from, and I told him I had been hiking and got into someone's barbed-wire fence. There was anger in his voice—it didn't feel like he cared that I was hurting myself but that he was going to punish me further. He didn't believe me, and he asked me more than once, but he finally stopped asking, and the cuts became long, unnaturally straight scars. They stand out more prominently when I get a tan, and any carefree time on a beach or in shorts is always tempered with the reminder of what I have inside me—an anguish that seeks an outlet. A wound that marks me as both victim and perpetrator. A pain that my children will notice in some form, no matter how well I hide it or how deeply it is buried beneath my love for them.

# CHAPTER 20

## *Say It Right*

I started smoking cigarettes when I was a freshman in college. I didn't realize they were cigarettes at first—James had introduced me to bidis when we were still in high school. The ones he got were usually strawberry flavored, and he told me they were an herbal blend wrapped in a large bay leaf. Eventually, when I picked up my own pack at the head shop in Lexington, the clerk laughed when I asked why he needed to see my ID if there was no tobacco in the bidis.

*These are the crack of the tobacco world.*

I had always hated that my mother smoked. My father smoked, too, but Mom was around us more and sometimes accidentally burned us with her cigarettes. Each time it happened, I felt slighted, unloved and unseen. I asked her to quit smoking for my birthday and Christmas presents. *I won't ask for anything else,* I would tell her. She would sigh and respond, *Something else. You have to ask for something else.* I didn't understand, then, how cigarettes were soothing her, giving her a comfort that no one and no other *thing* could as she tried to survive our father and young motherhood in our little corner of the world.

We always heard how Kentucky was twenty years behind the times, how everything was so much further along in places like California. We joked that the gap was even larger in our holler. Sometimes I watched movies where characters would go into New York City, finding themselves surrounded by emotionless throngs of people and by subways that moved too fast and taxis that moved too slow. The rest of the world looked so crowded to me, so loud and cluttered and clamoring. I didn't mind being twenty years or more behind everyone else when I watched the sunset, which happened at the mouth of the holler, so all the colors spread out in the widest part of the sky while the hills folded around me, darkening with a palpable tenderness toward foxes and deer and children.

When I went to Speech and Drama competitions in middle school, kids from other parts of the state mocked us sometimes, the way we said *pop* instead of *soda*. They mimicked our accents, the drawl and twang of eastern Kentucky I shared with all the kids in my county, no matter how much money they had. I was surprised that anyone from Kentucky would think themselves so different from the rest of us, that there could somehow be more ways to rank and categorize each other. I knew from Grandma Wright's television that the rest of the country saw us like *The Beverly Hillbillies*, ignorant and laughable. I knew the news sometimes provided captions when a hillbilly somehow found his way onto TV, trying to say things in a voice the rest of the world couldn't understand.

When I got to college, I thought that if I spoke carefully, I might be able to hide the shameful truth of exactly where I came from. I realized it was an uphill battle. My classmates didn't tell stories about dogs being whipped and shot by the creek. They didn't talk about how a father's laugh could turn your stomach or how his friends could look at you with some strange knowing in their eyes. They didn't know how it felt to live in the shadow of a valley that pulled you to it and hid you from the world and gave you so much beauty to adore but no protection from the men who wanted everything inside it.

You had to be smart to get into Berea College—and not just smart, but you had to be able to prove it on a test and have letters of recommendation and a grade point average that showed you could perform like a smart person for a long stretch of time. It's hard to do those things if you're worrying about money for milk and whether Dad is going to kill your mom or your grandparents or maybe even you. So, while I found myself surrounded by people who liked to take psychedelics and wanted to save the world from itself, and they thought it was just fine to be smart, there was once again a wall, an invisible barrier reminding me that I didn't quite fit in. I had spent most of my childhood learning to survive our home and very little of it learning to survive in society. I didn't know how to pretend that I felt good around people. I hardly knew how to *feel* good unless I had a substance to do that for me. I didn't know how to say the right things or read normal people—I could only recognize the ones who scared me.

To get into Berea, you also had to have financial need—it is a school for lower-income students, predominantly from Appalachia. It took a while for me to realize we hadn't all experienced what it meant to be *lower income* in the same way. At lunch one day, I took a handwritten list to the cafeteria with me and shared it with some people I knew, a young woman and older male student who were in my loosely defined friend group, but we weren't particularly close. My list was titled "Top Ten Reasons Why It's Good to Be Poor," or something along those lines. I had come up with a list of what I thought were irreverent, ironic reasons to enjoy poverty—and that included things like "You can't buy enough food to get fat on food stamps."

The young woman read my list and, with no small amount of disgust, told me how it was not funny and how poor people have a difficult time getting access to good food, how obesity was a serious health problem among the poor. The guy sitting next to her was also not amused. I didn't say anything, didn't respond to the chastising. I didn't know what to say—I thought it was somehow obvious that food stamps weren't enough to keep us fed all the time. I thought it was clear that my always being *too skinny* was tied to poverty. I thought everyone knew I was making jokes about myself and my own life, trying to laugh at the pain and absurdity. It hadn't occurred to me that not every other person going to Berea College experienced the same definition of poor. I thought that all poor people were the same—that we all feared our fathers and knew how to take a serious whipping without making a sound. I thought we all grew up afraid of hunger and accidentally drinking the snake venom in the fridge. But again, I found I was from a different world, and despite all of us falling below a certain financial threshold—at least on paper—I didn't understand these people. And they didn't understand me.

I didn't respond to her. I sat there, my mind racing through memories of cans of beans for dinner. My bed covered with marijuana and my father telling us that was our Christmas. My brother ridiculed for his cheap shoes. Me being ridiculed for just once having a shirt that wasn't cheap. I couldn't begin to say it all. I didn't know how to say that I had ached with shame for our food stamps, that I knew the hunger that marks us as wrong and revolting, and the people who call us such things.

I didn't know how to say any of it, so I said nothing.

After my second philosophy class, I declared my major in philosophy instead of English. My professor wanted me to be a philosophy major, and I told my English advisor that all I really cared about was getting to read and write, and doing those things a lot. There weren't many students majoring in philosophy, and no other females at the time. Most of my core classes had just a few students, which suited me well.

One of my philosophy courses was about the environment, and for the first time, I found myself in a class with a lot of my party friends. We usually had potlucks and went hiking, or James and other guys would play music for us while we danced and smoked weed or drank. We shared concerns about saving the environment and signed petitions to end labor abuses in far-flung countries that I couldn't pick out on a map. I didn't spend a lot of time talking about philosophy to most of the people in my friend group, but it seemed like we shared a lot of the same values.

One day in class, an active environmentalist I was often around stated that smokers shouldn't receive socialized health care if they ended up with cancer. I don't know how the conversation got to that point. It often seemed like so many of my friends couldn't distinguish between their values and logical thinking.

I waited for my other friends to disagree with the girl, who may have been arguing *for* socialized medicine—that was certainly a popular view among our group in the late nineties. But no one spoke up, no one challenged the idea that health care should only be available for *most people, most of the time*. I understood her point that smokers make choices known to lead to cancer, and how can we all be expected to pay for their mistakes? But I thought of my own mother and her smoking and wondered whether my friends would turn her away from a hospital in their utopian world.

I thought of the other choices people make—choices my family made, choices I made and was still making—and how ugly they look to the world. Smoking, drinking, my dad and his pills. Cutting myself. All the drugs I took—mostly handed to me, at least at first, until I felt they made life more bearable, even though I knew the risks. My mother's choice to marry a monster, her choice to have his children—was it a choice? Should we have been saved? Aborted? Would it have been better to never have been born at all?

And it suddenly seemed that the world they envisioned, a world with clean streams and free health care, with protections for workers and women and children, wasn't a place for our kind of people—people who smoked cigarettes to steady their nerves, who sometimes snorted a line of Lortabs with Dad because that was the most loving thing he ever offered. People who had babies they couldn't love with men who didn't love them. My liberal friend summed it up perfectly in class that day: *They made their choice. They have to live with it.*

# CHAPTER 21

## *To the City*

During my freshman year and the summer that followed, I worked at Denny's with a girl who had gone to Berea College for a time—Tanya was a cook and not at all the waitressing type. Since she didn't have a car, I gave her rides to and from work, and soon we were friends of sorts.

Tanya was hesitant to do meth as often as I did, but we smoked a little weed together and drank a little and stayed up all night. That summer, we decided to go to a music festival in Atlanta. We planned to leave after work one evening, drive through the night, and find a hotel down there. Taking my cue from my father, I brought a few Lortabs with us to help us stay up all night. We stopped at a Waffle House sometime around eleven that evening, already exhausted from working and being up for a regular day.

We took turns going into the bathroom to snort our Lortabs. We ate a little something, she drank coffee, and we got back on the road. We were driving the boxy white Ford that Granny had lent me—James had taken our car, which his grandparents bought us. We had sold my baby-blue Dodge Aries and bought something else, and that something else had died from a lack of oil—I had used a coupon for a free oil change, but the mechanic didn't tighten the oil filter.

I had brought as much money as I could, so I could buy something at the festival to bring back and resell—something psychedelic. I drove all night, minding my father's demand that I not let anyone else drive Granny's car. We got into Atlanta around four thirty in the morning and went to a shabby motel. While we were checking in, we saw some people our age getting out of a minivan at the entrance. They came in and booked a room, and we thought that though they didn't quite have the hippie look we expected, they might be going to the same festival. Their room was a few doors down from ours, so we managed to introduce ourselves as we all carried our stuff into our rooms, and before long, they offered to sell us some liquid LSD.

They had come to Atlanta from Florida not to attend the actual concert but to walk around the festival parking lot and sell their acid. I immediately bought a few doses, and they insisted we needed to get sugar cubes, so they could drop each dose onto a cube. I had dispensed the liquid into people's mouths before, but once accidentally gave someone three or four drops when he wanted one, so I knew the dangers of imprecise measurement.

We went driving around Atlanta as the sun rose, going into every all-night grocery store we could find. We seemed to be in a residential area, but next to nice-looking houses, prostitutes stood on the street corners while morning climbed into the sky. It was my first time in a real city, and looking around, I saw nothing that would make me want to come back.

We finally found sugar cubes and returned to our motel. Tanya and I took two drops apiece, and I bought some more to take home with us—one or two breath-freshener bottles filled with cinnamon-flavored LSD. It was about eight thirty in the morning by that time, and as soon as I took the acid, I decided I needed to sleep.

Sleeping doesn't normally come easily on LSD, and Tanya tried to convince me to stay awake. I couldn't, though, and we both lay down on our bed and quickly dropped off. When I awoke, I sat up and found the hotel room spinning. I was scared for a moment, then remembered what I had taken and tried to reassure myself that everything was okay. Tanya awoke then, and we decided to go to the motel pool, where we swam around a bit in the heat. In the water, I wondered whether I would drown or whether my body remembered swimming so well that it would keep itself alive even while I was in an altered state, like it had done when I faced my father's temper, or when I was pulled to the older boy's lap in church—kept alive despite all my desperate fears.

When we got out of the pool, we took a cab to the festival parking lot, so we wouldn't have to drive back. The parking lot was full of cars and buses and vans, and the heat bounced off the black asphalt at us, while the sun blazed down without clouds or winds to subdue it. Like everyone else, we walked around for hours, waiting for something good to happen, avoiding the cops that argued with people over their drinks or their dogs, and we especially avoided the cops who were searching through people's pockets and cars.

I started looking for a nitrous balloon right away. I had tried nitrous when I was sixteen and James took me to his friend's dorm room. I knelt at his friend's nitrous tank, taking it all in, and *went fishing*, meaning I had inhaled so much at once, depriving my brain of any oxygen, that I passed out and fell over, almost hitting my head on the concrete floor. After that first encounter with nitrous, I had walked away from campus and back toward my house feeling angry, thinking that something inside me had changed. I hoped it was not a permanent change, but part of me also thought that I didn't care about anything anymore. At that time, I didn't know my dad had a taste for nitrous himself and had paralyzed the woman while driving the oxygen truck, or that he sometimes had a tank in his and Mom's bedroom. He would tell me about it later.

When I was still sixteen, I tried nitrous again at another festival, and I discovered that people sold it in balloons, inflating them to unreasonable sizes, and I could walk around with a balloon in my mouth, inhaling the sickeningly sweet gas until my thoughts disappeared and everything felt less like pain and more like floating.

Tanya and I were still feeling the effects of the liquid LSD we had taken, which was powerful but not overwhelming. We walked and walked, waiting for the hours to pass until the show began. I wondered whether we would somehow have an exciting adventure. I did not feel at all capable of talking to the strangers in the parking lot, who all appeared to know what they were doing. They, it seemed, were part of the adult world, while I was somehow still part of a child world. Everyone else came across as knowing what they wanted and did not mind asking each other for it, even when most of us were looking for drugs. Tanya was unusually quiet where she was usually assertive, and I started thinking we were a bad pair—her confidence often made me feel even less sure of myself, and I wondered if my fear of people was bringing out her own lack of confidence.

Suddenly, a man walked up to her, and after a few words, they began kissing there in the parking lot, surrounded by people and me wondering what the hell had just happened. He had olive skin and black hair and a goatee. He talked to my friend while I stood there, dazed and uncertain what was going on. We followed him to a van, and he got something out of the back, then turned to Tanya and handed it to her. She ripped a piece of paper in half and told me to stick out my tongue. So I did.

*Okay, now leave that in your mouth for a while,* she said, and we started walking away from the exotic man and his van.

*Wait, what was that?* I asked.

*That was about twenty-five hits of acid,* she said. That scared me. I demanded to know what she was thinking, taking so much at once, and she told me to calm down, and I did. It was too late by that point anyway—the LSD had already absorbed into my tongue and was getting ready to have its way with my brain. Later, as we walked around and waited for the acid to kick in, she saw the man again and once more took what he handed her, ripped it in two, and put half on my tongue. This time, I didn't protest at all.

When the gates finally opened, we went in and found a place on the grassy lawn of the outdoor amphitheater. I tried to dance to the first band, which I had liked for a few years. The second band came on, and I gave up on dancing, which my body didn't seem to remember how to do. I lay on the grass, staring at a few clouds above me. As the music played, I watched the edges of the clouds swirl into fractals, like the endlessly recursive patterns of snowflakes and the Windows 95 screen saver. The headlining band came on, and I listened as the sky darkened. I was too affected by the LSD to stand most of the time, and I could hardly speak, it had hit me with such intensity. Once again, nothing made sense, but this time, it wasn't scary and confusing. I let the world wash over me for hours, bathing me in sound and color as if my mind had never grown used to such things.

When the show ended, we walked up the hill and out through the gate, back into the parking lot. People were everywhere, hawking their wares and laughing, calling out to one another and calling for their dogs. I knew I had to function but still wasn't sure how to, so I just followed Tanya. She wanted to hurry back to the motel, as the man with the powerful paper was supposed to call for her there. We hustled to the parking lot entrance, where a police officer directed the stream of traffic outward. All the cabs were spoken for, and finding an empty one seemed like a lost cause, so we started walking toward the closest building, which was almost a mile away. When we got there, we found a dilapidated garage with a few people sitting inside. I wondered why they were working at that hour and what kind of work they did in that strange garage, but they seemed decidedly indifferent to us as we used the phone to call a taxi service.

We walked back to the amphitheater parking lot and found an open taxi, though it wasn't the one we had called for. We jumped in the back, relieved to be off our feet. As we started moving, Tanya yelled,

*Wait! Where's my wallet? What the fuck happened to my wallet? Somebody stole my wallet!* The cabbie stopped the taxi under the traffic light we had inched beneath, turned around, and demanded to know who had the money to pay the fare—he wasn't driving anybody anywhere unless they could pay.

As he was yelling about the fare and Tanya was frantically searching for her wallet, a policeman started banging on the hood of the cab, yelling at the cabbie to move the car out of the intersection—all the traffic in front of us had moved on, and we sat there, in the middle of everything, everyone waiting for us to go. Tanya jumped out of the taxi and started running down the sidewalk, so I jumped out and followed her. She ran toward the garage, and we made it almost the whole way running, until the cigarettes and the meth and maybe even the nitrous slowed us down, and we walked as quickly as we could the rest of the way. We burst in, and everyone looked at us with the same disinterest as before. My friend hurriedly started talking about her wallet and went to the phone, where she had laid her wallet down and it had sat the whole time, unnoticed and undisturbed.

Wallet in hand, we went back to the parking lot, where we got a cab once again. When we arrived at the motel, she started talking about the man she had met, how they had locked eyes in the parking lot and that she felt it was something special, something incredible she had to pursue when he called for her. The next morning, when she was dropped off back at our room, I was glad I had stayed.

Her new soul mate had taken her back to his hotel room, where his wife and their three children were staying. She slept in the bed with them, the man's wife separating her from her new love. He spent the night reaching over his wife and trying to touch my friend, and his wife spent the night pushing him back to his spot on the bed.

How can so many lonely people be in one place together? Each of us reaching out, over and over, slapped away or left behind, hungry in a way that always seems to be our very own.

# CHAPTER 22

## *Faithful*

After we got back, James started spending time with Tanya, who ended up with a roommate named Rebecca. One day, I came home to find that my six-pack of Samuel Adams Cherry Wheat was missing, and a wet towel was hanging on the shower rod. When I confronted James a couple of days later, it turned out he had let himself in—I usually didn't lock the door—and taken a shower, then took the beer with him as a thank-you to the girls for letting him crash at their apartment. I began locking my door so he couldn't take anything, but soon, I came home to find the television missing—he had climbed in through an unlocked window and taken it so they could watch a movie. I resorted to putting a board in the window to keep him from climbing in.

Rebecca had started working with us at Denny's, and I was still the only one of us with a car, so I would often give the other two girls a ride, and the three of us would hang out sometimes. I didn't know Rebecca well, but one day, when I brought Tanya home, we all stood around chatting, and I noticed Rebecca had a pained look on her face. Eventually, I asked what was wrong, and Tanya told me, *She's afraid you're going to be mad at her because she slept with James.*

After a shocked silence, I told Rebecca no, it was fine—James was single, and they were adults and free to make their own choices. I hated it, but I knew I had no right to be upset. I assured her there were no hard feelings, but I did put two and two together that he had brought my beer to her, and they shared it, as well as some LSD, prior to their rendezvous. The girls didn't realize it was my beer he brought over that day and assured me they wouldn't let him do that again.

A few days later, I decided to call James. He had gone to stay at his mom's in Lexington. When she put him on the phone, I told him that I was sorry for my part in what had happened between us and that I would always care about him.

I felt so guilty about being a bad wife, and undeserving of a right to be angry with him, to ever be angry with anyone but myself. I felt I needed to rid myself of all those *lower-consciousness* feelings and focus on the best ones. Like the religion of my childhood, all that I read or learned about living a good life, being a good person, I interpreted as confirmation that something was wrong with me. I just had to try harder. It made me feel better, though, to tell him, *Everything is okay, you are okay.* I knew that my anger with him was at least partially justified, but I was happy to give him the *forgiveness* I thought he must be wanting. It was the same story I had always told myself about my father—that deep down he knew he was doing wrong and that, with my love, he could be the good person he truly was inside.

James responded that he would always care about me, too, and I told him that I knew he was enjoying being single but that I missed him and hoped the best for him.

*What do you mean, enjoying being single?*

*Well, you know, you're single now, and you're a good-looking guy, so I'm sure you're going to have some fun. You know what I mean.*

He insisted he didn't know what I meant, so finally I told him, *Come on, it's okay. I know you slept with Rebecca.*

No, he insisted—that absolutely did not happen. He was horrified they had told me that, and said both of those girls were sick, twisted people to do such a cruel thing to me. He told me to please stop hanging out with them, since they were obviously trying to hurt me. Eventually we hung up, and I sat there, once again, in shock.

We all worked together the next day, and Rebecca was especially friendly. I didn't tell them what James had said but observed them for a couple of days to see whether I could detect any psychotic tendencies. One night, one of our mutual friends, someone James had played with in a band for a while, came over to play chess, and I told him all about it. I was confused about who to believe and didn't understand why the girls would lie to me.

With a sigh, he told me no, they weren't lying to me, that it was James who was lying. I asked him how he knew, and he told me he knew because James was dating my best friend and didn't want her to find out about him sleeping with Rebecca.

I had met my best friend in the argumentation and debate class. On the first day of class, our professor told us to pair up for our first debate exercise, and she and I locked eyes. A boy asked me whether I wanted to be partners, while another boy asked her the same thing. I stumbled over my words, saying I thought she and I were going to be partners, and eventually moved close enough to her desk to ask, and she had the same experience of stumbling over how to say no to the guy who asked her.

From then on, we were inseparable. People thought we were sisters, and we would sometimes tell them that we were and even that we were twins. We soon discovered we had also both experienced weird things growing up—weird fathers and strange families. Fragments of memories and feelings that didn't quite make sense. She was willing to try most drugs that I tried, but she didn't seek them out or use them as often as I did. I thought of her as the more wholesome of the two of us. She certainly didn't come off as being as wild as I was. We both looked, at least on the outside, like happy, somewhat-ditzy hippie girls.

We had drifted apart toward the end of the school year—I had grown impatient with her naivete. Arguing about rocks having souls, impassioned pleas to protect box turtles from four-wheelers—all this seemed less and less important to me as I had become more critical of my own ideas. And though she was highly tolerant of my endless experiments with drugs, I imagine that my near-constant use of crystal meth at that point didn't help.

I'm not sure I could even tell you now exactly what I felt when I arranged to meet James and my best friend in the parking lot of a vegetarian café in Lexington to clear the air, as he suggested. I had decided I wanted to go ahead and clear everything, so I brought Rebecca and Tanya. There was a little bit of confrontation between the girls and James, a little bit of us all looking lost, and I bid the new lovers farewell.

Soon after that, a woman who was eating at Denny's asked me whether I would like to work at the local health-food store, which I jumped at. Soon I was high on crystal meth at the store, not so carefully rationing my paycheck for organic vegannaise and nutritional yeast, as well as the meth. I cleaned, ran the cash register, and soon began closing the store. I remember sweeping next to the cooler, fully immersed in my resentment, until one day a voice told me, *You have every right to your anger. Nobody will ever take that away from you. But it is hurting only you.*

So I tried to stop. I tried to forgive, to love my husband, ex-husband to be. To love my friend, who surely was only giving love the chance it deserves, no matter the circumstances. I failed.

I didn't know how to forgive someone while still honoring myself. And despite reading so much about the value of forgiveness as a child, I never felt like I really understood what that meant. What happens when one forgives? I was always so eager for the person I forgave to love me, I couldn't hold anyone accountable for their choices. I just wanted *everything to be okay*, and I didn't have the wherewithal to think of myself in that equation, of my own right to *be okay*, to approve of the way others treated me. I was convinced, at every step, that whoever seemed to love me would be the last person to actually do so. I had to hold on to the relationship no matter what.

Despite my whole bucketful of flaws, there was a nice boy, a friend in our group, who talked to me at work one day and wanted to go for a walk with me. When we strolled down the trail behind the college, crossing the wooden bridge, I wondered aloud about how the first people to ever hold hands would have come up with that idea. Since he didn't know the answer, he suggested we could be the last people to hold hands, at least for a minute, and so we held hands and walked. *Okay, we're probably not the last ones anymore,* he said with a smile, but we kept holding hands.

Less than a week later, I informed him James was coming back, and he asked whether I had told James that was okay. I said yes, I had, and with the most gentle disapproval I had ever seen cross someone's face, he told me he hoped I would be happy with my choice. I didn't know how to tell him that I hadn't made a choice, that after a childhood of having no control, I couldn't stand in front of a man and recognize what a choice was—I was just going to let James say his piece, and I didn't know what would happen after that. Of course, I had made a choice. I didn't understand that letting someone else decide for me was still a choice, that I could have said no. And I didn't know how to make this nice boy understand, so I didn't say anything to try to explain.

At the time, what I didn't understand was our spending time together and getting to know each other. I couldn't tell him how ugly I felt and that it never occurred to me he would find me attractive. I couldn't pinpoint exactly what inside made me feel so dirty and used—I didn't even have the words to describe that yet. I just knew he seemed nice, and he felt safe and smart and kind and healthy.

*Kind* is a relative term, of course.

He was never very friendly after I told him James wanted to come back. Even long after my relationship with James ended, when I ran into this former friend at a farmers' market—both of us real-live adults, him a lawyer, me a single mother—I was shocked at how condescending he seemed, how unkind it felt. There were a lot of things I couldn't explain back then, when we were in college, and maybe we could have been a couple. It didn't occur to me until years later that he liked me romantically. At the time, I thought he contacted me and visited me and wanted to hold my hand out of friendship—I didn't recognize a display of interest as courtship.

He was like so many other people I had met and thought were *my people*—my new people, not the people I was born to. I thought these new people could see and love the parts of myself that I had invented without my family's influence—the parts I liked so much better than the self I felt my family had forced upon me. For so long after I left my hometown, I thought that I had found *community* and that we all cared about the same things: *sustainability, equality, spirituality.* But I broke the rules too much, stepped out of line too often. I didn't know how to act like those people, how to talk like them. Quite often in early adulthood, I was still acting out the terrible lessons I had been taught as a child, and though I did not steal, and I'm pretty sure any hurting I did was minimal, I was clearly not one of them.

Once again, I learned there are unspoken rules to follow, and they have everything to do with your class, your gender, your education. I wasn't quick to learn those rules, although I tried really hard to mimic the college kids around me who seemed like such adults. But when you try to go where you don't belong, there is always hell to pay.

# CHAPTER 23

## *With You*

That same summer, I went to another concert with Tanya, as well as Rebecca, who finally convinced me that she had slept with my husband. There was more LSD, more of what was left of the Grateful Dead, and when I came back, there were somewhere around fifteen messages on my answering machine. Only the last message had any real information.

*Please answer my call. I need to talk to you.*

*Son of a bitch,* I thought. *He's calling me for money.*

James and my former best friend had gone to a Rainbow Gathering out west, something idyllic and serene, and I just knew he had run out of money and was calling me to wire him some, certain I would do so. But this was before cell phones, and I didn't have caller ID. He was calling me from a pay phone, so I couldn't call him back. The next day, though, the phone rang and I was home. It was him. He asked whether he could come home, and puzzled, I told him of course, he could go to his mother's, which was what I thought he meant by *home. No,* he said. *With you. That's my home.*

I wasn't so sure about that. I had just begun loving my freedom, my independence, the happiness and ease I felt on my own. I told him we could talk when he got back, but I just didn't know. *Where is she?* I asked, and he told me she was outside the phone booth. I couldn't believe he had her waiting for him, watching him as he called me to tell me he wanted to come back to me. *Does she know what you're telling me?* Yes, she knew. He had a dream in which he was with me, and that was a sign. She knew.

About a week later, I came home one evening, and my living room light was on. I had left the door unlocked again because I had gotten used to no one coming into my apartment and helping themselves to my beer or taking showers and leaving dirty towels behind. There was James, buck naked, sitting on my couch with a full erection.

*What are you doing?*

*I thought this was the best way to get your attention.*

*Put your clothes on.*

We talked a little, and I think we slept on the living room floor that night—I didn't want him in my bed, wasn't ready to have sex with him. I wasn't happy to see him, but he told me about his dream and about how he knew that he should stay married like his grandfather had, loyal to his wife always.

I let him move back in.

He was my husband. I had made a vow, a sacred vow, and I needed to uphold it. And I desperately wanted to be like his grandparents. Maybe there was still a chance for me to be loved and loving, content in some quiet routine, normal.

A day or two later, before he had finished unpacking, he said something about how he missed my old best friend, and I started throwing his stuff back into the half-empty boxes sitting around the apartment. Then he opened the Bible and told me about a verse he read, something to do with unity or marriage or love or who even knows. We unpacked the boxes.

Over the next year, he would disappear sometimes, and later I would find out he went to see her at her dorm. He finally got a job, and one day, his boss called the house, asking where he was. I thought he was at work, but he was with her. Later, he told me that during this time, he heard a mockingbird sing and knew he should go home to me. Something about what the other girl had told him as far as mockingbirds and their songs.

Inside, I wanted to laugh at that idea. Birds and their songs—why would that matter when you're hiding the truth from someone? None of it struck me as making any sense, but I quickly felt confused. I had always given him so much credit for knowing more than I did—he seemed so confident. And I knew that I came from a dysfunctional family but that his family had always been kind to me. Every time I found myself upset with him, I ended up thinking it must be something wrong with me. And so when he expressed this love, this devotion that rang false, I thought that it must be true and that I was somehow at fault for just not understanding.

They weren't sleeping together. At least, that's what she told me. Regardless, the back and forth was starting to make me feel crazy, and eventually I sat down with both of them and told them I didn't care if they wanted to be together, but if so, they had to tell the truth and leave me alone. No more lies, no more secrets. She said she wanted nothing to do with him and only to repair our friendship. I don't remember what he said.

They stopped meeting up, but I was still angry. She would appear at our house sometimes—by that point, we had a roommate, and there were constant parties. I was shocked she had the nerve to show up, but it didn't occur to me to tell her to leave. Eventually, I decided the only logical course of action would be for the two of us to go to a Rainbow Gathering the following summer. I walked with her to the same woods where I had held hands with a nice boy and, for a brief moment, we were the last couple to ever do so. I told her I wanted to forgive her, really forgive her, and the only thing I could think of was to take a trip like that together.

We did, and it was amazing. She came back with a boyfriend, and I came back and broke up with James for good. But from then on, my newly forgiven friend was afraid I would try to steal her boyfriend, to seek vengeance and do to her what she had done to me, and so we grew apart after all. It didn't matter that I didn't blame her for the breakup—I knew that wasn't her fault, or if it was in any way, it didn't compare to the other fractures in my marriage.

So much of my adult life would oscillate like this: some form of spiritual focus and hope, a good job or loving friends and maybe a boyfriend or husband who adored me for a time; next, a darkness. I would periodically discover I was taking too many drugs or drinking too much, or I would find bruises on my neck from a drunken argument with my lover. Then I would run to the light, to music and hiking in forests, to poetry and moderation, but the darkness inside me always drew me back, away from the flirtation with normalcy and stability. I couldn't pretend to fit into the world around me, which I so desperately wanted to feel part of.

# CHAPTER 24

## *The Cathedral*

When I moved away from home, Granny and I wrote a few letters back and forth. Actually, she wrote fairly often, and I responded a few times. I didn't yet know what it felt like to lose someone you love. I didn't know that I would one day—many days—dream about her house and my simple childhood moments there. Eating watermelon on the picnic table between her house and the garden in the summer. Running through the fields, trying not to step in the cow patties. Playing in the creek. Sitting down to her table.

I wish I had written her back more.

I didn't know how often I would later tell God that I would give all the money I had just to go to her house and lie in her arms, beg her to hold me, please hold me and let me be her little girl. Although well-meaning people sometimes told me I should cherish those days with her and not take them for granted, I took them for granted anyway. I didn't run to her when I could have. I often brought a boy with me when I visited, hoping for her approval but precluding any chance of lying in her lap and letting her pet my head and tell me she loved me and always, always would.

The Christmas before James and I split up for good, we went to her house for our family celebration. I had stayed awake for at least twenty-four hours, making stained-glass candleholders for family members while smoking meth to stay awake, cutting myself over and over on the little, beautiful pieces of glass as my fine-motor skills went from bad to worse. At Granny's house, I felt like everyone was looking at me, like everyone knew that I hadn't slept and that something was not quite right. There was hardly anything I would eat—I was still vegan, mind you—and I did not have much of an appetite anyway. Granny fussed at me for not eating, and I tried to stand my ground without being disrespectful.

Soon afterward, I wrote her a letter and told her I wanted to be able to come to family gatherings without such a negative focus on what I would and would not eat. I told her I was not so concerned about the meals but wanted to enjoy the moments that we could be together, which were so valuable. Of course, I mostly just didn't want anyone to look at me in a way that made me wonder whether I was paranoid or my drug-induced state was so obvious. She responded and told me that she knew better than I how valuable those moments were. Three years prior, she had been diagnosed with heart disease and was told she would probably die within a year. So, as I quickly caught on, she had outlived her timeline already. And, as she clearly stated, all she wanted was to provide for me in the same way she had always provided for me: with food.

I sighed. I would eat meat with my granny, for my granny, and only for her, cooked only by her. Preferably only from animals killed by her. I wrote her a letter and told her. When I visited a couple of weekends later, I thought the event would be a special occasion between us, a time when we realized that we had formed our own language of love, that fried chicken meant devotion and over-easy eggs meant adoration and the act of eating itself was worship.

Instead, Granny served me some country ham she had fixed the previous day. The event was clearly not monumental to her. Since I often promised to visit and never showed up, she did not go to the trouble of making a special dinner. She warmed up some green beans that she had canned from the garden and fried me some little round hoecakes, and I ate alone at the table, talking to her in between bites, my husband sitting with Papaw in the front room.

Granny had always favored me and made no attempt to hide that fact from anyone. She told me I was *special*, and though I wasn't sure what she meant, I believed her. Growing up, I got used to hearing that I was *smart*, but I would only ever count Granny's opinion as having mattered. Her calling me special was the only real compliment. When I was around nine or ten, she gave me her mother's jewelry box that still played music, and it contained a crown-shaped pin set with the birthstones of my great-grandmother's twelve children. My older cousin protested because I was younger, and she did not understand why she shouldn't be entrusted with the jewelry box. I'm not sure, either, but I think it could have been that Granny knew I would treasure it in some way no one else could.

When I became a young adult, Granny gave me her kitchen table, made of heavy oak. Again, it had belonged to her mother, and it also served as the place where the adults of my life had eaten every Christmas, Thanksgiving, Easter, and birthday dinner since I was born. It was the same table at which my father had eaten those meals, along with every other meal, from the time he was born. My granny ate and prayed at that table just about every day of her life. The gift of the table upset even more of the family, as my father informed me, since each of his adult siblings had expected to receive it in my grandparents' will, if not before their deaths.

Granny didn't talk about how much she loved us. She never pinched our cheeks or patted us and didn't smile a lot. In the winter, she put on thick gloves to carry in wood from her front porch, and she stacked it next to the woodstove close to where Papaw's recliner sat, where he watched Kentucky Educational Television and whatever else they were able to get—somehow, their reception was a little better than ours, but we hardly ever watched television there.

Junior and I wandered down to her house all the time, roaming around her yard and creeks as if they were our own. She often put us into a bath—sometimes in the washtub she canned vegetables in, or with some dish soap in a small kiddie pool in the backyard. We seemed to always look in need of tending. Other times, she sent me to her bathtub, and I would sit in the stillness, soaking it in. She would bring me a thick slice of fresh cabbage, which I loved, and I would eat in the tepid bathwater, the soothing quiet like a blanket that surrounded her home and protected us whenever we were there.

I took in the details of her bathroom each time I entered—the water heater on the other side of the shower wall, the oval mirror placed in front of a window that looked into the backyard, their towels and washcloths on a shelf above the toilet. The clean laundry that never sat for too long. The simple hook lock that slid into an eye to lock the door.

Granny didn't play music at her house—maybe gospel every once in a while, but not often enough to recall. Her house was clean, and it felt old and solid. The wooden steps that we loved to play on, and that she didn't want us to play on, were painted maroon. There was a window toward the bottom of the steps, which faced toward the mouth of the holler. Granny had a small mirror there and would put Oil of Olay on her face while sitting on the steps. She kept her round hairbrush on the windowsill.

Everything there was holy.

Granny had a flock of chickens at all times—of course, Dad sent me down for eggs when I was little. After I stopped being vegan, Granny started giving me eggs by the dozen, and I discovered their yolks were a deep orange-yellow, rich from the bugs and worms the chickens must have found as they explored Granny's yard and fields. When we were small, my brother, younger cousin, and I watched while Granny killed one of the chickens. She wrung its neck, twisting the head right off, but the chicken's body still hopped around for a while. I stood behind the screen door of the kitchen, horrified and frightened, but awed by my granny's strength. My brother and our little cousin shrieked with laughter and ran around the yard. Granny's face revealed nothing about how she felt. She cleaned and cut up the chicken, cooked it with dumplings, and fed us all, as she so often did.

When we spent the night at Granny's house, she made us go to bed early—in the summertime, it was still light out. She and Papaw knelt by Granny's bed together—they hadn't slept in the same room since I was born, as far as I knew—and they prayed, heads bowed. Sometimes they both prayed out loud at the same time, words overlapping like waves coming ashore almost together, one looking for the other. Granny often cried like she did at the altar. Sometimes I listened to them quietly, but if Granny was praying by herself, she had me kneel beside her, clasp my hands, and bow at the side of her bed with her. She prayed for us all, and from what I could tell, she prayed for us every day.

I wish sometimes that I could have the strength she had, with nothing but her prayers to comfort her. Granny had the only kind of power a woman in that time and place *could* have—the power to transmute pain into comfort, absorbing untold sorrow and giving her family a safe haven. It was alchemy.

I didn't know that we went to an evangelical church from a Pentecostal tradition. The Pentecostals I knew would speak in tongues and sometimes dance in the aisle, which made me laugh behind my hand because *What are these grown-ups doing?* Our church grown-ups mostly said *hallelujah* a lot, and there was some crying and the anointing with oil, which came with prayers that spilled onto me in a rushing, falling-apart voice that made me think someone was maybe going to do something wrong.

When I became a teenager, I asked Papaw questions about the contradictions I found in the Bible—I had read plenty of it on my own and quite a bit in church. I never got to talk with anyone about the things that didn't make sense to me, but Papaw seemed safe enough to ask my questions now and then. I never argued with him, though. I didn't want to find out where his patience ended and his anger began. Papaw corrected me as to why Jesus turned water into wine—not because it's okay to drink wine now but because the water wasn't sanitary back then. And when I asked about Daniel, the most famous vegetarian in the Bible, he told me that story was about living excessively, not the harm of eating meat. I wanted to shake his conservative interpretations, but it was enough to have an adult talk to me like I could understand what they said.

No matter how conservative their views may have been, neither he nor Granny talked about going to Hell or who should marry and who should not. They didn't talk about politicians or race or the sin of dancing. They fed us and worked. Papaw hunted squirrel and picked blackberries. Granny cooked and prayed and gave us money that we didn't deserve.

And though later I couldn't go to church or believe in a literal interpretation of the Bible, and it would take years to undo some of the harm done in the church—if it can ever be undone—I knew my granny and papaw to be the kind of Christians some politicians claim to be, the kind of people any of us could want to be. But there is no faking that kind of humility. You can't pretend to love and give and forgive like my granny did. She didn't go around telling people how much faith she had, or how good God was to her. I heard it in her quiet prayers. I tasted it in the food she grew, canned, killed, and cooked. I felt it in the softness of her skin, which grew loose and spotted with age, unprotected and unadorned. It filled her house and spilled into the creeks and waiting hillsides, it wrapped itself around me, and I held on to that when there was nothing else.

# CHAPTER 25

## *The Canary in the Coal Mine*

I've worried a lot about my father and how he became so cruel, so indifferent to those of us who loved him and looked for his love. I listened to him intently, always trying to learn what I could do to make everything right, and what I must not do so I could stay safe. No matter how many drugs he did, he told stories. He repeated many of them over the years, and it always seemed that he was a walking history book of our family, the holler, and all the triumphs and tragedies that covered four counties.

More than once, he told me about how he dropped out of school just a few days after turning sixteen. Some boys had been picking on him—they liked to pick on him because he was skinny and had glasses. He said they pushed him around until the day he brought a knife to school and threatened them all. He never went back.

Every time he told me that story, I felt sorry for him. I knew how it felt to be too small, to get picked on, to be vulnerable. Somehow, I thought feeling too small must have been harder for him and that he had hated it so much, he found a way to make himself scary to these guys. But maybe he didn't. Maybe the knife wasn't enough. Maybe he would have had to endure more, and maybe he knew that, and that's why he didn't go back. I never dared to ask. In his story, he won.

Dad would sometimes complain about how gentle Papaw was, and I asked him once whether Papaw was always that way. *No, he told me. Your papaw used to be a tough man, but Granny henpecked him to death. She kept dragging him to church, and as soon as he got saved, he changed. He's nothing like he used to be.* I wondered who it was that my granny fell in love with when she was a long-legged blonde and he was a young man in the military, wearing glasses and raising one eyebrow for the camera, his arms around his buddies.

After I was grown, my father told me one story about Papaw that complicated the person I had always imagined him to be. When my father was still just a little boy, they lived in a house closer to town. Papaw delivered milk for the dairy, starting each day at four in the morning. Their neighbors were what we would have called *no count*—they didn't have jobs and stayed up late, working on cars that never seemed to get fixed. They kept a dog tied up to their fence, and that unfortunate creature woke up my papaw with his relentless nighttime barking. One night, as he tried to fall asleep, Papaw lost his temper and went outside with his shotgun. He killed the dog and carried it from the fence to the neighbors' front door, which he kicked open. He threw the dog into the living room and went home, where he was arrested soon after. His boss bailed him out of jail, and not long after that, Papaw and Granny moved their family out to the holler.

What did that mean about Papaw? Is that where my father learned to shoot or neglect every dog that found its way to us? My father liked the man that he thought Papaw was then—a hard man, afraid of nothing, not even the law. I don't know what else I don't know. And I don't have any other history to help me understand who my grandparents were before they became the heroes of my childhood. I may never know what happened between them and my father, or between Granny and Papaw. But when he was a young man, when I was listening, my father created a story for that—Granny was the villain, the woman who weakened her husband like in one of those Bible stories. Papaw was the tragic hero who lost his power, all of it taken by Granny, sitting there in her pretty dress on a church pew. I guess it's easy to think of women as the enemy—I grew up with many of the same stories that he did: Delilah, Jezebel, Eve. All guilty of vanity, of not listening, of ruining everything for the heroic men around them. These characters set me up with the understanding that girls come into the world a little different from boys and that the men who simultaneously desire and revile women are the *real* victims, the only ones who were born with original innocence. With that kind of belief system, what kind of treatment wouldn't women deserve?

My father always liked the man that my great-grandfather was, though—the man who hardly raised his children because he was in and out of prison. The man who shot other men over petty arguments and to keep himself out of jail. My dad spent enough time around my great-grandfather to learn how to make moonshine and to hear his stories about selling it to Al Capone, prison wardens, and a president's father. My father still praises my great-grandfather and has endless stories about their conversations and adventures during my dad's teens and early twenties. I imagine my father learned a lot about what it meant to be a man from his grandfather, who died not long before I was born. My dad revered him and never seemed to think it mattered that Papaw was raised by *his* grandparents and not the man my father worshipped. Granny told me once not to ask Papaw questions about that, and the only clue I have about the people who raised my papaw is a black-and-white picture of them. I look at it sometimes and try to imagine their lives, their stories, and the history behind that simple photo.

But now that Papaw is gone, my dad seems to have respect for his father, too. Maybe Dad had to go through his own loss, see his children flee from him, before he could understand the value of the father that Papaw became. He certainly knows that Papaw worked tirelessly to give them everything they needed, and then some. I still ask for more stories, trying to uncover them all before it is too late.

Not long before she died, I asked Granny whether she still loved my papaw, hoping for some advice that would prepare me to work next to someone, suffer loss with them, endure great joy together.

*No,* she said. *I would have divorced him a long time ago if I had known then what I know now.*

We were driving the short distance to her house from my childhood home, which my father's friend would soon burn down. In my shock, I had little time to ask anything else. I couldn't believe she felt that way, with her faith in God and, I presumed, a sense of duty to stay married forever because of things the Bible said. It still makes me wonder what she experienced that left her so discontented in her seventies, as she grew soft with age in the only place I know to be heaven on earth. I still wish I had asked.

She never told me any stories about her life, and neither did my papaw. I absorbed my father's stories, grateful to hear those histories and characters with all their complexities. Along with the seemingly endless narratives he knew about everyone, my father also talked about the bank, about rich bankers and prosecuting attorneys, workers' comp attorneys—all these rich men who were out to get him. They were the enemy. I knew which kids at school had rich parents—my dad didn't like them, either. He was constantly trying to scam the system and talking about how rigged it is, how crooked the players are.

Looking back on Granny and Papaw and their life in the holler, it seems they almost lived in a different world than my parents did or than my siblings and I experienced. I have a lot of the old black-and-white photographs from Granny's house, and when my father grew up there, it looked almost exactly the same as when I was growing up. They took such good care of the house, it's still standing now, though a little worse for wear after Papaw passed away. Granny kept the house clean, and it always felt cool and peaceful there, like that feeling in the forest.

Why have I spent so much time trying to understand my father? Maybe it's a daughter's need. I know I always wished I could be *daddy's little girl.* It's hard to believe he turned out like he did after being raised by my grandparents. It's not that they were showy with love and affection—their goodness was just so evident to me through their actions, which stood in stark contrast to my father's. Still, parents can't help but be associated with their children's trauma; after all, the parents are there—or noticeably not there—the whole time.

Maybe he turned out as he did because of the guys who picked on him—maybe my father was like today's children, who also respond to bullying in often desperate, sometimes defensive ways. I could have easily been like that.

Or maybe my father was just a man of his time—the FBI's statistics on crime identify the 1980s and 1990s to have been some of the most violent decades in America, including the rate of domestic abuse. He could have been a victim of some environmental ill, of a society that encouraged violence in men, or maybe of both.

And then epigenetic research theorizes that some of our DNA is encoded from our ancestors' experiences and that our grandparents' lives have as much of an impact on us as those of our own parents. My father idolized his grandfather, the moonshining and lawless man who wasn't there for his kids very much. I idolized my granny, who made her kitchen the epicenter of her home and whose strength of will was more commanding than any law or social rule I know of. Perhaps we all, to some extent, carry these infinitesimal burdens with us always, lifetimes upon lifetimes of history and pain and triumph embedded into invisible and weightless, incomprehensible miracles of creation or chance that drive us, blindly, into passion.

Maybe my father is a sociopath or psychopath. I don't know what he is. For someone from his time and place, getting a mental-health diagnosis was rare, and mental-health treatment even rarer. After his hospitalization, nothing changed for him or us—there were no prescriptions or counseling, only a strange new word floating around our home that dad would bring up with a laugh, just as he laughed anytime someone tried to assess him. *I like to play games with them,* he would say. *Good luck trying to figure me out.* Like so many people from all socio-economic backgrounds, he simply kept on self-medicating, pushing away thoughts or fear or a darkness that had taken on a life of its own.

Maybe he's just a bad person. I can imagine saying cruel things to my children, and I wonder sometimes whether I'm a bad person for that. But I can't imagine doing some of the things he did to us, or to our mother, or to others around him. And yet, how do we know where the difference lies between realizing we could do bad things and choosing to do them? Where is that line? Surely most of us possess some capacity for cruelty, but then some people don't seem bad at all. Others clearly are. Who gets to decide?

Maybe there is also a sickness born of economic instability and pressure and helplessness that destroys lives all over the globe, and that sickness takes on a particular look and feel, depending on the landscape. Whatever happened to my father, and to so many other fathers I grew up around, seemed to spread to the mothers in my generation—now there's often no strong woman to hold the family together in hills and hollers, bringing children and grandchildren to the table with the reminder that we belong to one another. Hollers seem more empty even as they fill up with trailers and television reception.

But I don't think we are the only ones who have watched this generational carnage unfold. Such destruction occurs in regions throughout America and throughout the world, as the most vulnerable populations have suffered and continue to endure compounding losses, as their land or minds have been colonized. Sometimes financial poverty does not go hand in hand with a poverty of the mind and the spirit. A lack of *things* does not necessarily mean hopelessness and desperation. Being poor in the holler—or anywhere—does not require cruelty or decay or drug addiction.

However, that might be the logical end, after so much pain.

These are all theories, of course—the musings of a daughter who wants to make sense of why she wasn't loved. For much of my life, that thought made me sad, but now I can see myself as another person born into this world, born to people unprepared and possibly unable to love me, to fully *see me*. Maybe if I can make sense of it, I can make it mine.

But the hero of the story is always the storyteller. The storyteller is the one with power.

# CHAPTER 26

## *About Love*

For my nineteenth birthday, my father came to visit me in my apartment, which I subleased from another girl for the summer. James was living in Lexington again, and I had my own place for the first time. I was once more working for the college that summer and was surprised to find I could pay my bills, and did so on time. My meth dealer, a chemistry major at the college, had moved away after dropping out of school again. My apartment was on the top floor of an old house, and I loved to climb out of the living room window onto the roof of the second story. I would sit there and smoke cigarettes—always *natural* or *organic* tobacco because I was still trying to be healthy. I watched the sunset from there and listened to the train. In some ways, I was at peace.

Soon after he arrived, my father crushed a Lortab and Ritalin and mixed them together and offered me a rolled-up dollar bill to snort a couple of the lines with. I wondered how I could accept such a gift. It was expensive, I knew—the pills cost more than anyone can truly afford. The pharmaceutical companies have not only made billions of dollars every year since they hit the Appalachian jackpot; they also have a growing list of families and children and souls in their profit column. I know that people who want to escape will find a way to get high, get drunk, or whatever else, and Eli Lilly didn't pull my father from a path of righteousness. But you have to wonder how much was being done to guard against abuse when the only things at stake were these hicks and hillbillies, these rednecks and backwoods inbreeders. Balance that against the stock prices, the yachts and cruises, the Cuban cigars—and our history shows that time and time again, poor people just can't compete.

I've watched my generation turn into people like my father—in and out of jail, their children being raised by grandparents, their babies going to foster care. As the taste for painkillers has spread from the poor to the middle class, a collective agony has been uncovered. The poor used to be hidden so well, and now it seems that everywhere I go in my small town, or in the larger town I commute to—and on the interstate in between—there is someone carrying everything they own in a garbage bag, wearing clothes that don't fit.

I spent years wanting to escape my own body, to get some relief from the inner hell that would never just let me be. Now I look into my father's vacant eyes, hear the slur in his voice, and I know he found a way out of whatever hell was keeping him company. I see it all around me in the sunken, wild eyes I avoid in the grocery store. I see it in the way many addicts walk, a certain looseness I've come to recognize in the lost. It's so easy to escape the sinister harvest we now face after decades upon decades of exploitation and its attendant social ills: poor health, broken schools, broken homes. But the escape only lasts for a few hours at a time.

I took the rolled-up dollar bill from my father and snorted the burning powder, telling myself I could not reject what I thought was the only way he could show me love. It would be a long time before I felt like I deserved a love that didn't hurt.

That word—*love*—how does one begin to define it? For the longest time, I relied on the power of definition through negation. *I am not in love. I could never love a child as a mother should.* Now I tell my son of my love for him, how it will outlast us both. He asks me about my family—don't I love our family as much I love him? I tell him no, I love him above all else.

I used to define *love* in my romantic relationships with men, then finally realized I was just not yet equipped to do so. I loved men by waiting for them. The further they were from me, the stronger my devotion.

Almost always, I loved them by having sex with them when they wanted me, by not saying anything when I found their porn or figured out how drunk they had gotten, and I forgave them when they dismissed me, showed violence, cheated. It was all I knew to do, in the absence of tenderness and carefulness and devotion and all the other words that appear inside Hallmark cards—there, they are so often nouns, like objects that you can pick up or point to. As verbs they are much more elusive—where is the act of devotion? It seems to be not one act but a series of actions, and not just a series of actions but a manner in which one performs those actions. It's the noun, the verb, the adjective, the adverb—it defies the sentence diagrams I loved in tenth grade, when language and words were so easy, when they fit into categories and branched off with lines and always went in the right order at the right time.

I met Jacob when I was married to James, when James and I decided to go stay in a holler where a group of Rainbow hippies lived in their hand-built cabins. Jacob lived in a teepee on the property of a mutual friend. I hugged him when I met him sitting outside our friend's cabin. Had the hug lasted too long? James and I didn't end up staying in our tent out there for very long, and I didn't see Jacob again until after James and I split up for good.

One day, I drove toward my apartment and saw him sitting outside the public library with my dreadlocked friend who had lived with me a couple of times by that point. I pulled over in a hurry, ostensibly to say hello to my friend, and invited them both over for dinner—I had always thought Jacob was cute. We spent that night together, and then most others after that.

That first night, though, he found a used condom on the floor of my bedroom that I somehow had missed. And I had to tell him the whole story.

A few weeks prior to that, I had met a new guy, Wes, who was kicking a Hacky Sack on campus, though he wasn't a student. He had nice eyes and a gentle voice, and I invited him to a party. I had played my favorite records for him at my apartment, and he came over to my house and brought me a record that he bought from one of my favorite antique stores in town.

We didn't use a condom the first time we had sex, and he insisted later that I get tested and show him the results because, he said, I must have been lying when the nurse told me over the phone they were negative. Wes eventually apologized, and I invited him to come to another party with me. That night, two guys at the party latched onto me, though I was surrounded by friends. Why did they choose me? I was surprised at the time—I didn't try to flirt and didn't get drunk. There's a quality some people see in the vulnerable, a marker that's recognized only by the kind of people who want to prey on them. One had dreadlocks and a hippie nickname and knew several of my friends. The other was a friend of his, visiting from Colorado. They wanted my number, *in case you want to hang out later*, and I gave it to them, confused. When I left with Wes, they asked whether I wanted them to stop by, and I said I didn't think so.

When we got back to my apartment, they called and asked whether I wanted them to come over. *No,* I said. *We're going to bed.*

Wes wanted to know why I gave them my number in the first place, and I told him I didn't know. And I didn't—I didn't know why they wanted it, didn't know why they called, and didn't know anything other than I wanted him to hold me and be sweet to me and to fall asleep in my bed.

But he put his coat on and stood in the kitchen while I sat at the table, once again ashamed for whatever had led me to fail again so quickly. *I didn't realize you were so sexual,* he said. It didn't matter that I had told them not to come over.

We heard someone come up the stairs. There was a knock at the door, and he opened it. It was the dreadlocks guy. *Do you all want to hang out?* he asked. *No!* I said, this time not trying to hide my frustration. He said okay and quickly bounded back down the stairs.

Wes looked at me and told me that the dreadlocks guy left only because he was there and that the other guy was intimidated by him.

*Good,* I said. *Please don't go.*

But he left, and it was clear that he thought me a whore.

The doorknob lock was broken where James had tried to let himself in a few weeks before that. He had tried to persuade me to share my student grant money with him, since he thought I was receiving it due to us still being married. He stood over me, with what I sensed as a hint of threat in his voice, until I told him I would give him several hundred dollars. Which I did, once I received my financial aid.

After Wes walked out, I put the chain lock on the door, turned off the lights, and crawled into bed, crying into my pillow. Suddenly, someone pushed open my door until the chain caught. It was the guys from the party.

*We just wanted to see whether you needed some company.*

*No,* I said. *I'm going to sleep.* But they held the door open as far as the chain would allow.

*Let us in, and we'll keep you company.*

I didn't know what to do, so I grabbed my clothes off the floor and turned on the light. I opened the door, tears still rolling down my face.

*What happened?* they asked, so concerned.

I told them, expressing my confusion and how hurt I was, and they started massaging my shoulders and arms. They were big men, fit and strong. The one from Colorado was an outdoorsman, he said. They were older than me, and if I had met them under different circumstances, I'm sure I would have thought they were cool guys. One of them started to take my shirt off, and I pulled it back down. But then he tried again, and the other went for my shorts. It was then that I realized there were two strange men in my house, and though I kept saying, *No, please,* they weren't stopping. They moved me onto the floor and took their clothes off.

*No, please,* I said, but they weren't the kind of men who would acknowledge the word *stop.*

A day or two later, I told my friend who had held the party about what happened. *What the fuck, they were giving Lindsey a ride home. She was in the van downstairs while they did that.* It turned out our mutual friend had fallen asleep and didn't know they stopped at my house.

They waited for my date to leave. They had seen Wes standing in his coat, and they pretended to go. They sat in their van and watched him walk away. Did he see them, too? When later demanding to know what happened that night, he claimed that he didn't. He had heard that something happened and came to my house to ask me if it was true. I knew what he would say. There would be no sympathy for me. So I simply told him, *It wasn't as bad as it could have been.*

I did think Jacob would have some sympathy when I recounted the story for him so he would know why I had failed to pick up a condom that one of the men had apparently tossed aside before each of them said, *I'll be right back,* walked downstairs, and never returned. Jacob was a feminist, and he had told me about his favorite porn star, who was all about female sexuality and being empowered. He had told me all about his last girlfriend, too. She turned out to be a young runaway, and they traveled around doing Food Not Bombs activist work, living under bridges, until he decided to move back to his parents' house next to the golf course.

It shook me to hear he had dated someone who was underage. I knew he would be angry if I questioned him, so I tucked away my concerns, telling myself there was probably something wrong with my judgment—like I always did when a man's behavior made me uncomfortable. Looking back, I wish I had known that the too-young girlfriend might be a sign of how much he liked to have authority, a certain kind of power that is easy to claim when one person has so much more experience than the other. A runaway, at that—someone who had no security or stability to turn to. I didn't know that I wasn't too terribly different from her in some ways.

After I finished telling him my story, he asked, *Why did you let them in?*

I felt my stomach sink.

*Why didn't you kick them in the balls?* He was angry. I didn't even know what to say.

I had gotten out condoms, thinking it quite likely that these guys were disease ridden and that if they wouldn't stop when I said *please, no*, and if watching me cry the whole time wasn't a turnoff, at least I could try to keep them from impregnating or infecting me. I knew my physical odds of escape should they have decided to restrain me or punish me. I weighed about ninety-five pounds and had never kicked anyone in the balls or slapped anyone. I had never escaped any violence. I made the choice to submit, the impossible choice that garners no sympathy.

And there was none. I couldn't bring myself to tell my professors why I was suddenly late all the time and that I was afraid to leave my apartment. My mentor let me go from my teaching-assistant position at the end of the fall, and when I asked whether I could work for him in the spring semester, he just said, *No*—no explanation given, none really needed. I had stopped working hard and setting a good example for the students in his classes. I didn't know how to tell him what had happened, why I changed. How I was nervous to walk down the street now, and how every man with a shaved head looked like one of the men from that night, and I was full of anger and fear around any man with that appearance—especially the one in my professor's class. When Jacob wanted me again, he eventually let it go. A couple of women asked me whether I would call the police, and I said no, knowing what justice looks like for women like me, poor women with crazy fathers who grow up in hollers.

# CHAPTER 27

## *The Gift*

I had been vegan for a little over two years when I met Jacob, but he told me I was being ridiculous, so I began eating fish soon after he started staying with me. One evening, I asked whether he wanted to go out to eat—one of his favorite things to do. But that night, he accused me of trying to spend all his grandfather's money—the inheritance that he had partially lived on while in his teepee out in the woods and now used while unofficially living at my apartment. He had insisted on buying a VCR so we could watch movies together—I had only watched *The Simpsons* on my friend's small TV that she left in the apartment. He had offered to help pay utilities and my rent, but I told him no, I wanted this place to be my own, and he was my guest. Still, he recounted how many thousands of dollars he had somehow spent because of me.

Soon after we got together, Jacob told me how obnoxious I was when I was drinking, particularly when I had three beers on a New Year's Eve. Jacob said he used to drink too much, so he stopped drinking before I met him. I had sat on another guy's lap that night—I thought of him as a brother, but that probably doesn't work for many men at all. Jacob said his problem was not with me sitting on the guy's lap, but with how *drunk* I was. So *out of control*. So I stopped drinking beer with my friends.

Jacob hadn't finished college. He started at a private college, one of the most highly acclaimed private colleges in the South. Then he went to a state university and dropped out of that one as well. Jacob thought all my effort toward college was ridiculous.

I had friends who worked at the local coffee shop, and I would go there between classes, or sometimes after class, and socialize and occasionally get free or discounted drinks. Jacob thought my friends at the coffee shop were ridiculous, too.

Before a year had passed, he decided to buy land in an adjacent county and told me that if I didn't move down there with him, we wouldn't see each other or be able to stay together. So I moved down to his property in Rockcastle County, which we didn't yet know was actually 213 acres, since the deed said 75 acres, more or less. It was just about an entire holler. There were two waterfalls on the property and fallow fields all over. An unfinished house sat next to a queenly maple tree, and we lived in that house, sharing the space sometimes with rats and other times with snakes. A black snake lived in the maple tree, a copperhead in the compost pile at the corner of the porch. One black snake lived in the addition to the house, even less finished than the house itself, which boasted a painted chipboard subfloor and a pink insulation board ceiling. Little holes in the subfloor were scattered here and there, allowing you to see the ground below.

The house had been built in the passive-solar style, allowing heat to come in through the south-facing windows, especially in the wintertime, but the windows were too large and too many—the south-facing wall was made of much more glass than it should have been, so the house heated up far too much and lost too much heat in the winter. The summer was just hot, all around.

There were two lofts, one with stairs so rickety that I stopped going up them once I was a few months pregnant. The bathroom had a sink and a white enameled bathtub. A water hose ran from the plastic water tank outside to the sink, allowing us to turn on the water just about anytime. The house came with a woodstove that got way too hot some-times, and that's where we heated water for baths or washing dishes, until a friend from another eastern-Kentucky holler insisted on giving us a gas hot plate to use for the summer. We moved into the house in a chilly spring but still didn't have wood cut for the fall and winter, so when it got cold, neighbors sold or gave us wood sometimes, and my dad brought loads down a couple of times, too—mostly pine, which filled the pipe with creosote and smoked up the house, or half-rotten wood that also filled the house with smoke. I would learn how to make a fire out of damn near anything after my son was born.

The road was almost impassable without four-wheel drive, but some folks tried anyway. Several vehicles were ruined by the bouncing, and the road itself was as much chunks of conglomerate rock as it was dirt and gravel. You had to know where to put your tires, and due to rain or snow, that kept changing. For a while, I still had my little Volkswagen Fox, the first car I bought by myself, with a standard transmission. It couldn't make the trip down into the holler, so I had to park it at the top of the mile-long driveway and walk down to the house.

I didn't know it when Jacob bought the house, but the couple who sold it to him did so in part because one of the rednecks who lived around there told the husband he had seen the wife naked through his gun scope one day, so the wife was no longer willing to live there. During my pregnancy, that redneck and several others would periodi-cally ride their four-wheelers through our property, sometimes when I was alone, and I would wonder whether I could fight them off with nothing but the ax I kept next to the futon mattress on the floor while I slept.

There was electric at the barn, so Granny gave me a minifridge to keep food there after the big refrigerator that came with the farm died. She told me not to lift it, but I was stubborn and unloaded it anyway, alone in that empty holler after I drove it back. There was a solar-electric system at the house, but it wasn't set up well, or the batteries were too old or had gotten too cold—I never really understood why it wouldn't work. We couldn't have more than one thing on at a time, so if you wanted to listen to the radio during the summer, you had to turn the fan off. And at night, if you wanted to use a lamp, you couldn't have the fan or the television on.

Rainwater fell from the roof into a gutter and then into the plastic water-storage tank. Sometimes the water turned green, so we added bleach to it and went on with our bathing and teeth brushing. We carried water from the spring in five-gallon jugs, even after we found a six-inch parasitic worm whipping about in one of the jugs we drank from when I was just a month or two pregnant.

~

When I was fifteen, I started thinking I wouldn't live past the age of nineteen—at the time, nineteen seemed like an old age, and I thought I would be through with all this living by that time. I spent a lot of time with my new little brother, who was about two years old when I moved away from Morehead. My dad had married a woman just eight years older than me, and he started over as a father. I hoped that, somehow, he would be gentler with the younger kids than he was with Junior and me. Two-year-old William would spend the night with me, sometimes up to a week at a time. People thought he was my child, and though I loved him and changed his diapers and it felt right to take care of him, I was horrified at the idea of being a mother.

By the time I was seventeen, I told my family I would never have children of my own. I did not want the responsibility of having a child, but I also thought I was incapable of loving someone enough to be a mother. In my young wisdom, I thought that the universe, or God, or anyone else who might have a say in the matter, would not allow me to get pregnant, that I was as good as barren.

So when my period was late for the first time, I thought it was because I had abandoned my vegan diet, and the dairy I was consuming had somehow altered my hormones. I thought that my body was readjusting to the new food, even though I only consumed dairy from cows who didn't receive extra hormones. When I mentioned my theory to a friend, she looked at me with raised eyebrows and asked whether I could be pregnant. I had always been so convinced that I couldn't be a mother, the thought had truly never occurred to me, though I was not on birth control.

Jacob and I went to a Rite Aid in Lexington and got a pregnancy test. As soon as the results showed up positive, he said I needed to decide whether to keep it or not, which I thought was surprising because, although I had debated about abortion in my philosophy classes, I knew it to be a thing good girls don't do. We drove to the Henry Clay Estate and sat on a bench in the garden, surrounded by hedges and looking out at an array of rosebushes. It was beautiful, unlike anything I had ever seen. We talked, and with little thought, I decided I wanted to have the baby.

We had to get married, Jacob said. His family was Catholic and would consider our child a bastard if I didn't marry him. They were true southerners, with the accents and money and not-sweet corn bread to prove it. They approved of me somewhat because I had gotten into a good college with no help from my family. I decided to marry him even though I had told him, when we started dating, that I didn't want to get remarried anytime soon. When I was little, one of my aunts had read my palm and told me I would be married and divorced three times. I was determined never to let that happen, since three failed marriages sounded like a hard way to live. But more than that, I didn't want my child to be scorned by his father's family, so I agreed to it.

We were riding through town in his little red pickup truck one day, my feet propped up against the dashboard. He reached over and grabbed one of my toes and pulled it toward him, bending it the wrong way, smiling at me. I told him to stop, *That really hurts,* and he did it for a moment longer before letting go. I reached over and gave him a push, checking my anger at the last second to be sure I was playful and not aggressive. He didn't like that, though. He pulled the truck into a parking lot and, with visible anger, ordered, *Never touch me like that again.* I tried to explain that it was playful, whereas he had really hurt me. I felt like a fool for trying to make a joke out of the anger I had rightfully felt, giving him this ammunition against me. He told me that he wasn't sure he wanted to marry me and that he would leave me in the parking lot if I weren't pregnant. Eventually, he decided to forgive me, and we drove away.

I should have known it was a bad sign when Jacob accused me of being selfish like his mother in the first few months of dating. He hated that they had raised him next to a golf course and had shoved a golf club into his hands. They were materialistic, especially his mom, and he was determined not to be. When we officially lived together—when I moved into the house he bought—we disagreed over money, but I lost all those arguments since his money was not mine to spend, and the little I received for school needed to go toward our family.

We visited some of Jacob's friends in Tennessee, who ran a specialized greenhouse and nursery, and he later told me they lived on five thousand dollars a year, and he wanted to get to that point. *I grew up so poor,* I told him, panic rising inside me. *I don't want to be poor again—I want a better life.* But Jacob said he knew what it was like to be poor, too. He had lived on fifty dollars a month and had lived under bridges with the young girlfriend.

*Who bought you that truck?* I asked.

He had bought it himself with money from selling his car.

*Who bought you the car?*

His parents.

*And where did you get that fifty dollars a month?*

His parents.

*Where did you go when you didn't want to live under a bridge anymore?*
To his parents.

I tried to explain that being poor means there is no car to sell, no
certainty in any income. And most of all, there is nowhere to go when
things get too hard or you get too tired. There is no one to call, no saving grace. Just the fear of losing your children or your home, the fear of
freezing or starving. Dignity is far from important, and in the throes of
poverty, the need to survive outweighs all else except the need to forget
your misery.

Over the next few months, doubts about motherhood crept into
my mind without rest. Morning sickness had kicked in a couple of days
after the pregnancy test, immediately after I drank a shot of wheat-
grass juice and walked around the health-food store, dazed, for hours.
I researched herbs and home birth and read everything I could find
about women's bodies, unborn babies, vitamins, and breastfeeding. In
the back of my mind, though, was the thought that I did not have to
have the baby, that maybe I wasn't ready after all. I wondered how my
body would change, whether I would be big forever afterward, when
I was used to being small. I wondered whether my breasts would sag,
whether I would suddenly look like mothers appeared to me, with their
unflattering clothes and tired bodies.

One morning, Jacob sat up in bed and turned to me as I awoke. He
said the spirits had told him that I had to decide whether I wanted the
baby or not, that if I did not decide, the baby was not going to come.

*I know,* I said. I thought about it all day. I thought about it while
swinging in my hammock chair, in the hot, damp air of that summer.
I thought about it while reading. I thought about the alternative, and
that scared me more than the thought of giving up all the control I
had over my body at that time. I decided to brave the stretch marks,
to brave gravity, and to brave the great breaking open I knew would
happen when the baby finally came. And I said, *Yes, I choose this baby, I*

*want this baby, please let him come,* though I knew I did not know what that meant.

~

After that, I was certain I would have a son with blond hair and blue eyes. I picked out a boy name, and as soon as I saw it, I knew the meaning was for him. His father came to agree, and although we gave a girl's name a little thought, I did not want a daughter, and I secretly prayed I would not have one. I was not ready, I thought, to have a girl—I was not ready to love a girl, not sure what that meant. I felt like I could take care of a boy, having spent so much of my life trying to earn my father's love and trying to protect my brother. I knew I could serve my son in a way that I could not serve a daughter.

Throughout my pregnancy, I gained seventeen pounds, though technically I probably lost some muscle weight and gained weight in fat, so the baby had more to work with than what it seemed. On a bright and cold February day, eight days after the estimated due date, I was awoken by a sharp contraction at about six in the morning. I told Jacob, and he encouraged me to go back to sleep. I woke up again around nine and had contractions steadily throughout the day. It was the first stage of labor, all very bearable and somewhat pleasant. I called my mother and told her my labor had started, and she tried to convince me one last time to go to a hospital, but I dismissed her concern. She was afraid, she said, for me to experience so much pain and not have any relief from it.

I wasn't afraid, because I didn't think any physical pain could rival the emotional pain I had known to that point.

Natural childbirth would mark my first memorable experience with physical pain, and it would surely establish a new reference point that I would use from then on.

My midwife showed up that evening, when the contractions were no longer somewhat pleasant. She brought an assistant with her, who was the same woman she had apprenticed under and who had attended over six hundred births. That woman had retired, but my midwife asked her for this favor, knowing we were an hour's drive from a hospital and no ambulance could reach us.

By eleven o'clock that night, it was clear the baby was nowhere near ready to make his entrance. My midwife had me take a bath to try to relax and ease the contractions. When that didn't work, she had me drink half of a home-brewed beer, again hoping it would slow the contractions and allow me to sleep for a little while that evening.

Everyone else went to sleep—the midwives and my friends who came to help found places to sleep downstairs near the woodstove, and the father of my child in our bed in the loft. One friend was a massage therapist, the other a student and friend of mine who majored in art and photography and would photograph the birth. I sat in a rocking chair next to an enormous window in the loft and rocked silently through my contractions all night. I labored in the dreamland of maternal solitude. I did not count contractions or minutes or anything else, and we did not have a clock to watch anyway. There were no lights on anywhere, inside or out, and no noises except the occasional creak of wood beneath me, the sound of someone moving in their sleep next to me, worlds away. In the darkness, I watched the moon travel in its arc over the sky as my child and body worked together toward a new life for us both. When the sun rose, I decided it was time to vocalize my suffering.

I let myself moan with each contraction throughout the morning. I wanted to be left alone in the ocean of pain that kept pulling me further away from the world.

My midwife checked me around noon and found I was ready, though my water had not broken. I asked her to rupture the membranes artificially—to break the caul that surrounded my unborn son and that held him in blissful suspension, in sublime safety. She did, using a tool that looked like a crochet needle, but to my surprise, it did not hurt. After that, things got interesting.

My irritation with the people around me was completely obliterated. I had felt distracted when I heard their talking downstairs, and though I wanted to be comforted, I did not want to have to speak or hear any voices. After the water poured out of me, I entered a new world, the kind of world that sets your body and your mind adrift and shows you why the Crucifixion of Christ is also called *the Passion*. My midwife reached inside me to push my bones apart and allow my son's head to descend. The indentations we all have in our lower backs—the two dimples that sit several inches apart—mark the width of the ischial spines, where yet-unborn heads must first arrive before coming to the light of day. My ischial spines, it turns out, were quite narrow, and though we did not know it yet, my son's head was relatively large.

If I had bellowed through my contractions as the sun rose, I could only scream when my bones were forced outward. The midwife was gentle, careful, respectful—but the goal was to move something farther than it wished to move, and resistance like that, of course, is a force to be reckoned with.

When my son's head was finally visible, it was a small, wrinkled bit that my midwife encouraged me to view with a mirror. I found it alarming, though, and failed to see the beauty in that first glimpse. After reading books about natural childbirth, unassisted childbirth, water births, and everything in between, I had thought I would give birth in a squatting position, aided by gravity and with a nod to my tribal ancestors, who understood the efficiency of such an irresistible force. I found myself instead lying on my back, my photographer friend behind me to help me arch my spine into a *C*. My husband held my right leg, and my massage-therapist friend held my left leg in the air. My midwife knelt between my legs, trying to coax my son out, once and for all.

My son's head crowned for an hour, on the verge of slipping into this world and giving him his first breath of air, his first view of his mother, his first opportunity to cry. But he stayed inside, so my midwife reached for her scissors. It had to be done.

By this point, the other midwife was kneeling beside me, her hands on the top of my still-pregnant belly, pushing downward to help force the baby out. Finally, my son's head emerged and he cried out.

Another moment later, his body followed, and my son was born. Sometime later, Jacob would bury the placenta in a hole where he planted a tree for our son.

I got my first tattoo about a year later. One morning, while I was lying in bed with my son and enjoying the first few weeks of his life, dazed and soaked with the various essences of human life, I thought that my stretch marks looked like lightning bolts, and I considered it an apt symbol for my son's birth, as well as for my experience of birth, though the man who did my tattoo executed an image that was markedly different from what he had sketched for me.

*Pain* is a place, a substance, a state of being: *I am in pain.* We say *hurt*, and we mean *like that baseball that hit me in the face when I was twelve.* Or we say *excruciating*, and we mean *like giving birth and the stitches that follow.* We say *broken* and mean *my arm* or *my heart* or *something else I clearly need to be whole.*

Suffer enough, and if we are lucky, you and I decide *something has to change*, and somehow, sooner or later, it does.

# CHAPTER 28

## *Cyclical*

I spent my first six weeks with the baby down in the holler, leaving only to have him examined by a local doctor who was sympathetic to home birth—there was a fairly large Mennonite community nearby who took their babies to him. The rest of that time, I held and nursed my baby and discovered my capacity for love in a new, sacred dreamworld. I couldn't fathom leaving the protective hills then—I carried my son at my chest when he wasn't eating or sleeping, and there was nothing else in the world for me that mattered. It seemed all I did was nurse him and change his cloth diapers while my body slowly healed from the tearing apart.

That holler was so much like the one where I came from, with its breathtaking beauty, its carpets of wildflowers, the furled fronds of the ferns taking invisible breaths as they revealed themselves to a waiting forest. But for all the beauty such places hide, they hide everything else as well. Those hills are hallowed, the terrain unyielding, like a church whose walls write secrets upon the hearts of the trembling.

And that holler was equally severe. We boiled the rainwater from the roof in five-gallon pots on the woodstove, fifteen minutes for each pot—one pot at a time, usually—so I could bathe in clean water. Somehow, that didn't prove clean enough, and within a few weeks of giving birth, my postbirth blood turned rancid. For a couple of days, I wondered what was wrong and finally asked Jacob to bring me the thermometer from the bathroom.

*You're fine, you don't have a fever.*

He refused, so I walked gingerly down the loft stairs, rough-cut boards with no railing. I made my way to the bathroom, mindful of the stitches that must not come apart, and took my temperature. It was 102.5. Jacob went outside and came back with an echinacea root that he rinsed off and handed to me.

*Chew this and swallow the juices.*

I did what he said, and the juice was bitter and burning all at once. But I chewed the entire root, and a couple of days later, the infection cleared. When I felt well enough to walk outside, I used my cell phone on the one spot it worked in the holler—standing on the corner of the porch, facing the barn. I called my midwife, and with evident frustration, she told me I had had a uterine infection and, if it happened again, to make him take me to the doctor. I looked it up and found that a uterine infection is the same as *childbed fever*, the malady that has taken so many women without clean water, without proper care. I was more careful then and took no more sitting baths until I healed, though I was almost always covered in sour milk and spit-up.

Jacob worked on weekends and was gone the entire weekend, coming back on Monday afternoon with our weekly groceries. I think he stayed home with us for two weeks or so before going back to work. I slept with an ax between me and the loft stairs and kept my baby close. Winter gave way to spring, and my enchantment was punctured only by the reality of how cold the house could be. I learned to build a fire out of anything—we occasionally had a nice load of red oak, but at other times, it was wet and rotten wood that I coaxed into burning while the baby lay safely nearby. I wondered whether it was possible to freeze in that house, like our eggs and lettuce had done in the cabinet on the porch—a ramshackle, makeshift icebox that spared us from walking to the barn several times a day.

Thankfully, the chilly spring gave way to warmth and a hot summer. The failed passive-solar design ensured that the house was always hot, and we kept a box fan running when we could, moving the damp, heavy air through the living room space. There were few walls within the house, so the fan did what little it could to provide some relief. The baby and I were always covered in milk and sweat, and I did what little I could to keep him cool and dry. We often walked to the waterfalls before they dried up for the season, and I relished the cool, trickling streams.

I had taken off the spring semester from college and had the summer off as well, and would then have just my senior year to finish before I graduated. As the summer wore on, though, I worried about how I would make it to class. The trip out of the holler took time and care, and it was another thirty minutes or so to get to campus after reaching the road. With his unflagging criticism of the idea of college, I began to suspect that Jacob wouldn't make it easy for me to leave the holler and do the work I needed to do to finish.

One afternoon, I realized I hadn't brushed my hair in a few days, and I was suddenly frustrated with how little time I had to take care of myself. I asked Jacob to watch the baby while I went downstairs—I wanted to brush my teeth as well. He lay next to the baby on our mattress and rubbed the baby's back as he started fussing. Standing beneath the loft, I knew what the baby's cries meant as they intensified: *Pick me up. Hold me. Let's walk around.*

I stepped out of the bathroom and looked up and said something like, *Can you calm him down?*

*I've got this, we're fine,* Jacob replied.

I brushed my teeth, and the baby began to cry in earnest. I again stepped out and looked up, and this time, I did not hide my irritation. *Can you take care of him?*

Jacob stood up and came downstairs, leaving the baby on the mattress. I don't remember whether he said anything, but he was clearly angry, and I went upstairs to pick up the baby and then brought him back down. Jacob kicked the baby's walker, and it flew across the floor before hitting something else that stopped it. I grabbed my little zippered purse, the phone and charger, and the diaper bag and hurried to the old Toyota 4Runner we had bought with some of the wedding gift money Jacob's parents had given us.

I buckled the baby into his car seat in the front passenger seat—why it wasn't in the back seat, I can't say. I locked the door as I always did, a measure of precaution in a time when most car doors—especially the older cars—didn't have automatic locks. As I buckled myself into the driver's seat, Jacob came to the passenger door, tried to open it, and then just stood looking at the baby. I thought he wanted to give the baby a kiss or say a little goodbye, because clearly I needed to leave him alone for a while, and this was no time to talk about what had just happened.

But when I unlocked the door, he immediately began unbuckling the baby, and I reached out in horror—*What are you doing? You can't take him, you can't keep him here.* I held on to the baby as gently as I could, suddenly afraid in a way that I had never been before.

*Please let me go,* I said. *Please don't do this. I won't take anything, you can have everything. Just let me leave.*

Finally, saying nothing, he stepped back, and I shut and locked the door again, my heart racing. I started the engine and looked in the rearview mirror, ready to back up and turn around near the old shed at the corner of the dirt driveway. Jacob stood at the back of the vehicle, reaching his arms to the top of it. A couple of times, I asked him to move; he finally did, and I could see him walking into the house as I drove away.

Then I was seized by a new fear. Would he follow me? Try to stop me again? He had the white pickup that I had clutch-started during my pregnancy. Of course I would not leave him without a vehicle. There was no way to drive up the hill quickly—you had to be so careful as you negotiated the chunks of rock that jutted this way and that from the dirt of the driveway. To be careless or drive too fast meant that something would be knocked loose under the hood, as several people came to find out. Part of the way, someone could walk faster than driving up.

I reached the top of the hill, breathless with fear, but he never appeared in my rearview mirror. I made it to a friend's house and stayed for a night or two. Jacob called me and said he wanted to talk, and I met him in a parking lot, hoping it was a safe and smart thing to do.

When we argued, Jacob would tell me I was like my father. I had told him some of the stories about my childhood, and early in our relationship, I related every story of my shame and mistakes—I thought that's what it meant to be honest, to be vulnerable and trusting within a relationship. When the first signs of his disapproval surfaced, he compared me to his mother: selfish, materialistic. But after a while, it was my father he saw in me—at least, the version of my father I had shared with him: *violent, full of anger, fucked up.* I believed him, already so convinced of my flaws, so certain that any anger I ever felt was a sign I had failed to escape fate. I feared becoming like my father, and comparing me to him was a keen weapon.

In the parking lot where we met, Jacob told me it was my fault he had acted like he did. Somehow, it was a drama he felt forced to play, and the role of my father had been forced upon him. But he wanted me to come back. *You belong at home, and so does our son,* he told me.

I took another day or two to think about what he said. I couldn't wrap my mind around what had happened, it seemed so surreal. Just after he kicked the walker, part of me wanted to stop and talk to Jacob, to say, *Okay, this is ridiculous, we don't have to do this, this is not who you are.* Like the time I thought I could stop my father from whipping me, when I realized that I had done nothing wrong and that it was unfair. I had thought better of my father than he thought of himself—I believed his reckless violence was beneath him and not his true nature.

None of it made sense to me, but maybe I had subconsciously provoked Jacob. I was always filled with so much guilt, I accepted that I had magically orchestrated everything he ever disliked about his life. I was lost inside myself, certain of nothing good about me other than the fierce and selfless love I felt for my baby. To my friend's dismay, I went back.

# CHAPTER 29

## *The Whore*

Within a few weeks of the fall semester starting, I found that I was right to be concerned about getting to my classes. My childhood fear returned, that of being trapped and not allowed to leave, isolated from the rest of the world in a beautiful prison. One day we were in town, and I had someone watch the baby while Jacob and I ate at the Mexican restaurant. We walked down the street afterward, holding hands, and things felt so pleasant, I thought he might understand what I told him next.

I had used some of my student grant money to put down a deposit on an apartment in town, within walking distance of the college. Jacob dropped my hand and stopped walking as I explained—I wouldn't be able to get to classes from the holler, and it was so important to me to finish my degree. No, I wasn't sure what I would do with a bachelor's degree in philosophy. Yes, it was just a piece of paper. But for whatever reason, I felt like it was necessary that I finish, that I prove myself.

I told Jacob he could live in the apartment with us if he wanted, and we could just go back to Rockcastle County as we pleased, and after I graduated, we would be there for good. Or he could come and go as he wished, as my husband, staying in town sometimes and in the holler whenever he felt like it. He could take care of the baby while I went to class, or I would pay a babysitter—he didn't have to do anything. Eventually, he seemed to accept the arrangement, though he was not happy about it.

One of his best friends, Greg, was living near me with his wife and their child, who was born just before ours. Jacob arranged for them to watch the baby sometimes, and I would drop him off on my way to class. I brought the baby's food already cut into pieces so no one would accidentally give him too big of a bite. When I could, I came back between classes to nurse him, and I pumped milk so he would have bottles when I couldn't be there. Jacob showed up to watch the baby less and less, so when I didn't have anything else arranged, I often ended up taking him to class with me in a baby backpack. He grew so big, people constantly remarked that he was bigger than me.

My professors were as understanding as possible. I brought him to my weight-lifting class one day when Jacob didn't show up, and the coach sent me outside to walk laps around the track with my son pulling my hair and drooling on me. He was quickly bored, so I bounced around the track, trying to keep him entertained, wondering how I was going to make it work. I brought him to my senior-seminar class another time, and he fussed so much, I ended up nursing him to keep him quiet and to not have to leave the room. There were two other students in the seminar—both male—and our professor was male. I was well covered while I nursed, but they kept their eyes fixed to mine, and they took everything I said about Wittgenstein seriously, which almost kept me from being embarrassed. I was a research assistant for another philosophy professor that year and once nursed the baby in his office during a meeting—the baby only nursed briefly but then spat it all back up onto the professor's carpet. The professor refused to let me clean it, and I didn't cry until I was outside his office again.

Jacob still came over and spent the night, usually a couple of days a week. During one of the many arguments that seemed to always happen, I looked at our son's face and saw he was still playing happily, unaware and unaffected. I just kept washing the dishes. I decided in that moment that I wouldn't fight with Jacob and that I would never again let our son hear us arguing.

I wanted to go out on Halloween that year—I hadn't spent much time with friends in a long while, especially without the baby. He agreed to watch the baby so I could go to a Halloween party, but when I returned, he was back at it, telling me how I was a terrible person, a horrible mother. I told him if I was such a negative person in his life, he should leave me. By that point, I couldn't think of any reason he would want to be with me. I knew he wanted to hurt my feelings, but I didn't understand how he could hate me so much. I had done everything I knew to be a good wife.

He stood up and told me he would leave me. For a moment, I thought about everything that meant and then said, *Okay.* He walked out and came right back, pleading with me to *work this out.* I told him that he deserved better, that I was making him miserable. I wasn't sure I was so bad, but he had been so insistent just moments earlier, I figured agreeing with him and apologizing would be the quickest way to end the painful evening. I was emotionally and mentally exhausted and didn't feel like I could do any more mental gymnastics to determine who was the worst of us, where all the blame for our lost love should be placed. And yet, we talked into the night.

I moved to a one-bedroom apartment soon after—I couldn't quite afford the two-bedroom apartment I was living in, and the downstairs neighbors were young men who loved heavy-metal music and who didn't care how many times I banged on the floor or went to their door, asking them to be quiet. Jacob kept a few things at my new apartment until I finally told him to take them home—his nice kitchen knives, a cookbook, that sort of thing.

He was over one day before work, and I began vomiting—I was too weak to walk to the bedroom, so I slept on the couch in between vomiting. He put the baby to sleep in the playpen in my bedroom—the playpen served as a crib—and started to leave. *Please don't leave me, call in to work—I can't take care of the baby like this.*

But he would not miss work. When the baby woke up, I was too weak to stand, and I crawled to his playpen, trying to comfort him. My downstairs neighbors knocked on the door at the top of the stairs between their apartment and mine—we shared a washer and dryer that sat on their floor, at the bottom of those stairs. I crawled to the door, the baby crying in earnest now.

*Do you need help with your baby?* They had never heard him cry so much. I told them, *Yes, please—he just wants to be held,* and the woman came in and picked him up and soothed him, then took him to the far end of the living room, which I had set up as a play area with toys and bright pictures to counter the dark wood paneling of the apartment. I don't remember her name, but I wish I could find her and thank her for that. I could often hear her boyfriend's booming voice—he always seemed to be yelling at her—but she came into my house that evening and wasn't a bit worried about getting sick herself.

Jacob and I were no longer together, but he came to my apartment one day and found another young man there—he was a friend, and we had been intimate once, but that's not why he was there. Still, Jacob was mad at me and asked, *So this is who you leave me for? That boy?* He also read my journal when he got a chance and had nothing but disdain for me.

During the first year after I moved out of Jacob's house—he was always clear that it was his house, his money—the people around me seemed to change. I had lived in Berea for almost four years and had my college friends who were mostly my age, but I also had a group of older, hippieish friends who were involved in sustainable living. I had met most of them when I was a freshman and had always been welcome to go swimming with them in their private ponds, and to attend their potlucks and parties.

But after I first moved out, before we really split up, Jacob told me that he and his lesbian friends had discussed my leaving him, and they all decided I must be a lesbian. These were women I knew, a couple that I had thought of as matriarchs in the community, though they weren't that much older than me. I had not told anyone but my closest friends what he had done, the things he had said to me, but he apparently told all kinds of stories about me to anyone who would listen.

About a year later, one of those women happened to see me at a mutual friend's on a summer day. I brought my son with me to this older couple's house, quite a ways from town. They had a large, deep pond—more like a lake—and I was allowed to come there and swim whenever I wanted. When I arrived that Sunday afternoon, I found there were a lot of cars parked along the gravel driveway and quite a few people swimming. Some were naked, some were clothed, but I didn't own a bathing suit at the time and always swam in my friends' ponds naked, as did the owners. After we swam around for a little while, someone mentioned the trampoline that sat in the field and how much we would enjoy it, so I wrapped myself and my son in towels and went to the trampoline alone. I didn't bother with shoes—I loved feeling like I was part of nature again, and the path was mostly soft. I let him jump for a few minutes, and we were quickly dry, so I wrapped us both up and headed back toward the pond.

I had never been out to that field before and, until I was walking on gravel, didn't realize I had taken the path to the left, which led to the rest of the driveway and another small house, rather than the path on the right, which headed back to the pond. I suddenly found myself walking on sharp gravel, carrying my son, surrounded by a lot of people I knew and a few I did not. The house owners had thrown their annual party that weekend, and most of these people had spent the entire weekend there. The mood was relaxed and cheerful as people chatted, and some drank beers and smoked. The wife of the couple soon came up to me as I tried to walk down the gravel road and return to the pond.

*Are you naked under there?* she asked me.

*Yes, I'm really sorry. I took the wrong way back from the trampoline. I'm trying to get back to my clothes,* I told her.

*Oh no, honey—we don't mind that kind of thing a bit here. You look like Eve in the Garden of Eden. Go sit down—I'll get your clothes and shoes for you.*

And with that, she walked off, and I was free to put my son down, a one-year-old who was big for his age. The guys on the porch offered me a chair, and I sat, relieved and embarrassed, but also heartened to hear the owner's compliment. After a few minutes of sitting and drinking a beer, I thought it was reasonable to take my towel off and sit naked, rather than pretending I wasn't basically naked already. I chatted with some of the guys, and plenty of people wandered about. My son played in the dirt, and for a moment, I thought I was in some kind of heaven—where being *natural* was not just accepted but encouraged. The men kept their eyes aimed toward my face, and since I thought I was so ugly, it never occurred to me that anyone would think anything about me other than I was a tomboy who happened to be naked, but so were a bunch of other people at the pond, and most of those people had seen each other swimming around naked anyway.

I was wrong. Jacob's lesbian friend showed up at the party and was all of a sudden walking down the same road that I had come up, heading to the field with a few other people. She turned and looked at me, said hi, and turned back around without stopping. A couple of days later, Jacob said, *She told me she saw you out there, naked and sprawled out for all the men to see what they could have if they wanted it.* I didn't know how to defend myself, didn't have the words to say, *I was like Eve in the Garden, not a whore. I thought that was freedom. And didn't you all decide I was a lesbian anyway?*

Some months later, I was buying a couple of groceries in the health-food store—the same one I had worked in for a time—and I ran into Jacob's friend Greg, whose wife had babysat for me. Greg walked up to me, and my stomach knotted with dread, but he told me he owed me an apology.

*For what?* I asked.

*Jacob told us that you were such a bitch, and we believed him. He said you wanted to sleep with other men but didn't want him to sleep with other women, and that's why you split up. He said that you were a terrible mother and that you didn't care at all about the baby.* Soon after, Greg's wife echoed what he had said and told me, *I believed him for a while, but you were always there for the baby, bringing his food already cut up*—she laughed—*I told my husband that this is not a woman who doesn't love her child.*

I called Jacob and asked him whether he had said all those things, and he said yes. I told him he knew that wasn't true—I had never wanted to be with anyone else when we were together. He reminded me that I had told him I thought an open relationship was a good idea.

*I told you I believed that when I was seventeen, and it didn't work for me.*

*Well, I can't help what people say about you,* he responded.

*Yes you can, if you stop telling them lies and tell them what you said isn't true.*

But of course, that was not going to happen. For that first year or two, I lost one round of friends. *That's okay, they weren't my friends anyway,* I told myself. But I missed being able to go to the potlucks and the outdoor parties with the other hippies and homesteaders.

There would be another wave of loss later, when I tried to fight for my son in court. When I was ready to file for divorce, Jacob told me he wanted to keep the baby half the time and not pay child support. I didn't know then that he had gotten that idea from another man, someone I would end up dating. Jacob had been giving me a couple hundred dollars each month, which I had thought was really good. But he had insisted that I couldn't keep either of the vehicles that we bought with the five thousand dollars from his parents' wedding gift—that money was going into the land and would stay there. He agreed to give me seven hundred dollars, and other than some fancy CorningWare baking dishes, that's all I got of the property we owned together.

I signed up for legal aid, a free attorney who would represent me in court, and refused to take my granny's money when she begged me to go hire a good lawyer. I felt like I had taken so much, it didn't make sense to spend her money on a lawyer when I could get a perfectly good one for free. I didn't want Jacob to take our son back to the ramshackle house in Rockcastle County overnight, so far away, but he insisted. When he brought him back, I asked how it went, and with an edge to his voice he told me they were fine but would say no more. When Jacob first mentioned keeping our son half the time, I insisted he couldn't because the baby was still nursing, but after spending some nights away from me, he quickly weaned himself.

Soon after the baby turned one, Jacob told me that his dad had advised him to just take the baby and move back down to Atlanta, where they were from. I asked him what his mother thought of that idea, and he said she didn't approve of taking the baby away from me—I was glad, since I had spent that past Christmas with them just so Jacob wouldn't be away from his son for *his* first Christmas—but I got the message loud and clear that I was in no position to fight Jacob, who had his parents' money at his disposal. I met with a couple of lawyers for consultations—not the free lawyer, because there was a long waiting list—and they told me that in Kentucky, since we were still married and there was no custody agreement, Jacob could take the baby whenever he wanted, wherever he wanted, and not give him back to me. And if he did that, it could be a year or more before I saw my child again. So I agreed to the equal time sharing and began drinking when my son was away, trying to drown my grief.

# CHAPTER 30

## *Pretending*

The day I graduated from Berea College, Jacob held the baby while I sat through the ceremony. My mother and stepfather came, and my granny came with my dad. After it was over, I got my son and looked for the rest of my family. I found Granny and Dad, and they told me they were leaving—though it was early afternoon, Granny didn't want it to get any later before they drove the hour and a half home. I never found my mother, but when I called her later, she said they left immediately after the ceremony ended, so she wouldn't run into my father. I walked out of the gym, where my friends and classmates were hugging their families and taking pictures, and went home with my baby.

I was scared after I graduated—I realized I needed to find work immediately but had no idea what I could do or how to land a real job besides waitressing. My stepdad told me I should go to a temp agency in Lexington, so I did, and I was able to work a couple of short-term jobs through them and made enough money to pay the bills. One of those short-term jobs led to a long-term, but still temporary, position as an administrative assistant in Lexington.

I felt like I didn't know how to do anything, so I worked as hard and fast as I could at everything. The director of the department found out that I liked to write, so she had me help edit the newsletters the company sent out to customers, and soon I was drafting articles and learned to do the layout as well. I picked up on how to write macros in Excel, and anytime someone asked whether I could do something I couldn't do, I said yes, then learned how to do it. Eventually, they offered me a full-time job.

I constantly worried about how to make ends meet and wondered what would happen to me and my son if I failed to make it in this new world—the world of working and babysitters and commuting and flat tires on the interstate. Since the time I had moved out when I was seventeen, my mother had given me money only once—when one of the struts broke on my car. I was surprised—she usually wouldn't even lend me money, but she and my stepdad paid the garage that fixed it, so I could drive my car to work. At other times I asked for help, and if they lent me money, I had to tell them the exact date I would pay it all back. When another of my cars spewed oil everywhere right before I started a new job, they wouldn't lend me their extra vehicle—*neither a lender nor a borrower be,* my stepfather reminded me.

I knew I couldn't move back in with them if I couldn't survive as an adult—now a parent myself, with someone else to care for. I tried to hide my fear at work, and I kept my face as expressionless as possible—an essential key to survival, as I had learned when my dad whipped me for crying, and at other times for smiling, or when, all those years ago, I saw Granny talk to my dad like her grandchildren and our mother weren't crouched on the floorboard of Papaw's truck, holding our breaths.

Eventually, I became friends with another woman there, who told me she had thought I was *haughty* due to how disinterested I looked all the time. I hadn't thought I was better than my coworkers, but as in the past, I found that I couldn't relate to them, that what I did to survive somehow made me wrong in their eyes. They talked about watching *The Bachelor,* losing weight, and giving their husbands blow jobs. When I brought Indian food for lunch, they made faces, and the director asked me not to eat it at my desk. I didn't understand why they were content with fast-food cheeseburgers and fries, or how it mattered if one woman didn't like another.

Once I left Morehead, a lot of the people I met told me I didn't have an accent after they found out I was from eastern Kentucky, but anyone who heard me on the phone with my family commented on how my accent came right back. I had worked hard in college to say words the right way, enunciating the endings like we never did back home and quickly scanning my brain for different words when I wanted to say *wallering around* or *up in the holler* or *I reckon*. I didn't know anything about linguistics, and even when I did take a linguistics class in graduate school, it didn't dawn on me that my people had their own grammar. Like all cultures everywhere, there are unspoken rules for how certain sounds are pronounced, and for arranging those words, but it all follows a structure and has nothing to do with being ignorant or lazy—we were just country people talking like people from the country. Every group of people, everywhere, has a way of talking.

The mockery of Appalachia has evolved from *The Beverly Hillbillies* to concerts where musicians who've gotten rich off Appalachian music traditions don't mind making fun of toothless Kentuckians right here in Kentucky. Quiznos featured a "hillbilly hot tub" in one of their commercials, which was met with some disdain for the homoerotic undertones, but I never found any backlash at the ad's depiction of hillbillies as ignorant and mentally slow. Maybe I was the only person who boycotted Quiznos from then on. And I was horrified when I recently watched *The Simpsons*, and it featured a woman from Kentucky—she was a hopeless heroin addict who made beautiful music but who ultimately disappointed everyone by turning back to drugs and alcohol after Lisa tried to save her from herself. I knew when we were supposed to laugh, but all I could think of was the people I have loved and the mounting losses between us. The punchlines we're so good for.

Sometimes, when I was around my family, they would turn to each other when I used a word they didn't understand—*a five-dollar word, too rich for our blood*—and I would look away, knowing my new way of speaking marked me as an outsider. No matter what I did, I couldn't do good enough in someone's eyes. But I couldn't take back the education and years of reading poets and philosophers and history. And I couldn't tell them, *I am still one of you,* because in so many ways, I wasn't able to be. For a while, I thought I could show them what was so good about the education I had received, show them that the *going away and having your head filled with nonsense* our people had looked down on for so long was just wrong thinking, that there was so much good in those books and classrooms.

The years wore on, and each time Jacob was angry with me, another group of friends and acquaintances turned their scorn toward me. One friend who had told me, *He doesn't help at all with the baby,* later described him as one of her favorite people. Another friend, a man who had been as good as a brother to me, ended up telling me, *Jacob isn't so bad these days.* When Jacob told a story about me, no one ever asked me my side of what had happened, and I didn't volunteer it. If there's one thing you learn growing up as a girl in the country, it's not to air your dirty laundry in public.

I started to wonder, though, what would have happened if I had told all my stories to these people. Would they have believed me, would they have cared? Would they have turned their backs on Jacob in line at a restaurant, or have stopped inviting him to their parties? Would he have seen so many friendly faces close themselves to him, shut him out from the small-town social life of the farmers' market and elementary school events? And would Jacob have wondered what he had done wrong, how I had single-handedly taken a town—a chosen home— away from him? Or does that just happen to girls like me?

The answers don't actually matter. I didn't want him to feel lonely or abandoned, so I didn't tell the stories that would have led to him being judged by those people. The loneliness I carried for so much of my life, though, was deepened and sharpened, somehow a vast hollowness that left me bleeding and aching and wishing for comfort. And though I shared my stories with my closest friends, some of those people chose him, in the end. It took me years to realize that they couldn't love me and still celebrate the man who had belittled me. And even longer to realize that those people, with their talk about community and female empowerment and protecting children, could not see the disconnect between their theories and the world we live in. They did not want to see people like me, who *needed* the world they claimed to want.

I wasn't great at being an employee, as hard as I worked. Sometimes it was because I had bad luck—two flat tires in one month, a boyfriend living with me had a seizure and I *had* to stay home with him. Sometimes it was because I drank so much while my son was at his dad's, I drove in late or I had to sleep during my lunch break. Other times, I was clearly just sabotaging myself, and my boss had the kindness and good sense to point that out, but I didn't know how to fix it.

Because of my absences and lateness—you could have only five occurrences in a twelve-month period—they sent me to the employee assistance program. I soon found myself in a therapist's office, trying to figure out why I had a hard time enjoying my job and getting to work on time, and he asked me whether I believed in God. He seemed like a nice guy, but nice in the way that I felt like he couldn't understand a word I said, or he could be a really crazy person who would shock me with his own darkness. Either way, I didn't trust him. When he asked me to close my eyes and pretend I was telling Jesus why I was angry with him, I was even more concerned. It didn't seem worth it to try to explain that I didn't blame a god or Jesus for anything I had experienced but that I wasn't very happy with the people in the churches I knew.

I couldn't keep my eyes closed for long. I took about fifteen minutes to tell him what I thought had been most traumatic to me. Then I suggested I needed a female therapist, someone I could open up to a little more comfortably. He sent me to the in-house psychiatrist, who was, indeed, a woman, so I could get some medication for what he thought was post-traumatic stress disorder. That made sense to me—I could imagine what it meant to have PTSD but not due to war or famine. I hadn't thought about it before, but it made sense that enough scary experiences might have impacted me in ways I didn't understand, that I might be carrying some of that with me still.

It took a long time for me to feel safe enough to let go of my church-induced hellfire-and-damnation, born-into-sin fears. For a long time, I cast a glance upward and asked to be enlightened—either gently prodded or firmly reprimanded—if I was sorely mistaken in my views. But ultimately, no matter how afraid I felt of my own sinful nature, I saw God as a smiling benefactor, someone like Papaw Wright, who was quick to give us kids a quarter or a dollar, who always offered us his exotic cans of pineapple juice, and who never seemed drunk even though he always had a beer in hand after his workday was finished.

I found the Sufi notion of God more poetic and enjoyable—God as the Lover and the Friend, the ultimate companion. I found the Hindu gods particularly attractive—especially the trickster and seducer Krishna. I imagined myself in the woods, happening upon the beautiful, blue-skinned god as he played his flute. I could see myself going to him, disarmed by his gaze and enchanted by his music. I always thought that whatever consequences there would be in losing myself with one such as he, the ecstasy would surely be worth it.

I read and consumed whatever I could find in religion and philosophy, searching for a cohesive map to lay on top of the story of my life. I felt I could stitch discordant fragments of spiritual truth together or convert to Judaism, so long as it gave me the magic missing piece, like the prize from a cereal box that you set upon the jumbled picture, and it suddenly becomes clear, it suddenly makes sense.

After a twenty-minute question-and-answer session with the psychiatrist revealed I was prone to making bad decisions, they prescribed two different medications and scheduled my first appointment with the psychologist. I liked him—he wanted to sit outside and smoke cigarettes with me while we talked, and when I told him I had been praying for clarity, he told me how he had prayed for the same thing. And when I told him I was afraid of being alone, he said there would always be a man who would love me and my fine little body. The next time I expressed that fear, he said, *With that tight little ass? You'll be fine.* He had set me up with family medical leave due to my *condition*, and when I stopped using one of the medicines, he told me he would have to take away the benefits.

But I didn't want a therapist talking about my tight ass, and I didn't want a prescription to help me stop making bad decisions, so I stopped taking both medications and bid my family medical leave farewell. I decided to try to make better decisions more or less on my own. I broke up with my boyfriend and stopped drinking bourbon all the time, too. I had my birth control removed—the one that had kept me from having a period for years, by that point.

After three and a half years of working in the corporate world, I decided to go to graduate school. Now and then, I had fleeting thoughts that maybe my desire to be a writer would dwindle away, but instead, it seemed to eat at me, like a wolf that wouldn't leave its prey alone. I called my mother and stepfather to tell them the news.

*What will you do with an English degree?*

*Maybe I'll be an English teacher.*

*The world has enough English teachers. You should move to Vegas and deal blackjack—that's where the real money is.*

I loved graduate school, though—especially literary theory class. We looked at so many different theories—*lenses of perception,* I thought— and each one made sense, each was so valuable and good. One day in class, our professor asked me how old I was. *Twenty-eight,* I told her.

*You're gonna be all right,* she said.

For one of my comprehensive exams, I decided to explore Walt Whitman's *Leaves of Grass* through feminist theory—it seemed easy, really, but fun. Years later, I found myself standing in the coffee shop where I had bought coffee and brownies and sandwiches for twenty years. Our local prominent feminist stood beside me, a woman who had written plenty of books and essays on all aspects of what it means to be female and how race intersects. She was one of Jacob's best friends. To that point, she had been friendly with me, though I never got to talk to her in a real conversation, as I had asked Jacob to introduce us, but he had not. She loved my son, though, and made that clear, doting on him anytime she saw him. She had chatted with me and introduced me to her sister, and I was glad to finally be able to form my own connection with her.

This time, though, was just after Jacob had grown angry with me again—our son wanted to live with me full time and wasn't happy with Jacob's home. We had *blindsided* Jacob by asking to meet at a restaurant to talk, and he didn't even want to know what schedule our son was suggesting. He told our fifteen-year-old that if the schedule involved less time at their house, he didn't even need to hear it.

In the coffee shop, the prominent feminist author turned away, instead of acknowledging me, and gave my son a cold *hello* instead of her usual affection—she had told me more than once how wonderful he was. I stood in line behind another friend a few days later—a woman I had known for nearly twenty years—and she and her husband looked at me before turning away, silent.

It was then that I understood the difference between theory and life. It was then that I realized I could never go home to the women like my mother—like me—and tell them feminists were working for them by writing essays or books or songs. I finally understood that the same people who sign petitions for laborers across the world don't always love the laborers next to them. And that *health care for all* sometimes means *not the ones who smoke*. I realized that the feminists around me would still ask, *Why didn't you kick him in the balls?* because a woman should be able to fight off two men twice her size. A feminist can still say, *She was sprawled out for the men,* and an entire community will shut out a young woman who is trying to figure out how to survive and be a mother if her decisions don't meet their standards, if she doesn't control the story told about her. I finally understood that so much of what I did looked *ugly* to the people around me, and they were happy to accept whatever a man decided was ugly.

I had never asked myself what I thought feminism *should be.* I try not to worry too much about what people call themselves, or what nuances separate their ideas from mine. There are so many of us trying, striving through our imperfections to be *good.* But what would I tell a daughter who calls me one night, excited about the young man she has met, who knows so much about *everything* and is a *feminist who really cares about women's rights, Mom?*

I think I would tell her to see how he reacts when she doesn't please him, when she doesn't follow his unspoken rules. When she is too loud or accidentally breaks his favorite cup. When she wears something he doesn't like or gets excited about something he doesn't care about. *Does he talk out both sides of his mouth?* I'd ask. She'd know what I mean—does he find a way to make himself right when he's wrong? Does he charm people with his endless wit and wisdom, and where does he want her to sit while he does it?

And then there's the other women, so good at deciding when a woman's sexuality is her empowerment or her sluttiness. So wrapped up in keeping women in their place—whatever that place may look like—they forget that the rules they embrace are also their own bondage.

In my small world, I found myself more alone than ever and wondered whether any of these other worlds would ever truly want me, whether I could belong anywhere. I couldn't return to the holler where I grew up—my father lives there still, shut in my granny's house, all the old magic gone from a place now filled with the sorrow and torment of a man shooting up heroin that is somehow affordable to the hillbillies that once had to rely on Lortabs for such a high. The new home and family I thought I had—the family I chose, the ones who care about social justice and the environment—have abandoned me each time a man told them to, and I never know who is gone until I meet them in the grocery store or at a restaurant and they look at me, full of knowing, then turn away.

# CHAPTER 31

# *Handwritten*

After I graduated from college, one time I went to a party in Elliott County—the same county in which I had gone to court as a girl but never testified. The party was thrown by one of my college friends who was living on someone's lovely, rambling wooded property. When I first arrived, I went to the deck adjoined to the house and introduced myself to the owner. I knew he was an attorney in this godforsaken county, and I asked him what kind of law he practiced. He said he was a criminal-defense attorney, and I grinned.

*Criminal defense? You must know my father, then!*

I laughed a little at my joke, and he asked me my father's name. When I told him, his eyes widened, and he looked at me in disbelief. I stopped laughing and asked, *Do you know him?*

It turned out that not only did he know my father, but, as he said, he had kept my father out of prison.

*Which time?* I asked breezily.

It was the time my dad got caught stealing copper from railroads, when I was about six years old. I remember the fires he had by the creek, stacks of coiled wire burning and melting away the protective rubber casings. I don't know how he got caught, but like every other illegal thing he has done, he managed to stay out of prison—and here I was, looking at the man who kept him out of it that time, getting ready to eat a hamburger on his deck. As he stared at me, I grew nervous and wondered what he was thinking of me, this man who knew where I came from, who may have even seen me in his office fifteen or so years before that.

My mind raced through the same thought I've so often entertained, trying to understand how the hell my father has been in a courtroom and even in a jail cell so many times, and yet it was never for anything he did to me, my brother, or our mother. Like many poor people, I grew up learning not to trust the police, and nobody had to sit me down to tell me why. I knew that poor people had a good chance of getting into more trouble if they called the police—you might have a warrant for unpaid traffic fines, or maybe the baby has a bruise and the police call Social Services. Maybe you had a drink or something to calm the nerves, and now your husband's come home to knock you into the wall a little. Call the cops—maybe you'll go to jail, maybe he will. Maybe both. It's harder to pretend when you're poor—harder to keep up the shiny veneer that tells the rest of the world that you're harmless and innocent, that you deserve protection.

I faked what I hoped was humble confidence and said, *I guess sometimes the apple does fall far from the tree.* I think I was hoping to reassure him that I was nothing like my father, that I wasn't going to steal from him or start a fight or kill any dogs while I camped on his property over the weekend.

*Looks like the apple rolled down a hill and into a creek and washed up on another bank, in this case.* He kept staring, but reassured me that he could perceive, even in that small amount of time, that I was, indeed, not my father. I was shaken, though, and spent the next few weeks wondering what would have happened if my father hadn't gotten such a competent lawyer. Who paid for the lawyer anyway? It was probably Granny, whose allegiance to her children always came first, right after

God but before the Law. And then us grandchildren—we took a place ahead of our parents, who she often had to protect us from.

I imagined what it would have been like if he had gone to prison, if my mother had raised us alone. Would she have stayed in that holler? Would she have worked, or would we have lived off welfare? Would she have divorced him sooner, or later, and would she have replaced him with someone else to dominate every facet of our lives? Or would we have found freedom, living in the midst of so much forest, and would there suddenly have been so much space in our lives to be loud, to be happy, to be children? Would the nightmares have ended sooner? Would we have visited him in prison? Would he have died there, knifed by someone he robbed or refused?

But there is no use in daydreaming about such things. His prison was always internal, and we were always right there with him—captor and captives, king and slaves.

Though I grew up reading everything I could get my hands on, our family didn't tell regular fairy tales. Our stories were of real people, with real villains and casualties—never the happy or meaningful endings of fiction. When I was about twenty-three years old, my dad told me how he ended up in rehab. He told me that he and his second wife were convicted for prescription-pill fraud. His wife went to prison, but he was allowed to stay in the county jail because his father was a Freemason, his brother was a Freemason, and the judge was a Freemason. He was even made the trustee in the county jail and carried keys to get in and out of various rooms; he mopped the floors and was able to stay well supplied with his pills. After being in the county jail for a bit, he went to the Hope Center in Lexington.

He had written me a letter or two while he was in the county jail—the only times he had ever written me, at that point. He would write me more letters from the same county jail years later, but they are all the same. His sprawling handwriting can't be contained within the lines. I can tell he presses the pencil down hard, as if he is struggling to put the words on the paper. He always says he wants to see me, he loves me. And he'll call me when he can—sometimes a collect call from jail and sometimes from a new cell phone number when he's out—and wonder aloud why I won't come see him, then tell me about the latest person to steal from him, or who he stole from last, or how he got a little money and wants to send me some, wants to send birthday money and Christmas money, but the cards never come, that money never arrives, and he doesn't call back.

But this was the first time he had gone to rehab, and I thought there was a chance that something was different this time. I wanted to see him and see what had changed, whether he had finally *hit bottom*, as many people have to, or whether he had been inspired to make a new life for himself. Maybe he just wanted to be a dad now—a real dad who could love us and see his grandkids, and we could meet for lunch on Saturdays like I saw other grown daughters doing. It had been fifteen years since I dreamt I had saved him, and I thought fifteen years wasn't too long to wait to see my father finally be *okay*. I arrived at the Hope Center with my son and went inside to the front desk. He showed up a few minutes later, grumbling about something and talking a little to the men around us, who opened and closed their lockers and looked at us with blank faces.

We went outside so he could smoke a cigarette, and I sat down next to him, ready to hear how he was getting his life straight and turning over a new leaf and that sort of thing. Instead, he told me another story. He told me about his buddy at the Hope Center and how he and his buddy went out one night, over to the edge of the field, and got the knife that another guy dropped there for him. Then he told me about the man who had tried to take his change when he bought something from the vending machine. But he and his buddy convinced that guy to walk to the train tracks with them a few days later, and that's when my dad pulled out the knife, and his buddy knocked the guy out—*a big ol' boy*, my dad said, with a laugh—and they put him in a train car and shut the door. It was June and hot. He'd wake up in Chicago or even farther, if he woke up at all, my dad mused, still laughing. I sat there quietly, grateful my son would not remember the conversation.

After that, I wondered whether my dad had ever killed anyone. Maybe he killed the man he put on the train—where would *he* be now? There was another story I remember from when I was very young, but the details were always murky to me. It seemed that a man was bothering my dad at the gas station he managed, where he worked for several years. I heard him talk several times about breaking an Ale-8 bottle and threatening the guy with it, but he also mentioned his brother being there to help him, and I don't know—maybe they cut the guy, maybe they didn't.

On one hand, my dad's stories instilled in me a sense of vigilante justice, of people taking care of each other in families and communities, not waiting for police to arrive and not settling matters in court. I loved watching *Bonnie and Clyde* and westerns with Clint Eastwood, stories about Jesse James and even the cartoon version of *Robin Hood*, where Robin Hood and Maid Marian are foxes.

On the other hand, it became clear over the years that Dad's black-market dealings, his law-of-the-land justice, his defiance of the system, none of that really translated into loyalty to family or protection of his children—to love. He even managed to sever his relationships with the men he traded guns and knives and old coins with, grew weed with, and sold pills to or snorted them with in the barn. Sooner or later, it seemed like everyone who knew him held a grudge against him. The last time he went to jail, I realized that he had a growing group of enemies, and people told my brother there was a price on Dad's head. I wondered how, in his state, he could manage to survive being in jail any longer, and particularly how he could still get the drugs he needed to survive at that point. That line of thinking quickly goes where I am not ready to go, so I leave it, not yet at the end point—not ready to lose that which has caused me so much harm.

While he and his wife were both in jail during one of those times, their kids in foster care, I visited his house. There was a dog there, worse off than any of the ones we watched come and go when I was little. This one, like all the dogs my father and his wife somehow ended up with, was tethered to a ramshackle doghouse by the creek, fed for a while, and then forgotten. The dog whined and strained at its chain, its cry broken for lack of water. I wanted to ignore its ribs and the parasites that must have feasted on it in the dusty, shadeless circle it inhabited, no more than thirty feet in diameter. I was scared to get close to it, but I felt implicated in its torment, as if eventually some day of reckoning might come, and I might be required to define *compassion: How much do you wish for? How much did you show?*

There was no dog food, of course, so I looked through the kitchen cabinets for acceptable substitutes. The refrigerator held nothing edible. Finally, I opened a can of baked beans. Looking at it, I tried to guess how long the dog had gone without food. Granny had little sympathy for the animals at this house, but she claimed she had fed it once or twice. I pulled another can of beans out of the cabinet and paused. Would my youngest brother and my sister return to this house? Would the beans be replaced? Was I taking food that might feed them, and if so, would there be other food for them? Was this a *choice*?

I opened the second can and muttered, *Fuck.* The dog went into hysterics as I approached, and I saw that he had an empty stainless steel bowl. I poured the beans onto the ground in as neat a pile as I could, and he lapped them up as if they were filet mignon, as if they were anything designed for his body. I laid the cans out of reach and quickly grabbed his bowl. The creek looked like it always had, but smaller. I dipped a bowlful of the clear water and watched a crawdad zip underneath a rock. I took the water up to the dog, and he rushed for it, lapping furiously until it was gone.

*Okay, okay.* I picked up the bowl, avoiding his paws, and refilled it while he returned to the spot where the beans had been, licking hopefully at the dirt. Standing by the creek for a moment, I wondered at the countless hours I had spent there. I had seen copperheads and a rabid fox; I had played in the barn where rats prowled the abandoned corncrib; I had crossed the swollen creek once during a flood, walking over a rotten log that hung suspended above it, holding on to the rusty barbed wire that formed the rest of the strange fence. Would anyone ever again love that place as I did?

I carried the bowl to the dog and set it before him. I turned away as quickly as I could, grabbed the cans, and took them to the garbage pile by the creek, a mound of trash bags and refuse that only the desperate seem to be able to produce. As I drove away, I realized that I could have freed the dog, and wondered what it was that kept me from doing so.

# CHAPTER 32

## *Silver Dollars*

Around that time, Dad finally lost the house I grew up in. He couldn't hustle for the payments while he was in jail, so the bank finally got what it had hovered over for twenty years. As he promised all my life, though, the house burned down before anybody else could live in it. Granny and I had gone in there not long beforehand. Someone had moved nearly everything somewhere else, most of it never to be seen again. I found a paper grocery bag full of weed under his bed and shoved it back under when Granny noticed it. We both pretended we didn't know what it was.

I got a few things that day—my dad's knife and coin collections and an antique railroad lantern—that were the fixtures of my childhood. I would often ask him to show me his knives and coins, fascinated by the history they represented. The railroad lantern came from my great-grandfather who sold moonshine in Chicago during the Depression. He was a drunk and a murderer and mostly in prison, but there are fascinating stories about him, some of which make my father look like an upright citizen. That lantern was my night-light when I was very young; it hung in my bedroom and cast a strange blue-green light from two of the glass lenses, a harsh red light from the other two. It was never a comforting, soft kind of night-light, but it was the light I had, so I treasured it. Why didn't the person who took everything else also take those things? They were set carefully in what used to be my father's closet, not forgotten or overlooked. Maybe someone knew I would want them, somehow knew I would come.

My father was my first storyteller, and though his stories never reflected what might be called "traditional values," they still comforted me, and I could sense the magic with which they were infused, like all other icons of childhood. There wasn't a lot that I could thank my father for, but there was a tenderness in his desire to tell me stories, which were so much more like the original *Grimm's Fairy Tales* than the *happily ever afters* I could have heard. I didn't grow up believing he loved me, but he did think I was worth giving these histories to, and I cherished them.

He kept boxes full of newspapers and newspaper clippings, preserving the news of an arrest, a death, or a scandal. He showed me one clipping of my great-grandfather, for whom my papaw and brother were named, standing in a prison next to Al Capone. The men stood in their boxer shorts, arms slung over one another's shoulders. My great-grandfather, Dad said, became friends with Capone while running moonshine to Chicago. Because the prison warden was one of his customers, my great-grandfather spent most of his time doing as he pleased, enjoying the fruits of corruption while paying the price for his lawlessness.

There was the story about the sheriff of Carter County, who tried to find my great-grandfather and his moonshine still one too many times and ended up shot and dead at the end of my great-grandfather's gun. My dad laughed at the end of all his stories, including the one about my great-grandmother's father, whom my great-grandfather shot during dinner, after they argued over who made better moonshine. I didn't find that one as amusing, and I wondered afterward how my great-grandmother must have felt, having her father killed by her husband while sitting down for a dinner she must have cooked.

She favored her youngest son, my father said, who was conceived while her husband was in prison. In the end, he got everything she left to her children, and my father said that youngest son swindled Papaw Conn out of his inheritance. My papaw would hardly talk about it when I asked, but expressed his conviction that the money and the property were not worth bearing a grudge.

Papaw was particularly good at not holding a grudge. He had worked for a dairy for about twenty-five years and was ready to retire when they suddenly let him go. He used to take us in his milk truck sometimes, riding around in those dark, early mornings, and we would get a little chocolate milk if we could stay awake long enough to drink it. I asked why they had let him go, and someone told me it was so they didn't have to pay his retirement. An enormous clock from the dairy hung above the bureau in Granny and Papaw's dining room, and Granny took it down after that happened. I asked Papaw about it one day, expecting his righteous indignation—like my father so often expressed. Instead, he looked away. *There's no use in dwelling on these things.* But I grieved for how unfair they had been to him. Instead of resenting it himself, Papaw just worked at the county roads department for another fifteen or twenty years, tirelessly.

My great-grandfather died the year before I was born. I wonder whether he ever imagined that he would become the hero of my father's stories and the legend of my childhood. I wonder whether he realized at some point that my father idolized him, and whether he ever recognized the influence he had in shaping my father. I wonder whether he loved his wife, or regretted his absence from his children's lives, or regretted killing his father-in-law, or the sheriff, or whether he thought much at all about such things.

My great-grandmother outlived him by many years, and we would go visit her in Bath County. She lived in a light-yellow house that some of her sons built for her and that sat immediately next to the house where she had raised those sons—the two doorways were about twenty feet apart from one another, facing each other diagonally. She had short white-gray hair and was very large in my memory, always sitting in her chair and watching the small television that sat high on a shelf in the living room. The living room was filled with stacks of newspapers and other strange collections. She had dolls everywhere, and several of the largest ones stood as sentries next to her chair, their lifeless eyes staring always, their hair perfectly colored and cut, their clothes nicer than anything I owned.

Her house had a funny smell, and it wasn't until I bought mothballs some twenty years later that I recognized the familiar scent. It filled each room—the cramped and cluttered kitchen, the spare bedroom that housed most of the dolls, the strange bathroom with a soft toilet seat. When we visited, I would go directly to hug Great-Grandma in her chair and stand around for a few minutes, waiting to see whether she would give me a two-dollar bill, a half dollar, or, rarest of all, a silver dollar from her collection.

Outside her house was an exotic array of plants that grew around the perimeter. There were grapevines in a corner, touch-me-nots that I touched over and over, watching the little seed pods explode, and lush islands of color scattered around. My brother and I explored the vines and the gardens through overgrown grass, stepping away from snakes whenever we found them curling and sliding through their paradise.

My favorite place at her home—and perhaps anywhere else—was the abandoned house of her childbearing years. It sat two stories high and was a slate-gray color, weathered and worn. It smelled even older than the house she lived in, and must have been home to many creatures by that time, but it was filled to the brim with the objects from her past and from her children's pasts. My father and grandparents would sit inside the yellow house with my great-grandmother, visiting for hours, while I moved through the old house, searching for treasures.

At the end of each visit, I would go to Great-Grandma with whatever I had found, asking her whether I could keep the items. She let me take the 1905 *Sears, Roebuck & Co. Catalogue* that was about three inches thick. I was seven or eight years old when I acquired the catalog, and I would sit on my bed, turning through the pages carefully so as to preserve them. The catalog reminded me of the books I read by John D. Fitzgerald, the Great Brain series. I longed for things like Radio Flyer wagons and Tinkertoys, though I did not know what they were. I thought about how it would feel to get an apple and an orange in my Christmas stocking, and somehow, that seemed much better than the toys I received. I imagined simple holidays with a rare Christmas bird—perhaps even a goose, like in the stories—and savoring treats like roasted nuts. I didn't know why, but I was fully enamored with my conception of the past and longed to experience it. Maybe, like so many people, I thought all the terrible things I had seen and felt and heard only existed due to inventions—in our case, pharmaceuticals. Maybe guns, every now and then. As if no one was beating or raping women before that. As if every adult had behaved before gunpowder came along.

The floorboards in the old house were rotten or broken in places, and I would climb the stairs with some fear, knowing I had been warned not to go up them. Upstairs would have been a room for a child—or two or three children—and it seemed that the objects there had been abandoned for even longer. I picked up fewer things, afraid I would find a snake or worse in the hot darkness. I felt the presence of the children who had grown up there, though—their games, their arguments, their hiding beneath hand-sewn quilts. I felt like they were still there, all around me—not the adult siblings of my papaw, and not quite ghosts—and it was vital to leave their things undisturbed, so they could return someday and find everything where it belonged, waiting for them in an endless childhood.

I felt comfortable throughout the downstairs and ventured around as even my father hesitated to do. The rooms held dishes, newspapers, clothes, and furniture; it seemed as if Great-Grandma had simply stepped out of the house and walked into her new one at some point, leaving everything behind and accumulating a new houseful of things. I was an explorer, and I sometimes brought her things that she had long forgotten but was glad to have moved into her new house. Once, I found a collection of coins, all organized in books with labels. I immediately recognized their value, as my father's coin collections had instilled in me a great awe for the uncommon currency.

She kept those coins, and I wonder now what happened to them when she died. Perhaps another relative asked for them before that point, and she gave them away. Maybe they went to another great-grandchild, someone not in my papaw's line. Who went through her things, parceling out the riches I had longed for in childhood?

Another time, I thought to look behind the door that always stood open, the one between the dining room and the living room. Behind it, I found a vodka bottle that was about one-third full. When my dad came into the house to look for me and perhaps find something for himself, I showed him the bottle where it sat, hoping he would be impressed by my grown-up discovery.

*Look, Dad, I found a bottle of vodka.* He picked up the bottle and unscrewed the lid, then smelled the alcohol inside.

*That's not vodka,* he said. *That's your great-grandfather's moonshine. Don't tell Great-Grandma you found this.* He tucked the bottle inside the jacket he was wearing and managed to save it for several years, until one day shortly after my mother left him for the last time. I was spending the night at his house, and he was particularly happy and cheerful. He bought us a pizza and gave me and Junior permission to watch movies, then disappeared for hours. Later, he told me he had gone into the woods with that bottle and drank every bit of the twenty-year-old moonshine inside it, roving around the forest in the dark, missing my mother terribly.

I must have inherited some of my sentimentality from my father. Every chance I got, I took our family pictures from his house, telling myself that they would someday be lost and squandered like everything else. One of the pictures I rescued/stole is a reprint dated 1953, of a black-and-white picture that was probably taken in the early 1900s. My father once told me that the youngest boy in the picture, who is almost lying down in someone's lap, is my great-grandfather. On the back of the picture are names I do not recognize, though, so I wonder now whether he was right. Either way, they are my ancestors—men with handlebar mustaches and sharp jawbones; women with their hair pulled back into buns, even the young ones looking haunted; the younger people almost indistinguishable from their parents; nobody smiling—the image of all I've inherited.

I've never known anything about my great-grandfather's father, about his story and how he became an outlaw. He was the only real hero I ever heard of as a child, and his legacy still haunts us. I wonder whether any of our men were ever good, whether any of them ever loved their children or touched their wives with tenderness. I wonder whether the women were gentle, or whether their hollow expressions accurately reflect their despair, their loneliness, their sense of futility. I wonder what they passed down to me—my blurred vision, my thin frame, my long fingers, my penchant for superstition, my longing for green hills and cliff faces?

I want their stories, so I can write my backstory. I want their names, their loves, their longings, their addictions, and their brutalities. I want them to whisper to me their heroic moments, their indiscretions, their final regrets, and the recognitions that filled their eyes in the moments before death.

But the storyteller was always my father, the original unreliable narrator. Drunk, drugged, lost.

# CHAPTER 33

## *The Brokenness of Everything*

Granny called to tell me when the house burned down. *You better come up here,* she said. I was dating the same young man I had loved in high school, when I was dating James, and he came with me. We stopped at Granny's, and she remarked, *He's pretty,* in her usual fashion—men were never handsome or cute, always pretty. We drove up to what used to be my home, and sure enough, there were ashes and some pieces of cinder-block foundation, but all the house and every beautiful, sad detail about it was gone. So was the dog.

There were still two or three old cars sitting by the creek—when did he start letting people park junk cars there? I hated the way they looked, abandoned and worthless, such a cliché symbol of *white trash.* We had always had the beauty of the creek and hills, if nothing else, and the cars seemed to take something away from that. I found a tire iron and went about smashing every window of the cars, wondering for a moment whether anyone would mind but quickly deciding I didn't care. I climbed onto the hoods of the cars, so I could smash the wind-shields properly, while my boyfriend stood there, learning more about me and my grief than probably anyone else ever had. Thick glass flew everywhere, and I picked little pieces off me and felt some twinge of regret that the glass was on the ground. It was too late to worry about it now, though.

The one thing that survived the fire was a millstone that had always leaned up against the side of the house, in a little flower bed. Junior and I would buy planting flowers for my mom at a sale at our elementary school every Mother's Day. I took great care in picking out what I thought were the most beautiful flowers I could afford with my few dollars. I don't know where the millstone came from, but I decided it was coming home with me, this last fixture of childhood that somehow hadn't been plundered or destroyed by my father. Some of the tar paper from the house had melted onto it and it was covered in ash, so I tried to roll it, but it wouldn't roll properly, and I picked it up. My boyfriend offered to carry it for me, but I told him no, I had to do it. I washed myself off in the creek for the last time and knew I wouldn't be back.

When my father got out of jail, someone from the county court system—an attorney, I think—called me to come answer some questions about my father. My dad was there in the building, but I went into a room with the attorney, and he closed the door. He explained that there were marks all over the kids' legs, and someone thought it might be child abuse, but my father and stepmother said it was from the dog wrapping its chain around their legs when they tried to play with it. They wanted to know what I thought.

I was scared that someone would tell my father what I said, but I decided I had to tell this man the truth anyway. I had the chance to do for my siblings what so many adults in my life should have done for me. Maybe it wasn't too late to save them and their children and all those who would follow.

I told the attorney that I doubted my father had whipped the kids' legs with a chain—if he wanted to hit them, he would have done it where no one would see the marks. He was always smart enough for that. I never saw a bruise on my mother's face, and I don't believe anyone outside our home ever saw a bruise on me. But those marks could have easily been from switchings—the same thorny black locust trees still grew in that yard. Or maybe my father had grown sloppy as he aged, and he didn't think to hide things as well. No matter what had happened in that particular instance, I knew the kids needed to be protected.

*He's a terrible father,* I said. *He shouldn't be allowed to have children. Please, do not give these kids back to him.* The attorney wrote down everything I said, looking up at me with some strange expression on his face—surprise? Concern? Was he bored? All I know is that they gave the kids back, and I could not fathom why, other than maybe thinking it's always better to keep kids with their parents even when the eldest tries to convince you that a dog chain is the least of these kids' problems.

But several years later, my little sister would beg me to take them out of foster care, and I would tell them, *No, I'm sorry, I can't take you.* I would anguish over that choice and wonder how I could possibly save them when I was still trying so hard to save myself and my children.

My son was about five years old when we went to my father's rental house for a birthday dinner—Granny had asked me to come, so I did. My brother didn't show up; he was out with a girlfriend. We drove to my granny's first, and found that she had cooked an excessive amount of fried chicken, baked beans, and coleslaw, along with a chocolate cake and sweet tea. I had assumed the party would be there, but I followed Granny out to the house in Elliott County.

The house my father occupied then—you couldn't really call it living—looked like it would be a nice-enough place if it were completely emptied and sanitized. I pulled my car off the side of the road, into the yard where my dad directed me. At first, I tried to avoid running over garbage, but then I realized it was everywhere. The front porch was crowded with towers of useless and dirty appliances, clothes, toys, utensils, everything. A dead-looking car sat in the front yard. Flies swarmed everywhere. I said my *hellos* and *good to see yous.* Granny told me to come into the house, which looked like one of those commercials for a drug-free America, the ones that show a passed-out adult sitting in front of a blaring television while a baby screams in the background.

In this case, the television blared cartoons toward an empty twin bed in the living room. I walked through the house with my granny, wondering whether I should be outraged or just let myself cry. Who slept on that bed? They must have had an illegal cable connection, since they rarely paid the electric bill. My granny warned me, *This is really bad. I wasn't sure whether you should see it or not, but I wanted you to know what was going on.*

Sure. Let me soak it in, see what there is to see.

The house was bathed in darkness, which hid some of the trash but also made it look more sinister. I walked toward the kitchen, stepping around two black garbage bags whose tops gaped at me, spilling cigarette butts and food onto the floor. Scrambled eggs from two or three (four? more?) days previous rested patiently in a crusted frying pan, which sat on the hot plate they apparently used for cooking, when they cooked. I felt steeled for whatever came next. Why not? I opened the freezer door, and a stench hit me in the face. As I swung the door shut, I realized that nothing in the freezer was edible, or else it was beyond recognition.

*Come here. Look in the bedroom.*

I followed her to the bedroom. There were stairs leading to another bedroom, and what looked like a bathroom beyond the bed in front of me. I was putting it together: mounds of clothes and stacks of papers—that's my father's pack-rat nature at its worst, where nothing is worth keeping, and there's no real space for anything to claim, so everything sits out in the open. Ashtrays overflowed onto a bedside table and down to the carpet. I wondered whether they took their shoes off.

I searched my granny's eyes for some way to make sense of it. There was only one, which was to acknowledge that most of my father was gone, disappearing more each time he leaned over the table with a rolled-up dollar bill.

*You should look in the bathroom. Can you believe this?*

We went to another bathroom, and I peered inside, knowing already that the floor would be haphazardly covered in dog shit, that the toilet would be dirty and unusable, that I would fear for my siblings' mental health and mourn their existences.

We walked toward the door, realizing there was nothing to be said. My twelve-year-old brother came in and showed me his legs. *Look, Sis, these are flea bites. Don't stay in the living room too long, or you'll get eat up. These are Sissy's shoes—mine don't fit anymore. I really need some shoes, Sis.*

I put my hand on his shoulder and smiled at him. *Of course, honey. Let's go get you some shoes.* The three of us stepped onto the porch and into the heat. The sun bounced off the greasy water puddles in the yard and illuminated the brokenness of everything around us. *Let's see—we need some cups, don't we? And paper towels? I'll take the kids to get everything. Where's my dad?*

His wife responded with a lie. *He went with a man to check on a job.*

A job. That answer was supposed to protect Granny from the truth, but maybe at that point he thought I would believe it, too. I knew where they were, although I don't know whose house they were at, or how much money was being exchanged. I knew he would return either happier or more distant, depending on what he was able to buy and how quickly it would work through his bloodstream.

My young siblings, my son, and I walked to the dollar store that was visible from the house. I asked the kids what they wanted. My son wanted a Power Rangers toy. My brother wanted some shoes. My sister wanted nothing. I looked at my brother's clothes more closely and noticed his T-shirt was a man's large, and it used to be white. It had a small hole in the front. He was wearing some shapeless, baggy shorts that looked like they once belonged to a high school basketball player. I asked him whether he had clothes to wear to school; the school was always giving the kids clothes. *I do, but I can't find them. They're all dirty.*

That's the economy of the household: get something, use it once, watch it rot as it sinks into the torpor around you.

So we got him a nice pair of jean shorts, some sandals, and a shirt. He picked the shirt that said *Parents for sale: Buy one, get one free.* I convinced my sister to pick out a nice shirt for herself, and I told them, *I love you, you must do well in school, don't forget I love you.*

We went back to the house and ate on the front porch, swatting flies and sitting in old restaurant booths that at least seemed safer than the table inside the house. I wondered how my father had come down this road, how everything had gotten so much worse once he left the holler. Maybe it had been worse for a long time, and I had just not seen it. Maybe it was the shifting variety of drugs available to him as the pharmaceutical companies changed up formulas. Maybe it was just the way things were always going to go.

Later, as I'm driving away with my son, I worry that he won't understand what we've just seen. I realize he has no context for the decay in which my family is living, so I ask him what he thinks about it. He says everything was gross, but he liked the pocketknife my father gave him in lieu of the birthday card that was supposed to arrive in the mail four months ago. I see a teachable moment, a way to explain the dangers of drug abuse and discourage him from ever seeing pills as a form of recreation. I choke on my words, though, and sob as I drive. In the end, I plead with him, *Please, please don't ever take that chance. My father's mind is gone, it's somewhere else, and I could not live if I saw that happen to you.* From the back seat, as he looks up from his new Power Ranger, he assures me, *Don't worry, Mom. I will never do pills. I will never be like your dad.*

How can I create a different world for my children, one that does not lead to broke-down cars and crippling addiction and felonies? How can I even be a mother? How do I translate the language of my childhood into a language of adoration, of devotion, of caretaking? I constantly tried out new words and, like magic, drew phrases like *I love you* and *You're so good* from nowhere. Like a miracle.

Jacob had remarried a few years after we divorced. When he was still little, my son would tell me he wished we could all live together—his father and stepmother and me—and I said, *I know, I'm sorry we can't.* He asked me whether I loved his father, and I said, *Yes, of course, we're family.* He asks me what a family is, and I say, *Family is all of us who love you.* He seems to think that's good enough.

There are other words, too, that I've had to define in conversations with my son. When he didn't want to sleep and I comforted him in his bed, I told him he was safe. In one sense, I mean that the bad guys will not come into our home; no robbers will plunder our meager belongings. It means that the stove is not on, and I will get to him through any fire that could ever burn away those meager belongings. But as I tell him that I will protect him, I also think of how he isn't awakened to me begging a husband not to hit me again. How he won't learn the word *rape* from what his father does to his mother as she cries for him to stop.

I have no word for that.

A day or two after the birthday dinner, as I tuck him into bed for the night, he hugs me tightly and tells me, *We love each other so much. I'll always fix your heart, even when your dad breaks it.*

# CHAPTER 34

## *Strangers*

In many cultures and religions, naming a child constitutes a kind of defining, a way of determining the child's personality or destiny. For years, I looked for my own name in books and on little cards that are sold in souvenir shops. All I found was a reference to Robert, which means *bright fame*. I hated the maleness of that name, as well as the idea of fame—it didn't match my perception of myself. As an adult, I found more precise resources that identified my name as a diminutive of Barbara, from *barbaros*, the Greek word for a stranger, a traveler from a foreign land. A *barbarian*, it turns out, is *someone new and different*.

And finally, it made sense, this name that always felt right, but whose meaning never did. I am the stranger in my family, the one who left, who does not belong. It explains my difference, my not belonging. I would have thought I was adopted, if poor white people in hollers adopted babies they couldn't feed and didn't like just for the sake of having them. My name, this particular definition of me, gives me a location to fix my longing for another place, a home I've felt since childhood. It's what I found each time I ran to the woods, whether I was running from my father's rage, or exploring, or checking on the flowers and blackberries. It's the silent welcome I felt there, where I was free and wild.

I was named after my papaw Wright, whose name was spelled *Bobbie*, which is often the female spelling. I puzzled over that and once asked my mother about his side of the family. She explained that he had been adopted when he was very young, and then those parents died, so he was adopted again. His birth family was probably lost to us forever, and that troubled me. Who named him? Why did they spell it that way? Was someone out there wondering where he had gone, searching for their lost grandson or nephew or brother?

Since I can call myself a stranger, I understand why I see myself surrounded by strangers. I can write imaginary lives for this imaginary family. Define *brother*. Not by blood, or by cohabitation. By occupation: *My brother has been homeless and jobless. His children have been in foster care because he has sold pills to buy pills.* By shared history: *He was my companion in those times.* By his pleas: *Don't give up on me.*

Now there are thousands upon thousands of young men like my brother, and there's me praying to an unseen god to spare him from what our father gave us. No easy redemption awaits him, no surprise happy ending, and no simple kindness can survive his world. This sounds cynical, and perhaps it is. But I am humbled by my mother's own cynicism, as displayed immediately after the death of one of my cousins. His death was somehow woven with his addiction to prescription pills, though I never found out what was in the autopsy report. Perhaps he inadvertently committed suicide, but there were other people with him, and their stories never made sense when put together. After filling me in on what she knew, my mother sighed. *Oh well. Your brother will be next.*

What could I say? That comment immediately and permanently revised my definition of *cynical*. I can't hold a candle to that.

Junior started dating a girl when he was fifteen years old, and by the time he was twenty, they were having a baby. They got married and lived in a trailer. He worked in a factory, making decent money for a while. Then he got in trouble for pills—he had grown up watching our father do them, but living with him during his teen years probably changed his trajectory forever. Junior went to the county jail but got out on work release during the day and was able to keep his job. Until he was searched one day, coming back into jail from his job, and they found the pills he had taped around his waist. I don't know what he was thinking, but since he was high at work and high on his way back to jail, he probably did not think about the fact that he always got searched when reentering.

He lost his work release and then his job. For trying to smuggle in the pills, he was also charged with promoting contraband. He got out of jail for a while, and his wife had another baby around that time. I visited them when the new baby was born, and in the older girl's room, I found a pile of dog shit from the rottweiler they let run in and out of the house. Junior asked me about some of his baseball cards, which we both collected as children. I had taken his little book of Ken Griffey Jr. cards, as well as his yellow baby blanket, from our mother's storage shed, along with some of my own things. He wanted to know when he could get his cards back, and I told him he could have them whenever he wanted—he just had to come and get them. I thought to myself that I would keep them for him, as he was surely selling and trading most anything with value for pills.

Looking at their house, I could see the deterioration already setting in. The kids intent on the television, surrounded by filth. My brother had drug addicts and sellers coming around—it seemed like a perfect repetition of our childhood, with large, unattended dogs thrown in the mix. I worried for the children, but I figured that whatever happened to them, they would not be subjected to it for long. That kind of thinking is probably what kept most people from interfering with my father's treatment of us, and it is really an attractive thought for people who don't want to rock the boat. *Just stay out of it, hope the best for those kids, and surely this insanity won't continue for another year, or another ten years, or another eighteen. Surely the kids will have someone to teach them a better way than their parents are showing them. Surely this won't all get worse.*

Then my brother went to jail again, leaving two children with no father to care for them. When he got out, they came to live with him. Junior seemed to be doing well for a while, receiving assistance to help him provide a clean home for his daughters. Granny started telling me that she was helping pay his car insurance and some of his other bills. Next my mother told me she was paying all his utility bills, and I realized that with two people paying the same bills, he was doing something with the extra money that he did not want anyone to know about. I went to visit him around Christmas and found his trailer full of trash, with cigarette butts everywhere and ashes falling onto the carpet out of garbage bags that sat all around the living room and kitchen. I had brought presents for the girls and for him, and I said I would help clean. He was indifferent while I hurriedly bagged up the trash and took it outside. *Come on, Junior—you're better than this. You don't want to become our father, do you?*

Our younger cousin overdosed around that time. He was in Florida to visit a pain clinic and get oxycodone to bring back to Kentucky. Those trips are often financed by someone with a lot of money—someone who does not go to prison when they get caught, but who gets probation and maybe put under house arrest. They don't mingle with the petty criminals that go to prison so quickly and are in the county jails so frequently. I don't know how my cousin got involved in that world, but when he died, Granny was devastated.

Junior suddenly came down to my house for a few days, dropped off by another cousin and his girlfriend as they drove to Tennessee. I talked to him right away about the pills and the people he was around. We talked about our dad, and Junior told me that Dad had started shooting up some kind of pill. He would heat it up in a spoon and, when it melted, draw up the liquid with a syringe and shoot it into his arm. Later, Papaw Conn told me they took Dad to the hospital for an infection in his arm, which Papaw knew was from shooting up.

Dad wasn't being very careful, Junior said. When my brother first watched our father shoot up, Dad used the needle that two other men used right before him. Then he offered it to Junior. I asked Junior whether he took it, and he swore he didn't—I still pleaded with him not to.

When we got a phone call telling us that our cousin had died and that it had happened in a motel room with one of Junior's friends, I convinced Junior to stay with me and to let me tell everyone that I took him to a rehab facility in Lexington. His biggest concern at that time was our uncle, who had been estranged from his son and had not been allowed within a certain distance of him because of a restraining order, but who was now ready to kill someone over his son's death. This is the same uncle who had the gunfight with our father in our front yard and who helped our father beat various men throughout our lives. We knew he meant it. Junior's name had been mentioned one too many times, so we believed he was safest with me, far away from home.

I got him some herbs on the advice of my herbalist—stuff that would help ease the withdrawal symptoms. I got him Epsom salts so he could take hot baths and soothe his aching muscles. I made miso soup and sushi, which he hated, and fed him granola that he loved. I made him take out the trash, but other than that, the only thing I asked of him was that he not call anyone and not tell anyone where he was—I didn't trust any of his friends, and I especially did not want our dad to know where he was.

A few days into it, he seemed to be doing well. We watched movies together, and I tried to show him what my life was like—a life without people robbing each other and taking every chance they had to get fucked up. A life where you could enjoy simple pleasures and didn't have to be on guard constantly. A life focused on working for what you wanted to have in your life, and looking forward to the next achievement.

Then he called his best buddy, a man in his forties with no job and no teeth. I had heard him talk about Ben several times, and each time I told Junior that I didn't like the sound of him. Our mother talked about him as if he were Junior's guardian angel, helping him get on the straight and narrow path. But Junior had told me they did some pills together, yes, but Ben has it under control and isn't strung out—*You just don't understand, Sis.* I suspected that this man's interest in my brother was not at all altruistic and that he was calling Junior so much, asking where he was, for some other sort of reason. Junior answered his phone call one day when we were driving back from town. He told Ben he was staying with me, and as soon as he lost his cell phone signal on the winding country road to my house, I told him that he couldn't stay with me anymore, that he had broken the most important promise he made to me.

*Aw, come on, Sis—it's Ben! He's my buddy, he's got my back. There's nothing to worry about—I trust him.*

When his girlfriend called a few days later and wanted to pick him up, I took him to town and told him that he didn't have to do it, that he could go to rehab instead. He was in a bad mood and carrying everything he owned in a garbage bag, and he said he wanted to go home and *figure things out.* He didn't like it, he said, that he couldn't smoke inside my house or watch television in the living room as late as he wanted. It did not seem to occur to him that he was homeless and would not be going home to a television or a couch, but to someone else's house, where he would stay until things got too uncomfortable or too dangerous. He had me leave him in a Wendy's parking lot, and a girl picked him up a couple of hours later.

Shortly afterward, we all went to my cousin's funeral, and my brother was a pallbearer. There were young men at the funeral who looked like my brother looked in those days—vacant eyes, confused expression, and a general lack of presence about them. Junior talked to them, and I was pissed that they dared to show up at our family's funeral, but why wouldn't they? They probably thought they were all friends, in some sense. *Showing their respect.*

After the funeral, we had a dinner at the fellowship hall of the church I had gone to throughout childhood. Our father would hardly give us a minute to talk alone, but I managed to pull my brother away, saying we were going to look at our maternal great-grandmother's grave in the cemetery behind the church. When we got to the cemetery on the top of a little hill, I said to Junior, *You know that if you don't stop what you're doing, you're going to end up in the same place as our cousin, don't you?*

He didn't want to hear it and tried to tell me not to be so dramatic. I told him that he shouldn't think he could keep cheating death or prison as our father had done for so long—most people don't get to do that many drugs and be that destructive without worse consequences arriving much sooner. Junior talked about how he had been beaten up after getting out of the county jail recently, because he ran into someone our dad had ratted out.

I told Junior he had to leave, and leave fast. It was painfully clear that our dad would not stop calling him, or coming to wherever he lived, or doing *something* to pull Junior closer toward him and his own terrible life. Junior said that after he left my house, every drug addict he knew gave him free pills, knowing he had been deprived of them for a few days. Dad suddenly wanted him to buy pills, to drive to other states and buy pills—anything related to pills, while Junior said he wanted to try to keep from using them so heavily again. At the same time, Dad told Junior that if he didn't help get other people busted, Junior himself would have to go down. I never asked my father whether it was true, but I believed Junior. And all the while that our father was working with the law to stay out of prison, getting other people sent to jail for selling pills, he was still buying and selling them himself.

I promised Junior a plane ticket and a place to live on the other side of the country. I promised him that I had friends who would help him, who would get him a job and help him get on his feet, and that I would find help to get him through withdrawal. All he had to do was leave.

*I'll think about it,* he said. And we walked back down to the fellowship hall, which was almost empty by then. Standing in front of it, he reached into his pocket and showed me the drugs he had on him.

I told him he should throw them away, maybe keep the weed, but the other stuff kills people every day, and it was likely to kill him someday.

He left, unconvinced but still telling me what he thought I wanted to hear, that he would think about it. I told him that I wasn't making an indefinite offer, that I had money set aside and could make it happen soon, but if he waited until things got worse, it might be too late.

A few weeks later, he was arrested again. This time, he was facing trafficking charges for crack cocaine, unlawful possession of various pharmaceuticals, and who knows what else. The person who sent him there was his buddy Ben, who had been wearing a wire every time he asked Junior to score some pills for him. Junior had to listen to the conversations they had over their cell phones and in person, and then he went to the county jail for a while. Later, he went to trial and was offered a plea bargain—he could get a lighter sentence if he would rat on some other people, somehow portraying them as the *real criminals* that deserved to be in jail. Whether it was his sense of honor or a fear of retaliation, I'm not sure, but Junior chose to accept his fate, and he was sentenced to ten years in state prison.

I visited him in prison most Sundays, often bringing Orion and my new baby with me. At first, Junior just wanted me to buy him Mountain Dews and honey buns from the vending machines we were allowed to get snacks from. In the summer, the prison staff and some inmates would sometimes grill hamburgers outside, and we could buy those for lunch. Sitting at one of the round tables in the gymnasium during one of our earliest visits, I asked him what kind of programs there were that he could do while in prison. He told me that he was just there to sleep and eat and that his goal was to get out of there without doing anything else but those two things.

Frustrated, I told him, *You're going to get out of here in a few years if you get parole. No matter when it is, you can either leave this place the same way you came in, or you can leave with a certificate, some training, even just the respect of the people running programs. If you go back to your life the same way you came in, you probably won't stay out for very long.*

He dismissed me, and I decided I couldn't fix it. I also decided I wasn't buying him honey buns every time I visited, especially because he seemed to think I owed him something and hardly thanked me. But over the next few visits, his tone changed. He started taking some classes and got to work in the prison garden. He was good at it—he was always good at whatever he did—and his supervisor encouraged him. When he moved into a halfway house a couple of years later, he had recommendations that made it possible for him to get a job in a vet's office, and he was so good at that, they tried to convince him to go to veterinarian school.

Had I saved my brother with my lecture? Later in life, I asked him, and he said he needed that tough love to snap out of it, to stop feeling sorry for himself. But he also told me how, in that moment, he was *sick and tired* of feeling sick and tired. I had tried at other times to talk him into walking away from the world he was immersed in—I had asked him, *Do you want to be like Dad?* And of course he didn't want to be like our father, but he had to hit the proverbial rock bottom before he could really look at himself and take account of what his life had become. My words may have helped inspire him, but only because there was nowhere else to run. Thankfully, he was able to find hope in that moment, and support from the prison workers soon afterward, as they gave him a chance to prove himself while he stumbled along a new path.

Prison was probably the safest place for my brother to hit rock bottom. He wasn't willing to do what it took to get more drugs in there—he told me about the guy with pills and what he wanted in return for one. But I think about all the people who find their lowest point and can't pull themselves up, who have no way to muster enough self-worth to change. How many people find themselves facing the full weight of despair and disappointment in their lives and run from that grim reality? Why would anyone willingly choose to embrace self-awareness and the painful, difficult work of changing oneself from the inside, fully experiencing all the shame, guilt, and loneliness that one person can bear? When I lectured my brother, I hadn't even faced my own self yet. Despite how ugly some of my past had been, I hadn't found my own rock bottom.

We didn't stay in touch much after he left the halfway house. For a while, he wasn't allowed to leave Rowan County, where he had to go back to live. I was determined not to go there except for the occasional holiday—each time I took that interstate exit, I felt like I was driving into a dark cloud. Our father was always complaining to Junior that I never visited, never called.

I couldn't find the words to explain that I had fought so hard to build a new life, worked so hard for my college degrees and to just not be in a house where a man was beating me or humiliating me. I didn't know how to do that and stay in touch with the people who still lived where I came from. Our littlest brother and sister grew into teenagers and then adults, and I hardly ever knew how old they were. I would hear occasionally that my sister loved wearing makeup and shopping for clothes, that my youngest brother wasn't talking to Dad anymore. I worried about them from far away, wondering whether they could make it out of whatever desolate hell they had endured following what Junior and I had suffered.

But Junior was the only other person who knew what it was like to grow up as I did: in a beautiful holler, Granny's house so close and safe, our mother clinging to something she saw in our father or simply too afraid to leave. The nightmares that turned out to be real—pretending to be asleep so Dad wouldn't kill our grandparents or Mom or us. The sweet, wild berries and the cool streams. The joy of throwing walnuts against the tree in Granny's yard, next to the old well.

I grew up loving my family but knowing they didn't know me. We are all strangers. I can tell stories about them—they named me at birth, marked me, defined me. They determined my words and my meanings, bequeathed me their lexicon. But they also sent me running into the forest and into the pages of other worlds, where the chains of *little slut* and *whore* disappeared into a vast, infinitely variable realm of language.

The stories keep happening, and I wonder whether I can ever write them all. My granny, with her forgiving, boundless heart, eventually says, *I don't think I can make it . . .* My brother finally says, *I can't believe my own father would . . .* And at last I say, *Forgive us all, for we know not what we do.*

# CHAPTER 35

## *That Would Be Good*

One night, I dreamt that my granny was lying on her couch and I was sitting beside her, and I knew in my dream that she was dying. It was the couch in her living room, where she napped after fixing me Sunday supper for the first twelve years of my life. Where her school picture hung, forever portraying her as a seven-year-old girl with blond hair and serious eyes. An aerial photograph of their house hung above the couch, showing the gardens, the root cellar, the henhouse, the creek that flowed down the field behind their house and met up with Mill Branch. It captured the home and the land at its best—tranquil, well kept.

When I woke up from my dream, I called Granny—I was certain that it was an omen, a sign from whoever's in charge of signs these days. Without telling her my dream, I asked how she was doing and tried to pry beneath her standard *very well* response. She had had a kidney infection, she said, but the doctor gave her some medicine, and she thought it was almost gone. She was supposed to go to the hospital in Lexington to have a pacemaker inserted, but she didn't have a ride and would probably cancel her appointment.

*What? What do you mean, you don't have a ride?* I asked. Granny explained that my dad couldn't take her; he either didn't have a car or had something else to do—and besides, his driving scared her too much anyway. Her other son could not take her—he was in prison by this time, serving a forty-eight-year sentence for murder. Her daughter could not take her—she did not drive. And none of her other relatives could do it—none of her grandchildren, nieces, nephews, brothers, sisters-in-law—nobody. So she would have to cancel, she said.

By this time, I was teaching part time at a university, had given birth to a girl, and was again a single mother. I told Granny I would take her to her appointment, though it meant I would have to cancel a class I was teaching that day and, to get Granny to Lexington by eight in the morning, I would have to find child care for my one-year-old daughter so that I could leave my house by five thirty. Then I would need to take my daughter home until Granny was ready to go back to Morehead, when I would pick up Granny in Lexington and make the drive eastward once again, then southwest an hour and a half back to my house. She said it was too much, and I told her it was not enough—I could never begin to match the giving she had done in my life, but I could try.

So I did, and right away I was late arriving at her house, getting her to her appointment late. She was not allowed to eat prior to the procedure, so by the time they got around to taking her in, it was almost noon, and she was feeling out of sorts. She wanted me to go back with her and I did, sitting beside her in a chair while she lay on the hospital bed. This was going to be a relatively easy procedure, with the insertion going through her shoulder to place the pacemaker next to her heart. She told me she was scared, though, and I held her hand as we waited there. I told her that God loved her so much and would take care of her—offering her the same words she had given me so many times. I was allowed to stay until right before the procedure, and the nurses asked all their questions of her with me in the room.

At one point, a nurse asked her whether she had any other pains or problems, and she said no. When the nurse left, she told me that she actually did have a pain in her abdomen and that it had been there since around Christmas. She was afraid that if they knew, they might not give her the pacemaker. I convinced her to tell the nurse anyway, just in case, and when the nurse came back, she did. The nurse asked about her bowel movements and talked about stool softeners while I sat in my chair, silent but irritated at the medical field's pill-based model of care. But she did suggest that they do a scan of her abdomen, after the pacemaker insertion, to see whether there was a blockage, and Granny was happy with that.

I assured her that I would be in the waiting room for as long as possible while she had her procedure done and that, if I had to go, I would come back soon. I ended up leaving to get my daughter for a while, but then returned in the evening, after I called and they said she was awake. It was getting dark—past five in the evening, and she still had not eaten. When I arrived, she was angry with the nurses, who refused to bring her food until the doctor approved. I asked the various nurses, and they offered no solution, so finally, after almost twenty-four hours of not eating, my granny told me to go to the cafeteria and get her a hamburger. I didn't know what was worse—her continuing to go without food or eating a hamburger—but she was getting madder than a wet hen, so I got the food and brought it back. She was able to eat almost half of the burger and a few of the french fries but then said she had just gone too long without food, and we threw the rest away. She spent the night there, alone.

One of our other relatives—Granny's sister-in-law—picked her up the next day and took her home. When I called to check on her, she said that the pacemaker had made her feel really good the first couple of times it shocked her heart into beating faster, but it had started shocking her almost constantly, and it was wearing her down. She would soon be going to get it removed.

She went back to Lexington, and the heart specialist told her that one of her valves needed to be replaced, that it was too weak and wasn't efficiently pumping oxygenated blood in and used blood out. He explained it all in front of me, talking about the pig's valve that they would be using to replace her valve, how it was so much like a human valve and her body would take right to it. They were concerned, though, that her heart could be distressed by the surgery, and it might be too much. But, he said, it would most likely be fine, and she would feel like she was twenty years old again after the surgery.

You could see the doubt in her face as she looked down and said in her simple way, *Well, that would be good.*

They scheduled the heart-valve replacement close to Thanksgiving, and I wondered how Thanksgiving would be if Granny had not recovered enough by then to cook her usual feast. A lot of our relatives showed up at the hospital this time, and I wanted to stay away until she woke up. But my papaw convinced me that I needed to come up and try to be there when she awoke—it would mean so much to her, he said. My dad was there, wearing the nicest clothes he had. As soon as I walked into the waiting room, he came over to me and started talking about our relatives, how they looked down on him and were too good to talk to him. All those relatives *oohed* and *aahed* over my daughter, whom I had brought with me. I also brought food for my papaw and father, and they ate there in the waiting room while I tried to chat with relatives I had not seen in years.

I was glad to see so many people there for her—even my father. I knew that, in some way, she had cared for them all and had likely provided for each of them at some point. Who knows what all had passed between her and these other elders of mine, people whose wisdom I never heard but whom I can love because they loved her.

When I was little, my mother and my favorite cousin both called me *selfish* at different times. I didn't know why they thought that, and it hurt to hear it from them. I had always tried to show them that I deserved their love, that I would be good to them. Now I can see that when we are struggling to survive, a lot of things look selfish from the outside—we cling to the things that we believe are keeping us alive, and there is often no logic to that. At age seven or twelve, I couldn't have known better even if I tried—I couldn't have removed myself from my own experience, seen the need and want in another's life. Being called selfish at such a young age prepared me to hear it later in romantic relationships, where I dared to voice an opinion.

But I somehow knew my granny didn't worry about the selfishness in me. I think she saw, but didn't dwell on, the envy I felt for Junior. I didn't feel like she noticed my rotting teeth or my dirty hair or my clothes turned brown from the creek water we washed them in. When I was with her, I felt like she saw me without trying. Like she understood me without me pleading my case before her, working so hard to show her how much I deserved to be loved. She loved me before I understood that I deserved it, and I was grateful without understanding why.

There was a peace between us, the kind of peace that could make a person believe in God. It was a connection not with the previous generation, still reeling from their own traumas and doubts, but with a generation who had tried to love and who had been imperfect, who had lost, who had kept going for whatever good they could find.

And maybe she saw something of herself in me, though I hope she never felt the way I did. Maybe she just knew that she could pass along to me the simple joys of a simple life. Maybe it was something about how I knelt at the altar next to her, so scared of everything except being next to her and knowing that whatever we were praying for, we were praying together. Maybe that's just part of being a grandparent—giving this unconditional love that no one else can give, with a value that can't be understood.

I couldn't tell those people at the hospital any of this. I responded to their questions about my job and my children. I tried to smile when it was called for. None of that mattered as I watched my daughter, making sure she never touched the floor, making sure each person that held her was good.

# CHAPTER 36

## *Patron Saints*

When I was finally allowed to visit Granny in the intensive care unit, I thought at first that they had taken me to the wrong room. With the door and curtains wide open, my granny lay there, her mouth forced open by the tube that went down into her stomach. IVs tangled in and around her body. Her face was whiter than any face I had ever seen, and they had taken her false teeth out, so her cheeks were sunken. I started crying as the nurses came in and out, checking machines and injecting more drugs into her system.

I asked one nurse whether I could put a medallion on her—a Catholic medallion bearing the face of St. Jude on one side and St. Raphael on the other. I had been collecting medallions for years, finding them in antique and junk stores, then cleaning them up so I could read the names and prayers inscribed on them. When I found the first one I ever bought, I was immediately drawn to it. I paid two dollars, and when I examined it later, I found it was dated 1880. The print was tiny, but I used a magnifying glass to see that it bore two pictures with an inscription around each; the medallion itself was no more than a half inch in diameter. From then on, I bought them every chance I got, then began wearing them occasionally, on any necklaces I could string them onto.

I wore St. Jude and St. Raphael for about a year when I thought to look up the saints and see what they guard over. St. Jude, I found, is the patron saint of desperation and hopeless causes. St. Raphael is the patron saint of healing. When I found that out, I was struck by the irony—I had for so long felt like a hopeless cause, yet during that time I had tried using drugs and herbs and therapy to help me in some way—in any way.

I liked the idea of finding these old medallions, of them being infused with prayers and hopes and faith from all the people who had worn them or held them while praying or, like me, who had touched them unconsciously when uncertain and needing assurance. I thought that, no matter what else, the saintly medallions represented hope, and surely all of us praying and hoping and loving together could amount to something.

The nurse taped my medallion onto Granny's nightgown, and I left a Bible in there for her to see whenever she opened her eyes. A couple of days later, when she came to and was able to speak once again, I looked for her medallion and could not find it. It was gone, perhaps lost in the laundry or pocketed by whoever had changed her nightgown. Her wedding ring, her watch, and a spoon ring she had worn into the hospital also disappeared forever, after the nurse who prepped her for surgery placed them in a baggie and walked away as Granny was wheeled into the operating room. Though I called the hospital and spoke with nurses, supervisors, and even the company that washed the hospital's linens, I could never track down any of Granny's belongings.

When the doctor came to update the family, I was shocked to hear him say that he was surprised Granny made it through the surgery—he honestly had not expected her to live. Her heart was stronger than he had thought, and she should be feeling good before long, he promised. Her new valve would now be pumping fresh blood into her heart as the old one had not been for probably twenty years. He said she should have had the surgery many years ago, when she was stronger, but she had been afraid to have it done and put it off for so long. Her recovery would take longer, but she would have a higher quality of life from then on.

And then they did the scan of her abdomen.

The place in her side had been hurting for a year by this point. Thanksgiving passed, and she could hardly eat. Christmas came, and she was in pain. The scan showed a mass in her abdomen, and a rush of hospitalizations, tests, and delays ensued. I was driving to Lexington every other day, teaching classes at the university and a community college, attempting to stitch together a livable income, and trying to be a comfort to Granny. I would bring milkshakes for Papaw, who could hardly eat because of the myasthenia gravis and Parkinson's that had ravaged his body for almost a decade. I offered to read the Bible to Granny, or bring her food. The mass kept growing, and her stomach began to visibly swell. The larger it got, the angrier I grew.

I was angry with the hospital staff, who would one day send her fried chicken or soup beans and corn bread to eat, food that she could hardly touch, and the next day would have her on a liquid diet of Jell-O and iced tea—nothing to nourish and strengthen her. I was angry with my father, who would call me and tell me I needed to be there, *Go see your granny as much as you can, she won't be in this world much longer, I wish I could be there, but she thinks the world of you and you've got to be there for her,* and I thought, *Yes, I fucking know this already, but I am tired of being the only one of us who thinks she is worth being here for, and I don't want to watch her die, and I don't know what's happening in her body but it's scaring me, and there's no one left to make me feel like everything might be okay.*

But I just said, *Yes, I'm doing my best,* and I did my best, even when she wanted me to change her underwear for her, and I had to clean her like I had cleaned babies but never an adult, and I did not know whether her pride was hurt, or whether she was embarrassed like I was, or whether she could see the fear in my face, or whether she had just reached the point where such things don't matter anymore, where they fall away and what is left is the simple matter of being a human, having a body, and tending to it the best one can, knowing it has reached the end of its usefulness. I did my best when she wanted me to cut her fingernails that were long and yellowed, and beneath them was an unknown substance that was suddenly on my hands, and I was afraid something dirty was going to take over my body forever.

I did my best when she wanted me to lower her onto the bedside toilet, and she did not want me to call the nurses but to be there with her as she tried to shit, and nothing happened that needed to happen, nothing was working like she needed it to work. And I brought her watermelon one day, and she said, *This will probably be the last time I ever eat watermelon,* and I remembered eating watermelon at a picnic table outside her house so many times. And it seemed that bringing her that watermelon was the best thing I could have done, the only adequate expression I had while all the words stayed inside me, unspoken.

The nurses would not comment on her condition, and she was moved from one floor to another, then one wing to another. Finally, a doctor stood in her room, and I was there, and the doctor said, *It is cancer,* and Granny cried. The doctor told us the name of the cancer and ran through the short list of options: surgery was out because her heart wasn't strong enough; radiation might shrink it for a while, but the doctor was not sure whether Granny was strong enough for that; or, she suggested, *You could go home, and we can make you really comfortable while you enjoy the rest of your time with your loved ones.* I asked what she meant by *really comfortable,* and someone explained that Granny could have lots of pain medicine. No pain—wouldn't that be nice. Forty years of watching her son kill himself with pain medicine, losing her young grandson to pain medicine, another grandson in prison for *pain medicine.* There's no way, I thought, I could watch my granny spend the rest of her life in a fog of pain medicine, doped and delusional and absent. No.

Granny was discharged and went to the radiation clinic in Morehead. When she got there, they told her she was not strong enough to withstand the side effects, and they sent her home. In the end, though, the doctors did not make her *really comfortable* with a slew of pain medicines, and she was not able to die in her home, surrounded by loved ones, as I had always thought she would. They had her set up with a hospital bed in her house, but my papaw was the only person there to help her to the bathroom and back to the bed, to wash her, to bring her food and medicine—and before long, she was in the local hospital.

I called to check on her and found out she had been there for a couple of days—nobody called to tell me she was going, and I drove to the hospital right away, wondering how it was that no one in my family thought to communicate such basic information. When I got there, I found Granny in a quiet, dark room with flowers all around her. The nurses looked at me with sympathetic smiles as I went up there, and one of them finally said that she was dying.

*Oh, I'm so glad you're here,* Granny said when she came to. I was sitting beside her, not wanting to wake her but wanting her to feel my presence. We spoke for a few minutes, but she needed the quiet and had me shush my papaw and someone he was speaking with at the door. While we were talking, I asked her what she wanted me to do with the pictures I had taken from her house, the ones she lent me to make copies of but which I hadn't yet copied. *Keep them,* she said, *so they don't get lost. I want you to have my curio cabinet,* she said.

*I wish I had asked you to teach me more,* I told her. Like how to make biscuits, which she made from scratch, without looking at a recipe. She rolled them out and cut them into perfect circles with the mouth of a jelly jar or drinking glass. She made gravy that was never lumpy, never runny, and that was always better than anyone else's gravy I ever tried.

I should have helped her can some stuff, I told her. I need to know these things—how to prepare the tomatoes and green beans you put up. How to prepare the washtub with the hot water that you set the jars into, how long it takes. How to use that same washtub to bathe my grandchildren someday, how to give them baths that they will come to cherish, sitting in an old washtub in my backyard in the summertime. How to have a root cellar that keeps potatoes and jars of food cool all summer long, which will provide an endless supply of sustenance to my grandchildren and thus seem magical even though there might be snakes in there, so they have to watch out when they enter.

While she went back to sleep, I thought about the other things I had meant to ask, and the things I meant to tell her that I had never taken the time to do.

How frustrating it was to spend the night with her in the summer, when she would make us go to bed before the sun had set, and she forbade us to get up. How comforting it was that she always had Freedent or Wrigley's Spearmint gum and would give us a piece, or maybe just half a piece, in church. How I loved the tomato pie she made when I was little and how I didn't even mind the onions that were in it, because they were overpowered by sugar.

How I was always afraid of her chickens and never learned how to collect their eggs from beneath them, which Granny did effortlessly, and they let her do it as if they thanked her. How I knew she was the strongest person in our family, killing chickens and bringing in firewood and praying without fail, believing we were always worth her prayers and her money and her cooking.

How she told my father, *Don't you do that to my little girl,* and was the only person to ever say that.

My stepmother called me a little after eleven one night and left a message saying that my granny had just passed away. The coroner did not get there until after midnight, so her official date of death was the next day. I had been talking to her preacher, who came to the hospital to see her several times and prayed with all of us. I called him after she died, wanting to talk to him about her funeral. He would be speaking at the service, and I wanted to tell him how important it was that everyone know about her forgiveness. She had taken care of all of us for so long, feeding us, sharing everything she had, giving us vehicles and furniture and love that ignored how much we took, how little we gave. She forgave us for not calling as often as we should have, for not visiting as often as we should have, for using her savings to buy drugs or pay the rent because we had used our own money for drugs. She forgave us for not going to church, and she prayed for us each night and cried every Sunday.

I wanted everyone at the funeral to know these things, to know that Granny had defined *forgiveness*, and she did it in a way that many people could find fault with but that had finally taught at least one person about love that is not earned. The preacher already had a plan, though, and he dismissed me before I could tell him how important it was that we honor Granny's forgiveness. At the funeral, he read from the Bible and preached a little sermon and at the end gave everyone an opportunity to get saved by Jesus right then and there, just to the right of my granny's body.

My father sat in the front row, next to his sister. My uncle sat in the front row on the other side, in his orange jumpsuit, with handcuffs on. I sat on a pew three rows back, with my son on one side of me and no one to my left. At first, I wondered who I should sit next to, who could comfort me. But it seemed better, finally, to just bow my head and cry, and not look at anyone else or lean on them or have anyone whisper, *It's okay.* As everyone walked up the aisle to give their condolences and see her body, a few people stopped and told me how much she loved me. One of them was my dad's buddy who had held the knife against James's neck.

*Your granny sure loved you a lot,* he said. *She thought you were so special.* I noticed how his blue eyes sparkled and he smiled too widely, with a strange expression that I so often would have called love. It was how he had always looked at me, the look that made me wonder as a child what he knew about me, what secret of mine he had somehow discovered. I pulled my son closer. Church people consoled my father as my granny's body lay cool. And something came rushing into my waking memory as a shadow took form, as I realized my father's friend looked just like the man in my recurring nightmare, whom as a child I had compared to Brutus from the *Popeye* cartoon. I suddenly remembered what he had done to me, and my tears stopped falling.

# CHAPTER 37

## *The Long Night*

It was probably inevitable that I would grow up thinking about killing myself. When I was working in Lexington, I would look at the grassy area that dipped down to the left of the northbound lanes of the interstate, wondering whether I would die if I jerked my wheel hard enough to flip my car and roll down the little hill. It wasn't a sure thing, so I didn't take the chance. I thought about dying mostly as I drove, probably because that was the time I had alone—time to think before picking up a child and going home to fix dinner, wash clothes, clean toilets.

One day, I had just reached Berea and was thinking that I wanted to die. I didn't want to hurt my children, which is probably why I never followed through. But on some days, I felt they might be better off without me. I felt like my life had been a waste—too many mistakes, too much trauma—and maybe, despite my stubborn hopefulness, there isn't really a reason for all this suffering. Maybe there is no god and no angels and whispering trees. No ancestors whose stories matter, and our stories don't matter, no *beauty in the telling*. Just children struggling to survive their parents, the psychological and physical wounds growing with each generation.

As I crossed the train tracks, I heard, *Just wait. Wait and see. The day will come when you are glad to be alive.* Whether those words came from my own mind, or from Granny, or somewhere else, I'm not sure, but I agreed to give it a chance.

I remember the day I found myself truly grateful to be alive—it was a year or two later. I don't remember the circumstances now, but at the time, I thought, *This is it. This is the moment I have been waiting for, and you were right—it is worth it.* And there have been more since then.

When I became a mother, I made a conscious decision to devote myself to my child before he arrived. That's the kind of thing that seems to come naturally to a lot of people—they sure do say it, at least—but for me, I knew I was choosing something that I absolutely did not know how to do and that I would have to work at to do well. I understood the stakes, too—the missing piece that so many people seem to underestimate. I knew how it felt to not really be wanted and adored. I may not have been particularly *un*wanted, but I was not *wanted*, and there is a world of difference. And in the effort to save myself from all that entails, I looked everywhere—at church, in therapy, drugs, men. It turns out that putting someone back together is much more difficult than keeping them whole in the first place.

I got to feeling pretty confident once my son was around six years old. Orion was a beautiful child—blond hair and blue eyes, but also full of sweetness that he never hid. He brought me flowers and he cuddled kittens. He climbed trees and made his best growling-lion face. The people around us told me what a good mother I was, and I knew that I loved him, and I finally understood what people meant when they talked about dying for someone—I was probably already close to that on the birthing bed.

Around that time, I began reading a lot of Rūmī's poetry and was enthralled—he was a Sufi mystic, and his writing felt so much like what I felt in childhood, hearing stories about Jesus. Before long, I began praying in a new way, to a god who was a mix between my childhood understanding and this mystical, poetic understanding. In some ways, they were perfectly compatible. I saw myself as the kind of jewel Rūmī described—one with sharp corners that the jeweler, God himself, must carve away. I saw myself as the gold that must be purified by burning away the impurities. For once, I thought of myself as a child of God. I saw all my past suffering and all that I carried, all I had seen and felt and heard in the long night of my childhood.

~

My daughter was born right after my son turned seven. Rose is a leap-year baby, and every bit deserves the rarity of that day. Her birth took not quite as long as Orion's, but it was unexpectedly lengthy, given that I was in a hospital and hooked up to an IV full of Pitocin for a little more than twenty-four hours. She had stopped growing at around eight months, and my midwife told me that home birth was no longer an option. I was low in iron, too, so at a greater risk of hemorrhaging—and I had already hemorrhaged enough the first time for her to be concerned. Not being able to have my daughter at home seemed to fit—nothing was making sense at that time. I knew I wasn't bringing her into a good situation, but I couldn't sort out what fell on me and what fell elsewhere.

We had started the Pitocin drip at five o'clock the night before. It slowly took hold, and I knew from reading journals for doctors at college, and then at work, that Pitocin was contraindicated for pregnant women. Still, I understood what it was meant to do—set my uterus in motion, start the contractions, *get the baby out*. At noon the next day, I started worrying about what it meant to be here, in a hospital. I had an ultrasound before they admitted me—they were concerned, they said, and if I was their patient, they would give me twenty-four hours before inducing labor. But I could have forty-eight, and then I needed to come back if I wanted to have the baby there. I had thought I still had a couple of weeks left to get everything together but made sure to return within their time frame. I realized I wasn't progressing well, though— I asked the nurse to check me at noon, and she said I was about two centimeters dilated. I asked her to break my water. *Are you sure?* she asked. *Yes, I'm sure.* I knew I had been lucky not to have a C-section with Orion. I knew I couldn't labor with this baby for too long.

The nurse broke my water, and the serious contractions set in—the *real* contractions. These came on top of the medication-induced contractions from the Pitocin, so there was no relief, no break between them, and my body had not had time to prepare itself for this level of labor. Suddenly, my mother and stepfather arrived. Thankfully, I still had my hospital gown on. I greeted them and tolerated them for a bit, but then had someone ask them to leave—or maybe I did it myself. I couldn't really say.

My labor to bring Orion into the world had been filled with moans, but I was quiet through so much of it. Not this time. The nurse walked in at one point, and instead of my earlier smiling *yes, please,* and *yes, thank you,* she found me naked on my hands and knees, howling every obscenity I could think of. The nurse said, *Oh, how things change,* and even in my anguish, I could appreciate the wry truth of her remark.

I knew that the odds of pushing my baby out naturally would dwindle soon, and every muscle in my body was tensed with these contractions—there was no way to breathe through them. I wanted to climb outside myself, escape this unnatural pain, but instead I was crawling on a tiny hospital bed with an IV still in my arm, hooked to a pole. I asked the nurse what my options were for pain relief, and she offered an epidural or Stadol. I remember her quickly telling me that they could give Stadol only when there was at least another hour of labor left, because they didn't want the baby born with the drug in its bloodstream. She checked me—three centimeters—and said that I could have it if I wanted it, that it would make me feel drunk and give me about an hour of relief, but that I would still have contractions. My massage-therapist friend was there and reminded me, *You wanted a natural birth,* and I didn't bother telling her that at that point, I was just waiting for my midwife to arrive before asking for an epidural— I wanted to give my midwife a chance to give me any reason not to.

Though she couldn't assist in the birth, she had agreed to come to the hospital to support me.

They added the opioid to my IV, and almost immediately, I was able to sleep. I still had contractions that shook me from my slumber, but I moaned through those, and the anguish was gone. I dreamt during a lull between them: *I am walking through a forest, next to a tall man with brown, curly hair. There is a lovely cabin nearby. I tell him,* I can't do this, *and he says,* Yes you can, it's almost over.

I woke up and felt like I needed to shit, so I asked someone in the room—who, I don't remember—to help me to the toilet chair that sat beside my bed. The same nurse as before walked in at that moment and urged me back onto the bed while I insisted I had to shit, and she gently told me, *That's fine, just do it on the bed, I'll put something under you, just please get back on the bed.* The last thing I wanted was to lie in a bed and relieve myself when I was fully capable of sitting up, but I eased back onto it. I still had sense enough to cooperate.

It turns out the nurse knew her stuff, because in fact I didn't need to shit—it was time for the baby to come out.

I lay there pushing with each contraction, and someone told me, *Don't do that, wait until the doctor comes,* and I thought, *Fuck that,* and kept pushing. Soon, perched between my legs, there was a grouchy doctor I had never met—I found out later she was sick. Earlier, they had asked whether I would allow students to observe, and I said yes, but I didn't realize that when it was time for the baby to come, they would turn on spotlights aimed at my naked body and desperate face. I didn't expect the students to watch without expression, as if they had no idea that when we give birth, we flirt with the edge of death. I searched the room frantically for eyes to lock onto and finally found my midwife, present and full of care and love. I focused only on her eyes, and about forty-five minutes after I started pushing, my daughter was born.

She was so small, no one had to cut me, and she slipped out with so much less effort than Orion had taken. I was still feeling drunk from the Stadol when she was born, and she came so soon after the drug was injected into my IV, she was probably born with it in her bloodstream. What can I do but mourn that?

It was not the birth I wanted to have, nor what I wanted for my girl. I knew she was a girl when I felt the first difference in my body: my mouth watered too much one day. My herbalist said, *That's not a symptom,* but I knew. The pregnancy test came back negative that day, a Friday, so I drank as much beer as I could that night and sat alone, crying, knowing I would have a girl. I took another pregnancy test on Monday, and it was positive.

But looking at my daughter's face over the next days and weeks and years, I understood why people compare cheeks to apples. She doubled her birth weight in the first six weeks. I carried her everywhere, just as I had my son. I fell in love with her as I had never loved any other girl.

I didn't even love myself at that point. I still struggled with the guilt and shame of what I had experienced, what I had done in response. And there was so much I had been told about women—how catty we are, how manipulative—that I didn't acknowledge but believed to be true. I still carried the idea that everything that had happened to me was somehow my fault.

Rose was always sweet, but she was also fiery and wild. I found that I had to discipline her differently. I quickly saw that the tone of voice I sometimes used with Orion—to convey *I mean it* and *you'd better do what I say*—would crush her, and I knew what happened when a girl was crushed. I learned how difficult it is to take care of a wild and free girl, not to squelch her into obedience and silent resentment or, worse yet, self-loathing. I found that when I cared for her, though, it changed how I felt inside. I started thinking it was okay that my parents didn't love and adore me—I could love and adore *this girl*, and that was enough for the both of us. And when it was time to fight for her, I fought with everything I had and then some. I prayed to anyone who would listen to show me how to protect her and help her, and I think they answered.

# CHAPTER 38

## *Defiance*

Still, I stumbled as a parent. I used to spank Orion—my mother saw him act out once, when he was still in diapers. *You'd better start spanking him, or one day, he'll be bigger than you, and you won't be able to control him.* I knew what she meant, but I didn't want to believe it. I read everything I could find about raising children and discipline, knowing I needed a new model, an example that had never been shown to me and that I would have to patchwork together myself. I already loved him with such ferocity and knew our bond defied description. I was sure I could find the right care to give so he would be neither spoiled nor broken.

I flicked him on the hand when he was little, teaching him that my simple, calm *no* was something to listen to. He was exceedingly easy to teach, and I taught him *please* and *thank you*, and when he was difficult, I was the benevolent dictator of our household—authoritative, without being authoritarian. Loving, without being permissive.

I spanked him for a while. Once, he threw a handful of gravel at our neighbor's back as the neighbor and I chatted beneath a weeping willow tree. I told Orion to pick up a switch and go sit on the porch and wait for me. When I was pregnant with his sister, I found myself spanking him with anger that I knew had nothing to do with him. He started telling me the spankings didn't hurt, no matter how hard I smacked his bottom. That was when I decided I had to find a new way. I apologized to him when he was about sixteen, and I couldn't help but cry. *I'm sorry I ever spanked you, I didn't know what else to do. I did my best, but it wasn't good enough.* In his usual kind way, he said, *Oh, it's okay, Mom. I'm glad you spanked me. I needed it.* I told him no, he didn't, and no one did.

On the cusp of adulthood, he asked me what I really would have done if he had disobeyed me as a teenager—he didn't ask out of defiance, but with curiosity. And I told him that the most important thing we had was the love and trust between us, and though I could threaten him with any number of things, the loss of trust is worse than anything else. He agreed.

By the time my daughter was one and I was a single mother again, I moved my small family into an old, dark rental house that I could hardly afford. I had graduated from my master's program seven months pregnant. When Rose was six months old, I started teaching at the same university, as an adjunct professor, but didn't realize I would only have two classes in the spring, not three. I moved us into that dark house thinking I would have a third more income than I ended up with. But I took on extra work, and after getting the kids in bed, I would start again on whatever project I had scrounged for, working until midnight or one in the morning.

The house looked like I felt. An old fireplace dropped soot and god knows what else when the wind blew outside. A huge roach crawled into the living room once, prompting Orion to name our home *the Roach House* and prompting me to pay for an exterminator for the first time in my life. The light switches were not switches at all, but old-fashioned buttons you pressed to turn the lights on or off. There were no overhead lights in the living room or kitchen, ensuring that shadows flew through the spaces I most enjoyed—those rooms where my children and I communed together.

The house was heated by an old, stand-alone heater that glowed red, a few thin metal rods sitting in front of the elements, and there was nothing to protect a child's fingers or face from touching any of it. Rose was learning to walk and almost fell into it one day—how she never touched it I do not know, other than my constant watching and carrying her and maybe a guardian angel or two. Orion caught her from falling into it one day and then wrote a few paragraphs about it at school, and I worried that someone would see it as a reason to take my baby from me.

That's what happens when your house is unsafe and you can't afford anything better—you're called unfit, and nobody asks how you got to this place. That's why someone who used to be poor will, if they have it, lend money to a poor person to pay a bill—they know the stakes. That's why I eventually paid a friend's utility bill with a credit card. A broken water pipe in the yard had put the power bill too far out of reach for her. If just one of her kids had mentioned the lights being off, she could have lost all her children.

Spring came quickly, though, and my bedroom filled with roly-poly bugs that surrounded the head of my mattress and died there. The washer and dryer were in the basement, which was perpetually flooded. I had to put my daughter in a baby backpack and carry the laundry out the kitchen door, down the wooden stairs to the yard, and down the concrete steps into the basement, then make my way across some old wooden pallets someone had placed on the floor to keep feet dry on laundry day. A single, bare lightbulb illuminated the basement, and rickety shelves lined the sides, filled with dust and other forgotten things.

I worried over the baby touching the paint that flaked around the low windowsills—it probably had lead in it. Someone had come to fix a short in the wiring one day and looked at the ceiling in the third bedroom. *Don't put the baby in here—that ceiling probably has asbestos, and you don't want the dust falling onto her.* I put my computer in there instead, and when someone gave me a crib, I put the crib in my bedroom. I wouldn't realize until she started sleeping through the night that I hadn't slept through an entire night for three years, but you don't always see those things while they are happening.

Orion played soccer—I wanted him to do something active, and I knew that running would be good for him. It might even build his self-esteem, provide some measure of protection. I went to his practices and games, which were often in Richmond—around fifteen miles away—so that meant sometimes I drove up there twice a day. It didn't really matter where they were. Everywhere I went, I felt like I was coming apart. Every *thing* felt hard—driving to a soccer game, comforting the children, cooking meals, preparing for my classes. Opening the mail was torture—if I didn't recognize the sender but it looked like it could be a bill, I left it unopened, knowing I had no way to pay anything but the basics. I didn't know who else might be sending me bills, but I believed it was a very real possibility that there was always something else I owed, some other debt I couldn't manage. I just opened what it took to keep the lights and water on and a roof overhead—if you don't have those things, someone very likely *will* take your baby away from you.

Nearly all the time, I felt like my insides were on fire, and there was no relief.

I had moved to Lexington toward the end of my pregnancy, and when I came back to Berea with Rose and Orion, I thought my old friends would want to spend time together, hang out like we had always done. But many of them were getting married and settling into careers and not yet having babies. I tried to be friends with some of the other women living nearby—a couple of them were also single mothers—but it seemed as if they never really liked me. The support I had felt when Orion was a toddler disappeared, and the group of friends who welcomed him to every event and doted on him no longer wanted to see me so much. The people I had come to regard as my chosen family, with my usual stubborn and fierce devotion, were all but gone.

I walked around those days with my mind occupied by anger and fear, relieved only in the moments when my children reminded me of their sweetness. One day, as my mind ground away, asking *Why are things like this,* I had a new thought: every terrible relationship I ever had, had one thing in common—me. *Well shit,* I thought. I considered my last ex-boyfriend and how he didn't even try to convince me he loved me. It was I who did that. I thought of all the boyfriends and the couple of husbands over the previous fifteen years and suddenly understood that while they didn't look like my father, or talk like him, or try to scam the system like he did, they all *felt* like him, to me. I knew then that I couldn't trust myself to love a man, that something inside me drew me to the kind of men who wouldn't really love me but whose love I would desperately try to earn.

After that unpleasant realization, I wrestled for a while with the guilt I felt for making the same bad choice over and over—always in new packaging, because I tried so damn hard, but I couldn't escape the jailer within who kept me locked in a cage. I realized that no matter what else I accomplished, my cage wasn't so different from my mother's.

But I kept struggling with those feelings. I kept asking myself *why* and *how,* and as frustrated as I was with myself, I knew there had to be something better. I had seen beauty and felt joy. I was determined to claim some of it—if not for me, then for my children, who surely couldn't go through this, too. One day, a new thought hit me: although my life had not been my *fault,* I had reached the point at which I wanted my life to be wholly mine and not a constant reaction to the trauma I had known. There was no knight in shining armor coming to rescue me, to protect me from my father or any other man. I knew I had every right to be angry about the things I had experienced, but I also had to find a way to undo the damage that had been done, so I would never again choose the things that were bad for me. So I could stop being haunted by nightmares that belonged in the past.

I went to a financial counselor soon after that, knowing I had to figure out how to manage money if I was going to survive. It was a free service in Richmond, offered by the same people who ran the free bus. The financial counselor seemed much too normal to understand me, but she set me up with a spreadsheet, and we walked through all my bills, the due dates, and my spending. It turned out that I had no idea what I was spending—it usually seemed like there was no money at all, and then enough, and then none again. I wasn't buying anything extravagant, but it was the first time I thought about knowing *when* to spend. At the end of our session, the financial counselor suggested I find a one-bedroom apartment or someone's basement to live in. *Give the bedroom to your son. You can sleep in the living room with your daughter.*

I politely thanked her and thought, *No way in hell.* I decided to buy a house instead—I was paying $375 in rent, so I was certain I could find a mortgage I could afford. The mortgage officer at the first bank I went to told me about a government-subsidized mortgage program—she said she would be doing me a disservice not to tell me. Looking back, I know she was under some pressure to get me into a mortgage with the bank but chose to send me to that program instead. And I know that it was a dream to imagine I could buy a house at that point. There was no reason for me to succeed, on paper.

But around five months later, I bought a house that was nicer than anywhere I had ever lived, and though we hardly had any furniture, it felt like a palace. Just before we moved in, I started a new job—one day an old friend from my first job forwarded me an email and wondered whether I was interested. She was being asked to apply but had moved to another state. I applied and suddenly was making a middle-class income for the first time in my life. I lost the little bit of food stamps I was getting, and the kids' medical cards, and asked myself, *Can I really do this?*

There were so many things I knew were still broken inside me. *Orion filled the Jacuzzi tub with bubbles, and I yelled at him. I'm afraid I won't be able to keep the house clean, and it will turn into a nasty place with soap scum and dirty bathrooms, and I will fail my children, and they will feel like white trash, just like I did. I cussed at my two-year-old daughter today. I hate myself for it. I'm just exhausted by how much she needs, how much she demands. At the end of the day, I feel like a cigarette is the only comfort I have.*

I had romanticized self-awareness when I read *Be Here Now* by Ram Dass and smoked lots of weed and took all the LSD I could get my hands on. Back then, the idea of being self-aware was so romantic, so wrapped up in the feelings of magic and excitement I experienced with all those altered states. The goodness I felt and saw during my chemical escapes made me think I was really getting somewhere in my growth as a person. And maybe I did—I'm not sure what my outlook for survival would have been if I had not found some relief from my inner hell, some temporary respite. But by the time I grew up—*really grew up*—I realized I had just barely survived childhood and young adulthood. The only reason I survived motherhood was because I was so stubborn, I poured every bit of myself into it, unwilling to fail my children in the ways I had been failed.

But looking at myself as a thirty-year-old, knowing how much I had squandered, how little I had accomplished, was its own fresh hell. I gained a lot of empathy for the people around me who didn't seem at all interested in thinking about their lives and the choices they made. Taking an honest look at myself and what I had become was the most painful thing I ever experienced. I couldn't wait for my parents to love me, or for my granny to come back from her deathbed and remind me that I was lovable. The world I wanted would not pull me into it, not with me so accustomed to the hell I had come to think of as normal. I wanted something beautiful and magical to swoop down and save me, to show that it recognized how *special* I was, how *worth saving*. I was not excited or inspired when I discovered I had to be the one to save me.

After years of conscious work, I eventually realized my life had become different, that *I* had become different. Not perfect, of course. I still get upset when the kids leave things in our front yard, but I don't tell them it makes us look trashy and I'm afraid the neighbors will see me for what I really am. I don't let them eat on the couch, but I don't yell as I used to when I felt like every mess, every broken thing, every dollar wasted, was going to drag me back into childhood, where I would forever be helpless and afraid and poor and dirty. I tell them I love them and why I love them, and I listen to their made-up songs or the music they discovered and want me to hear. I go to their plays and concerts and games—I still don't feel at ease, but I don't always feel like something is clawing at my insides now, as I sit among so many people who might be enemies. To my surprise, I mean it when I smile and applaud.

In graduate school, I had written a story about my father and how he had sent me to my granny's house to call her a whore. I didn't think it would ever amount to much—there are so many people who want to write, and so many who have better stories or better luck. But it felt important, for some reason. The story had come as a surprise to me as I was earning a master's degree in English—I wanted to write poetry, but I didn't think I could fit all my words into a poem. After grad school, I kept working on my story and revising it, adding what needed to be said, finding God in the details along the way. I wrote it and rewrote it over the years to come, each time seeing more clearly that I had become the storyteller, that it was *my story* and that *I had to tell it.* With each revision, I understood that although many people had quieted me, even whipped me into silence, I still had words they could not take away from me. And while my words were in part the defiance and anger I had always been too afraid to voice, they were more than that, too.

As I wrote, I discovered words for what I felt in the forest, the sweet stillness that endures from countless hours in that holy place. I discovered that the words of the King James Bible that were sometimes used to frighten me still contain their own mystery and magic, and I can see what might have comforted and ignited my granny's inimitable heart. I beheld my granny and the poetry of her life, a life lived in quiet strength and selflessness—the life of a mountain woman whose power suffuses the kingdom within. I saw that every word I had to speak was the honoring of my history, the history of everyone I had ever loved, and the landscapes in which I had sought refuge, time and time again: first, the streams and forests of Kentucky, and then, every book I could get my hands on. And even when my story isn't pretty, or I wasn't, the living itself is. After all is said and done, I can't help but see the beauty we belong to.

I wrote from the time I was in middle school, even though my classmates ridiculed my imitation of the *Odyssey*. As an adult, I wrote and sent my work to professors and literary agents, asking over and over for their approval and affirmation, to be let into their world. Perhaps I just wanted someone to listen to all the words I had finally found the courage to bring to the light of day.

As I wrote, I understood myself as a character, as a person in a grand and vast story that endures far beyond me. I wrote and saw myself in a context beyond my family or place or time. I wrote my story again and again, until I came to love the little girl who survived it. I wrote to free her, to vindicate her, to give her justice. Writing was my best rebellion, my silent outcry, my ravaged testament to how much a person can love a world that does not suffer her. Writing my story became my duty, too—a duty to the grown and still-young children who stumble in the darkness, knowing there is something *good* but not believing that goodness is for them.

I wrote myself and found myself. I wrote nearly all the words I had swallowed for decades, passion transmuted.

# CHAPTER 39

## *Out of Line*

I grew up thinking there was something wrong with my family and especially with me. But I realize that, for the most part, the adults around me then felt like I feel now—childhood slips away without warning, and we find ourselves pretending to be grown, pretending we want to be part of this world with jobs and bills, but numbing ourselves with television or another glass of wine. We have our own children and see ourselves in them—we relive our teen years (*the best years of your life*), or we play out our unresolved conflicts while our own parents become grandparents and suddenly aren't so awful anymore.

For so many years—has it been decades?—I've felt misunderstood, and every time I thought someone truly saw me for who I was, for the *good girl* still inside me, I lapped up their attention like my father's dog devoured beans and dirt alike. I tried so hard to avoid dating or becoming my father. I didn't date anyone who did hard drugs (at least after my first marriage ended). I congratulated myself that no man ever hit me (*the bruises on my neck were more than ten years ago now, and that was only once*), though I never stopped being afraid of it, never stopped wondering whether it would happen if I dared say too much, if I let my face betray my true feelings. In the end, though, there was never a good set of rules to follow to protect myself.

My first husband and a later boyfriend were talented musicians, so I vowed not to date any guitar players. After my second husband and the guitarist boyfriend, I swore I wouldn't date a man who was a Cancer. After that, it was no guys who worked at bars. Then, no Capricorns. But the kind of men who will hurt women—especially women who have been deprived of love—are everywhere, and they look like everyone. In some ways, it's disappointing to know that bad men aren't just the ones who look like my father—raised in a holler, shooting guns, and making moonshine or dropping out of high school. For the longest time, that made it much more difficult to figure out who was *safe*.

It's more complicated, too, knowing that people who call themselves *feminists* and *social-rights activists* might turn their backs on the ones who need them: Women who are desperate to be loved, so they sleep with too many men. Men who are snorting pills or shooting up heroin or some mysterious opiate concoction, because being alive hurts so much, it is worth it to risk overdose and disease and losing everything you have, everyone who loves you, to escape the hell inside you, even for just a few hours. Poor people without the wherewithal to stop smoking or stop burning their trash by the creek, who would rather die in a coal mine than get free health care. How do you love people who look like this, who live like this? People like me, like my father, my brother, and my mother.

My brother—he is the one who was with me through it all, who saw and heard and felt everything alongside me. Did he not *feel like me*, too? What does he feel now, if he lets himself feel anything? I don't know, because we were never close again after he left prison and the halfway house. I wonder why he is somewhere else, not beside me as I write a new life for myself, not rejoicing in the freedom we gain from leaving behind the sins of our father.

I was so envious of him growing up. Everything seemed better for him, and I assumed it was because he was more lovable than I was. He had a cherubic face, and even though his baby teeth rotted at the same time mine did, he still had a beautiful, easy smile. It seemed like everyone wanted to take care of him—except our father, of course—and even I was willing to take a whipping to protect him from the pain our father subjected us to. Later, I was willing to wear the shoes I knew my classmates might mock, so I could protect my brother from the torment our peers subjected us to.

One time when we had both reached adulthood, I asked Junior what he remembered of our growing up. He had blocked some things out, he said—like our mother had—but he told me about the time he went to a cave with our father and how our father climbed onto a higher ledge while they were inside the cave, and he stepped on Junior's fingers. Junior yelped in pain, and Dad looked down at him with an empty expression, said nothing, and continued climbing or walking to wherever he was going. When Junior told me this story, he was still in wonder that a parent could hurt their child, even accidentally, and not feel remorse. Like me, Junior found it almost impossible to believe our father could really do the things he did, feel the way he felt toward us, over the years.

Unlike me, Junior had to *be a man* about these things. He learned on the school bus that the quickest way to escape abuse from other boys was to show them he could hurt them back. I'm not sure I ever really escaped, until my tormentors found more interesting things to do. I turned inward to seek a safe haven, and immersed myself in all the beauty I could find in books and nature and psychedelia. And in Granny, of course, and in what I could claim of church. I turned my anger inward, too, since I wasn't allowed to express it.

Junior didn't love reading like I did, and didn't do particularly well in school. He didn't seem to care about it, while I relished every bit of praise my teachers gave me. My love of reading and ability to perform well academically reinforced the positive feedback I received from adults at school. I came to want and need affirmation that I was smart, while Junior was rewarded for achieving less than I did. My achievements, though, gave me an easy route to a college degree without debt, and I had to leave my hometown in order to get it—the most vital step in escaping one's childhood hell, it seems.

And while I was subject to the whims and tempers of men who did not deserve the power they held, I sometimes wonder whether it would have been better or worse to be a boy, expected to *act like a man* in places where men are unpredictable, dangerous, forbidden to feel pain or fear. As a girl, I was yoked with the desire to please. As a boy, my brother was saddled with the command to dominate. For either of us, stepping out of line was met with brutality.

# CHAPTER 40

## *In the Holler*

When I hear people musing over the contradictions and sorrows that plague this region—Appalachia, with its unparalleled beauty—I want to remind them that it's always easy to see someone else's flaws, especially when the *other* doesn't have pretty clothes to hide behind. Whether it's addiction or racism or cycles of abuse, I want to tell them how *these are not just Appalachian problems*. We didn't invent fentanyl or Lortabs or OxyContin. It's not hillbillies who are getting rich off opioids—but just like this land's lumber and coal that fueled the economy for the rest of the country, someone is getting rich off our desperate and dying people, our last expendable resource.

And I cannot say what kind of hate is in anyone else's heart, but I know it is easy to turn a man to hate if you can convince him that the outsider is the cause of his problems. In a place like this, outsiders have taken away everything the people had—the very minerals from under their feet—time and time again. But just like the coal bosses brought in *scabs* to break the strikes, it is always someone at a higher pay grade who convinces workers to blame immigrants, people of color, and other poor people when the owner won't pay fair wages. In a land like this, people have *actually* been fighting for their lives—not figuratively or metaphorically—since they first decided to take their chances in this unforgiving Eden.

I've discovered that people of all classes fail their children—sometimes they abuse them, sometimes they neglect them. But if you can afford a good lawyer, you might not go to prison, and your kids probably won't be going to foster care. Sometimes judges even decide, *He's not well suited for prison,* so victims watch while abusers walk free because they themselves are too fragile to suffer the consequences of their choices.

These are rotten fruits we are reaping from conquerors who planted their flags in other people's homes and holy lands long ago.

When people ask, *What's wrong with eastern Kentucky?* all I know is *it's the same thing that's wrong with all of us.* My father was not the first man to hurt his children or his wife or his parents. My brother won't be the last to watch his children go into foster care while he—full of love as he is—chooses pills and prison. If we trace these heartbreaks back to some comprehensible root, we would probably find that somewhere along the way, some vital trust was broken.

It is bittersweet, finally knowing that I can't save my father—whether he's too far gone or had nothing to save in the first place, I may never know. I can't save any other men, either, no matter how lovable I see they are, and how I know they would be okay if they could feel the depth of my love for just one moment. I can't save my siblings, can't undo the things that broke inside them while our father filled them with fear and loss and pain. While their mothers watched.

I can't change anything that happened to my mother or take away any fear or loss that has haunted her. I can't give her vibrant youth back to her, nor the beauty in her high cheekbones and smooth skin. Without knowing it, I spent much of my young life longing for a new story with her, one in which we are close and she helps me understand motherhood, or how to be a strong woman. Maybe we get lunch together, just the two of us, or slip away for the weekend.

But perhaps like me, my mother wasn't ready to have a girl in her early twenties. And maybe my father loves me as much as he could ever love anyone, and loves himself least of all. There's nothing to be done with what happened. All I can do is write the future.

People tell me that my children look just like me. They were both born with almond eyes; my daughter's were deep and dreamlike for weeks, as if she were sent from another world that held part of her until they knew I was ready. My children's faces are symmetrical, their teeth straight. A babbling brook of confusion obscured my thoughts for most of their childhoods, but I still read books to them and sang songs and listened when they were sad or angry. I taught myself to apologize when I had wronged them. I taught them to apologize when they had wronged someone else. I know there is nothing I can tell them for certain, other than how I love them.

I tell my daughter bedtime stories about a certain girl who was sent down from Heaven because her mother wanted her so much. I tell my son stories about being wild and free in the woods, just like he got to be at times. I tell them both stories about Papaw and Granny, about meals and prayers that took place for generations at our kitchen table, about growing up in the holler. They ask for those stories over and over again—*my* stories, *our* stories—the threads of a story they will tell their children and grandchildren, who will someday savor those words.

When Papaw Conn was on his deathbed, I begged him to tell me some of his stories. *They don't matter now,* he told me. And I let it go, already mourning what I could never know of him and his life. But I discovered that our stories *do* matter—they tell us who we are, give us history and context that help us define ourselves. Some stories serve as a warning, while others are an endless source of hope. And there is always more to be written.

I look into my children's faces and see the best of myself, a reminder of how important it is to choose my best every day. I see life that springs forth and defies the cruelty we so often inflict. That I can give my children something better, give my *self* something better. That I must, come hell or high water. I feel the magic of childhood and the whispering strength of forests waiting for us. I see miracles incarnate. I hear the stories I tell my children, the stories of their births and how their lives are gifts to us all. I see myself and my parents, grandparents, generations I never knew but whose love and loss are bound into each thread of my being. I see the holler I was born to, as much as I was born to any person—a place and a symbol filled with power and knowledge, comfort and paradox.

I see my granny. We're sitting in the white glider on her front porch, a bucket of beans in front of us. She strings them with knowing hands, snapping off the ends without hesitation, breaking them into perfect pieces. I try to mimic her, carefully pulling the strings from each pod, knowing how they feel in your teeth once they're canned. She does not speak, and I do not need her to. I have watched her carry split wood from this porch—the fire never died in her house. I've watched her wring the chickens' necks and make pie out of just about anything you could ever want. I've watched her cry and pray and love when surely there was no reason to.

Not far from us is the creek I grew up playing in, full of pinching crawdads and the occasional copperhead. There's the forest with its guardians, oaks and maples who watched me as a child. Granny and I can hear the sound of the leaves moving in the distance. It's like a prayer she has taught me.

# EPILOGUE

## *Endless Revision*

At his high school graduation, Orion walked across the same stage I had crossed seventeen years earlier, when I received my college degree—his little school's gymnasium couldn't accommodate the ceremony. Orion earned the highest honors and received scholarships to various universities. Going to college was never even a question in his mind.

I took him to get his wisdom teeth out earlier in the week. We got home after that appointment, and I picked up his medicines a little later—an antibiotic and something for the pain, in case he needed it. I set them on the kitchen counter and didn't think about them until he picked them up.

*What's this?*

We looked at the labels.

*Oxycodone? I'm not taking this shit. Why would they prescribe that to me?*

*You're right,* I told him. *You don't need that. We'll use ibuprofen and Tylenol.* I wondered whether he remembered the time we went to my father's house and I cried in the car afterward, pleading with him not to ever take pills. Later, he said he didn't remember that specifically, but he knew how badly pills had affected so many people—he wasn't willing to take that chance.

I think about my own prescriptions—an opiate for pain from having teeth extracted so I could get my own teeth straightened after my kids both had braces. A muscle relaxer I was given following a car accident. They sit in a container high on a shelf, unopened.

During a thunderstorm, my daughter, now eleven, calls to me: *Come snuggle with me and the dog, Mama. You were made for comforting—we need you.* She doesn't share my love of thunderstorms, which cooled the thick heat in my childhood bedroom.

I look for every chance to show her I love her, though I sometimes feel so stretched for time, patience, energy. We go on mommy-daughter dates—usually just a simple meal. We go shopping sometimes, but we stick to what we really need and what she can buy with her small allowance.

Like Granny before me, I have largely hidden my emotional work and struggles from my children. All their lives, I have thought about how my choices will affect them, how they will remember all this, and what stories they might tell themselves about the life we are sharing. I force myself to speak gently when I just want everyone to be quiet. We say grace at the table to remind us all that there is always something to be grateful for. I try to find the balance between giving them everything and saving something for myself.

I put my arms around my daughter and pull her close.

*I wish everyone could have what we have,* she says. *I wish every family was like ours.*

When I sit alone at the end of the night, I realize this is my greatest triumph—to give my children the love and comfort I longed for, but which were not to be found in my childhood home. To give them a new world—one where they can thrive—without having first seen that world myself. What greater magic is there? Every day, I try to give my children the kind of life I know Granny wanted for me. And I do it without knowing quite how, writing a new story for us, revising until I get it right.

I think of my little-girl self, who is surely still inside me, and know I could tell her that she is good and that everything is going to be okay. I would tell her there are angels and spirits who have loved her since before she was born, and they have filled the forest with treasures that only she can find. I would tell her that everything she longs for is also looking for her, yearning to be found. Some of it is in the creek behind her house, hidden in the fossils and the sound the water makes as it caresses each stone. Some is at Granny's house and at her holy table, where love and sacrifice are made manifest. Some is in the books she loves to read, with characters whose lives she feels as if they were her own. Mostly, it is concealed within her own hopeful heart, just waiting for her to write her story.

# ACKNOWLEDGMENTS

I would like to thank Young Smith, my creative writing mentor, for being the first person to encourage me to write my story and for convincing me it was a story worth telling. I am forever grateful to Lois Giancola, who believed in me before I could believe in myself, and who has endlessly supported and encouraged me. Thanks to Adriann Ranta Zurhellen, Bianca Spriggs, and Hafizah Geter—three amazing women who helped this book be the best it could be and saw the value in bringing it to life. I thank my children for loving and accepting me throughout this project and during all our time together—to both of you, I love you most.

# ABOUT THE AUTHOR

*Photo © 2019 Erica Chambers Photography*

Bobi Conn was born in Morehead, Kentucky, and raised in a nearby holler, where she developed a deep connection with the land and her Appalachian roots. She obtained her bachelor's degree at Berea College, the first school in the American South to integrate racially and to teach men and women in the same classrooms. After struggling as a single mother, she worked five part-time jobs at once to support her son and to attend graduate school, where she earned a master's degree in English with an emphasis in creative writing. In addition to writing, Bobi loves playing pool, telling jokes, cooking, being in the woods, attempting to grow a garden, and spending time with her incredible children.